Hidden
Champions

Hidden Champions

Lessons from 500 of the World's Best Unknown Companies

Hermann Simon

Harvard Business School Press
Boston, Massachusetts

Printed in the United States of America

00 99 98 97 96   5 4 3 2 1

Library of Congress Cataloging-in-Publication Data

Simon, Hermann.
    Hidden champions : lessons from 500 of the world's best unknown
companies / Hermann Simon.
      p.   cm.
    Includes index.
    ISBN 0-87584-652-1
    1. Success in business—Case studies.   2. Small business—Management—
Case studies.   I. Title.
    HF5386.S54   1996
    338.7′4—dc20   95-43850
                                                CIP

The paper used in this publication meets the requirements of the American National
Standard for Permanence of Paper for Printed Library Materials Z39.49-1984.

Contents

Preface

U NTIL THE MID-1980s, I was not particularly interested in small and medium-size companies; rather, my attention as an academic was directed toward larger corporations. However, when I met Professor Theodore Levitt of the Harvard Business School in Düsseldorf in 1986, we entered into a discussion of the continuing international export success of Germany. We soon agreed that it couldn't be attributed primarily to the large German companies, since they don't seem to differ much from their international counterparts.

A major root of Germany's continuing export excellence, we supposed, must lie with small and medium-size companies, particularly in the category of firms that are worldwide leaders in their markets. While scarcely known, these smaller businesses have excelled throughout the world for decades. Intrigued, I determined to discover what these market leaders are doing differently and to investigate them more thoroughly. Over the years I collected their names and came to call them hidden champions. Hidden they are, and often prefer to be, but they are assuredly champions. The large number I found came as a great surprise to me—Germany alone is home to more than five hundred.

In the early years of my investigation, I thought that the hidden champion phenomenon was specifically German, rooted in a tradition of craftsmanship and pride in one's work. But in the course of time, I discovered such companies in almost every part of the world, ranging from the United States to Korea to South Africa to New Zealand. I learned that all are amazingly similar. The same principles seem to point to success and market leadership everywhere. Therefore the lessons I present in this book, which have been well received in all parts of the world, are likely to be useful for any company, irrespective of its location or national origin.

My experience with large corporations suggested that the hidden champions avoid most facets of the "big company" syndrome like inflexibility, bureaucracy, excessive division of labor, and remoteness from the customer. In my consulting work, as I tried to apply many of the insights gained from the hidden champion research to larger firms, I found that giants can learn a lot from the mighty dwarfs. While the usual path of learning runs from large to small companies, the findings encourage me to attempt to suggest a change of this direction. By the sheer fact that their strategies are widely known, large firms lose much of their competitive value. The approaches of hidden champions are mostly unknown and therefore may be more valuable for the conception of corporate strategy.

My increasing involvement with, numerous visits to, and repeated encounters with CEOs of the hidden champions led to a series of "Aha!" experiences. I was often deeply impressed by what these firms achieved in spite of their limited size and resources. I am convinced that the best companies in the world can be found among this group rather than among large corporations. I learned more about management from these hands-on experiences than from two decades of academic research. As a result, I take the liberty of sharing my subjective impressions and judgments as an academic and consultant with the reader. Not every point included in this book has been or can be verified scientifically. It may be that the characteristics least accessible to the scientific approach, for example, leadership, motivation, reliance on one's own strength, are the more important drivers of the success of the hidden champions.

The book is primarily addressed to practitioners who, I am sure, will appreciate the emphasis on practical relevance rather than on scientific rigor. Business researchers, finding some widely accepted views challenged will, I hope, be encouraged to delve more closely into these issues.

I owe thanks to the many who supported my work. First and foremost, I would like to thank the founders, owners, and managers of the hidden champions for granting me innumerable hours of stimulating discussions and learning experiences. I thank the German Research Foundation for generously supporting the project from 1993 to 1995. Eckart Schmitt, my research assistant, a highly competent, intellectual sparring partner, contributed immensely to the effort in all its phases, for which I am deeply indebted to him. I am also grateful to my colleagues at Simon, Kucher & Partners, Strategy & Marketing Consultants, for many inspiring, insightful, and challenging discussions on the strategic issues addressed in this book. The discussion with Nick Philipson of the Harvard Business School Press widened my perspective with regard to an international audience. Barbara Roth, the managing editor, guided me in a very professional way through the process of making this book publishable. Last, but not least, I offer my appreciation to Cecilia, Jeannine, and Patrick for their never-ending understanding that time is the scarcest of all resources.

Hermann Simon

1
The Hidden Champions: Who Are They?

We strongly prefer to remain hidden.

A VAST POPULATION of superbly successful business establishments has escaped the attention of those whose business it is to know everything—business magazines; to understand everything—business scholars; and to fix everything—business consultants. This is the sphere of world-class small and medium-size companies, the realm of the "hidden champions."

Buried deep below the headlines of sensational business successes and innovative breakthroughs lies a totally ignored source of management wisdom. A whole category of global competitors has remained hidden under a layer of inconspicuousness, invisibility, and even secrecy. Few practitioners, journalists, and academics know the names of these companies or are aware of the products they make, let alone the way they conduct business throughout the world. Their market dominance, however, belies their low profiles. Many of them enjoy world market shares of 70 to 90%, numbers that few giant multinationals can match. And many of these hidden champions were truly global long before the term "globalization" was coined.

This book reveals the secrets of success of the best of the best unknown companies. While they are largely uncelebrated, they deal in wares that constantly surround us. Quickly consider just a few.

- *Hauni:* The world market leader in cigarette machines, Hauni, literally the only supplier of complete systems for tobacco processing, has a world market share of nearly 90% in high-speed cigarette machines. All the filter cigarettes in the world are manufactured with a technology invented by Hauni.
- *Tetra:* If you own an aquarium, you are probably familiar with Tetramin. Tetra's share in the world market of tropical fish food is more than 50%.
- *Baader:* This hidden champion owns 90% of the world market for fish-processing equipment. Even in Vladivostok, you would encounter no problem buying Baader's products and service.
- *Hillebrand:* When you enjoy a Beaujolais Nouveau in Los Angeles merely a few days after the grapes were pressed in France, you're unlikely to wonder how the new wine arrived in California so quickly. There is a 60% chance that it was sent by Hillebrand, with offices in 60 countries the largest wine shipper in the world.
- *Webasto:* A double hidden champion, this company is the world leader in both sunroofs and auxiliary heating systems for cars.
- *Brita:* The market for point-of-use water filters was created by Brita. Continually fighting to defend its leading position, this pioneer enjoys a world market share of 85%.
- *Gerriets:* A maker of theatrical scrims and decorations, this company, as the sole manufacturer in the world of large neutral lighting cloths for stages, holds a global market share of 100%.
- *Stihl:* Its chain saws see action all over the world. A highly innovative company, Stihl claims a global share close to 30%, double that of its strongest competitor.
- *Barth:* As you drink a glass of beer, it would be most surprising if you ever give a thought to the origin of hops, an essential ingredient. Barth, the world market leader in hops and hops products, is run by one of the most truly international and polyglot staffs I have ever encountered.
- *SAT and Wirtgen:* Worldwide, road infrastructure is deteriorating and in need of renovation. At the same time, recycling and

environmental concerns are becoming increasingly important in many countries. Both these hidden champions take advantage of the opportunities arising from these trends. Wirtgen manufactures the machines and SAT supplies the services for on-site recycling of road surfaces. In their latest technology, known as cold repaving, the worn-out road surface is milled away, the material recycled on the spot without heat, and the road repaved in a single continuous process. Cold repaving is already being applied in countries like Australia, South Africa, and Israel and will soon be adopted for roads in colder regions.

- *Haribo:* Haribo's Gummi bears are equally popular in Europe and the United States. The company has been hugely successful in building a leadership position for these sweets throughout the world.

- *Würth:* Begun as a two-person outfit in the mid-1950s, Würth is by far the largest supplier of assembly products around the globe. Its strongest competitor is about one-fifth the size of Würth. With company-owned subsidiaries in forty-four countries, it continues to grow rapidly and further strengthen its global lead.

This list of hidden champions could go on for pages, detailing makers of products and suppliers of services like bookbinding textiles, skeletons, large living trees, model railways, metal filters, translation services for large conferences, poinsettia plants, measuring instruments for angles, buttons, nondestructive testing, large tent rentals, and potting soil. How have the hidden champions largely managed to escape the attention of the business press and researchers? There are several reasons. First, many of their products are inconspicuous or invisible, are used in manufacturing processes, or are subsumed in such end products as car sunroofs, perfume fragrances, and artificial hip joints. Some products are simply too unimportant to be noticed; we barely consider that someone has to supply, for example, buttons, pencils, screws, and labels for beverage bottles.

But an equally important reason for the low profile of these world market leaders is that they relish their obscurity. They shy away from publicity, some through explicit policies of not dealing with the press—or, by the way, with academic researchers! As an executive of a leading manufacturer of material processing equipment said, "We are not interested in revealing our success strategies and helping those who have recently neglected their business." Another hidden champion CEO wrote, "We don't want to be on your list. We strongly prefer to remain hidden." And the chief of the world market leader in a critical component for vibration control equipment remarked, "We want neither our competitors nor our customers to know our true market share." The young chief of a service company commented, "We have cherished our anonymity for years and feel very comfortable about it. Nobody has noticed our niche."

After a substantial research effort, the American journalist Philip Glouchevitch (1992, 51) resignedly stated that these "companies remain in many ways inscrutable—a deliberate characteristic." Quite a few of the candidates I identified did not answer my phone calls or letters nor were they available for interviews or a questionnaire survey. At L'tur—according to its advertising, number one in last-minute travel in Europe—I couldn't even get past the switchboard. It is still more difficult for me to arrange an appointment with a typical hidden champion CEO than with heads of large multinational corporations. What a 1994 *Fortune* article reported about Mars, the candy and pet food marketer, could be equally true of many hidden champions: "The privately owned company stays hidden, it grants no interviews, allows no pictures of executives. The enigma hints of contradiction, even weirdness" (Saporito 1994, 50).

But these companies have not remained totally undetected to outside observers. Porter (1990a), in *The Competitive Advantage of Nations*, describes several fields in which hidden champions play prominent roles, notably the German printing-press industry with Heidelberger Druckmaschinen, the world market leader in offset-printing machines, and Koenig & Bauer, the world champion in money-printing presses. He also mentions Claas, the world market leader in combines, and Cloos, a hidden champion in welding systems. Peters (1992), in *Liberation Management*, tells stories of "mighty dwarfs" and describes a few of the little known companies. Similarly, *Business Week* carried an article entitled "Think Small" (Schares and Templeman 1991), which portrayed some German hidden champions, and "The Little Giants" (Baker et al. 1993), a report about their American counterparts.

To penetrate the shield of secrecy of these bashful entities one has to earn their trust. Eventually, with some effort, I managed to persuade several hundred of their officers to be interviewed, to fill out a questionnaire, or to provide company brochures containing information on their strategies and management styles. Quite a few, however, were willing to cooperate only on the condition that I promise never to reveal their names or to mention them only in connection with certain citations and events. This attitude is understandable, because many operate in small markets where information may be directly conveyed to a specific supplier, customer, or competitor. Therefore, fully respecting this request for confidentiality, I do not identify those sources that prefer to remain anonymous.

CRITERIA FOR A HIDDEN CHAMPION

My decision to investigate hidden champions stems from a late-eighties discussion of international competitiveness. Further analysis revealed that Germany's impressive long-term export success is largely based on the strengths of medium-size companies. This insight led to my searching systematically for modest-size companies that occupy leading positions in their world markets. This perceptual framework offered a surprising result—over the years I unearthed more than five hundred candidates. Since there are no statistics for a hidden champion category, my collection is definitely not comprehensive, rather suggesting that many more must be ripe for discovery. Names came from many sources—newspaper and journal articles, seminars, individual conversations, and people who had read my articles on the subject. The deeper I looked into the phenomenon, the more it intrigued and fascinated me. Details of my first research project appeared in the *Harvard Business Review* (Simon 1992). In 1992, I started a much larger project, from which this book draws, as it also does from research of the past six years and my acquaintance with many of the hidden champions for which I have been consulting for a number of years.

To qualify as a hidden champion, a firm has to meet three criteria (see the following list and Exhibit 1.1):

- First, it must occupy the number one or number two position in its world market or the number one position in its European market. Ideally, market position is measured by market share, and almost all hidden champions are market leaders in those terms. But in the course of research, I also learned that firms do not always know their market share and that market leadership can go beyond the tallying of sales units. Some hidden champions that do not know their exact standing are nevertheless well aware that they are stronger than their competitors and among the leaders

Exhibit 1.1   **Criteria for a Hidden Champion**

- Number one or or two in a world market or number one in the European market in terms of market share; if market share is unknown, a company must be a leader relative to its strongest competitors
- Not more than $1 billion in sales revenue (except for a few; 4.4% of the sample companies exceed this limit)
- Low public visibility and awareness

in their markets. They play an active role in defining the rules of the game.

- Second, it must be small or medium in size and unfamiliar to the public. It should not generate more than approximately U.S. $1 billion in sales revenue, but a few larger companies that display the typical characteristics—for example, Würth—are included.
- Third, a hidden champion should have low public visibility. Thus, well-known companies—Porsche and Braun, for two—are excluded.

The definition of a number one or number two position in market share of course raises the problem of defining the market, a task left to the individual companies. It is discussed in detail in Chapter 3.

RESEARCH PROJECT AND DATA BASE

The research project and my sample focused on hidden champions in Germany. As the work progressed, my attention was drawn to similar companies in other countries, and I include qualitative insights gained from hidden champions in fourteen countries on all five continents. Believing that the lessons of the hidden champions are valid throughout the world, I elaborate on the non-German firms in Chapter 11.

Methodologically the project is based on the following five categories of data:

- Public information from magazine and newspaper articles, books, electronic media, and so forth.
- Printed company material such as annual reports, brochures, and catalogs.

- A mailed questionnaire survey.
- More than one hundred personal interviews, almost all conducted during scheduled visits to the companies. If the situation and the interviewee permitted, we tape-recorded and transcribed the sessions.
- Innumerable personal encounters with founders, CEOs, managers, and employees of the hidden champions in the context of consulting assignments, workshops, seminars, conferences, visits, and the like.

While a substantial portion of the information obtained, like sales revenue, number of employees, number of countries served, number of patents, and so on, consists of hard data, a larger segment contains soft and subjective data. The latter category includes data like the assessment of competitive advantages and customer requirements, information on employee motivation, and leadership. In quite a few cases, even the estimates on market size or market share are rather soft because they are not statistically supported. I wish to state clearly that I relied on the data provided by the champions themselves, because there is no realistic way to cross-check these data for hundreds of companies in dozens of countries. I had to believe that the respondents and those I interviewed told me the truth, which, as in all such studies, is of course subjective. However, I have no reason to assume that these people consciously deceived themselves or me in their assessments of markets, customers, and competitors. On the many occasions when I accidentally had the opportunity to talk to their customers or competitors, I found the self-assessments of the hidden champions strongly confirmed. My subjective impression is that they were biased toward being too modest rather than hyperbolic regarding their performance. In Chapter 11 I discuss how and why the lessons learned from them apply to firms all over the world.

In the quantitative analysis, I employed state-of-the-art methods of multivariate analysis to address measurement and causality problems. I refrain from going deeply into methodological issues, focusing instead on the managerially relevant findings of the research, since the primary audience is managers.

The comprehensive questionnaire, mailed to 457 companies, addressed all relevant aspects of competitive strategy. One hundred twenty-two questionnaires, usable for analytical purposes, were returned, a response rate of 26.7%. These and the interviews provide the main basis for the quantitative results. Of the sample companies, 78.6% reported being world market leaders or "one of the leaders," and 95.6% and 99.2% hold the leading positions in the European and German markets, respectively. The means of absolute and relative market shares in these three arenas are set forth in Table 1.1. The absolute market share is measured in percentage points and defined as company sales divided by total market sales. (All currency figures were converted at 1.50 deutsche marks to the U.S. dollar.) The relative market share is defined as a company's percentage share divided by the percentage share of its strongest competitor. A relative market share of 1.8 means that the company share is 80% higher than the share of its largest competitor. This is the case, for example, if the market leader has a 36% share and the second firm a 20% share. Only a market leader can have a relative share greater than one.

The means in Table 1.1 show that the hidden champions clearly dominate their markets. In the world market they have an average share of 30.2% and exceed the market share of their strongest competitor by 56%. In the smaller markets of Europe and Germany, the superiority is even more impressive.

Hidden champions can be found in almost all industries. In the sample, the largest industry is mechanical engineering and machinery, with 37%. The second largest segment is miscellaneous industries, including services, showing that smaller markets which do not have a specific slot in industry statistics are typical for hidden champions. Firms in the electrical/electronics sector comprise 11.8%, the metalworking industries, 10.1%. Chemistry, printing/paper, food, and textiles are other important branches.

Table 1.1   Mean Market Shares of the Hidden Champions

	Absolute Market Share	Share of Largest Competitor	Relative Market Share of Hidden Champion
World	30.2%	19.4%	1.56
Europe	36.7%	20.8%	1.76
Germany	44.4%	21.8%	2.04

The size of a typical hidden champion is reflected in median annual sales revenues of $130 million. Roughly one-third of the sample have revenues below $66 million, one-third between $66 million and $266 million, and one-third more than $266 million. The revenue of the smallest hidden champions is $3.33 million.

In spite of the recession, their 1989–1994 mean annual growth rate was 6.5%. In the boom years of the mid- to late-eighties it was 16%. Two-thirds of the respondents were satisfied or very satisfied with their growth-rate performance. Median hidden champions employ 735 people and, unlike large corporations, create many new jobs. In the late eighties, their numbers of employees increased rapidly, by 9% per year; even in the recession of the 1990s, their employment levels remained steady or increased slightly. Their products are primarily in the mature and growth stages of the life cycle, 67.3% and 28.2%, respectively, with only 2.7% and 1.8%, respectively, in the introductory and decline stages. This distribution points toward stable to moderate development.

The hidden champions are major exporters. On average, 51.4% of their sales revenue comes from direct exports. This figure does not include indirect exports, which involve the incorporation of one company's product in a finished product of another. Röhm, a maker of drill chucks, for one, engages in substantial direct exportation, but most of its products are shipped to foreign markets as components of the machines of others, for instance, Bosch and Black & Decker. The same holds true for Webasto sunroofs, which are exported in cars.

My sample hidden champions play an enormous role in Germany's trade position. Although small or medium in size, they contributed, on average, $66.5 million to Germany's exports in 1993. If we multiply this figure by all 500 hidden champions, they alone account for $33.3 billion of German exports, and these exports represent almost 200,000 well-paid jobs. While this calculation is somewhat speculative, it serves to illustrate the significance of such companies for a country's trade position and employment rate.

This insight has raised interest in hidden champions in many countries. For instance, Chris Schacht, the Australian minister of Science and Small Business, wrote in a March 24, 1994, letter: "Australian small and medium-size exporters tend not to have as strong an export presence as your hidden champions; nevertheless, many of the characteristics you have identified for export success also apply to Australia. Australian industry is now accepting this challenge and we are starting to see rises in Australian exports, particularly by small and medium-size enterprises."

The United States in particular could certainly improve its export performance by better developing and exploiting its hidden champion potential. Many of its small and medium-size companies have the internal strengths and resources to compete successfully in the world market. But with a huge domestic market, American companies of this size are not compelled or inclined to develop foreign markets for their products and services. They are bounded by their ignorance of these opportunities. Interestingly, some American corporations, detecting the promise of these German firms, have acquired or bought a stake in them. Thus, Tetra, the fish food marketer, is owned by Warner Lambert, and Glyco, a leading maker of glide bearings, is a unit of Federal Mogul, a large American automotive supplier.

Who owns the hidden champions? Of my sample companies, 76.5% are closely held, which usually means family owned; 21.1% belong to larger trusts, slightly more than half of them, like Tetra, parented by a foreign company. The remaining 2.4% are public. Of the total five hundred companies, about fifty—listed in Table 11.2—are publicly traded. The number of companies that go public has been increasing in the recent past. This trend is bound to continue, offering interesting investment opportunities. In 81.5% of the family-owned firms, a family member is part of the management team.

The age structure of the hidden champions deserves special attention. Their mean age of 67 is slightly misleading, since some companies are very old, driving up the arithmetic mean. The more significant median average is 47 years. The oldest firm was founded in 1753, and 7.6% of the hidden champions have been in existence more than 150 years. The age distribution has two maxima: a substantial group, representing 23.5% of the sample companies, was founded between 1845 and 1920; the largest group, 40.3%, came into being in the 1945–1969 growth period after World War II. About one-sixth are less than 25 years old. Their age distribution is shown in Figure 1.1.

The age structure is of particular interest because the sample contains both firms that have successfully survived several generations and others that are still in the first generation and have to prove that they can master the problem of succession, one of the biggest challenges they face.

Figure 1.1 **Age Structure of the Hidden Champions**

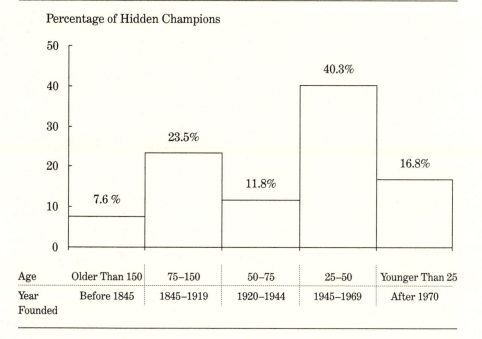

Percentage of Hidden Champions

Age	Older Than 150	75–150	50–75	25–50	Younger Than 25
Year Founded	Before 1845	1845–1919	1920–1944	1945–1969	After 1970

Table 1.2 summarizes the main characteristics of the sample hidden champions.

It is interesting to contrast these characteristics with those of the more spectacular success stories referred to at the beginning of this chapter. Compared with companies like Microsoft, Intel, Nintendo, Federal Express, and McCaw Cellular, the hidden champions

- grow more slowly;
- compete in more stable markets and depend less on fashion and boom cycles;
- have to grow by crossing borders from the very outset, since their market in any one country is small;
- may be longer lived;
- are family owned or closely held;
- remain relatively small or medium in size.

These traits contribute to a corporate culture that favors continuity, a steady rather than an explosive growth, and practices that are more down

Table 1.2 **Selected Statistical Characteristics of the Hidden Champions**

Revenues	$130 million
Growth	1989–1994 6.5% per annum
	1985–1989 16.2% per annum
Life Cycle Stage of Products	2.7% in introductory stage
	28.2% in growth stage
	67.3% in mature stage
	1.8% in decline stage
Number of Employees	735
Export Share	51.4%
Exports	$66.5 million
Ownership	76.5%, closely held/family owned
	21.1%, concern owned (of those, 59% foreign)
	2.4%, public
Age Structure	Mean: 67 years
	Median: 47 years

to earth than one might expect. Global leadership of this kind depends largely on vigilant attention to detail, incessant commitment to serving customers, and persistence.

ARE THE HIDDEN CHAMPIONS SUCCESSFUL?

This heading leads to a further question: What is success in business? Of course, as everyone knows, success depends on goals. If the goals are achieved or overachieved, a company is successful.

The most important and most challenging business goal is long-term survival, which even many huge corporations fail to achieve. Are the hidden champions successful survivors? The research doesn't strictly answer this question because survivors, as the sole representatives, are the only ones whose strategies I can analyze. The number of similar companies that fell by the wayside over the years is an unknown quantity, as is the answer to whether their operations differed from those that prospered. But the fact that 42.9% of the sample companies have been in business for more than 50 years, and 24.4% for more than 100 years, proves that many hidden champions have been successful in the perpetual Darwinian fight for survival of the fittest. This does not mean that they haven't occasionally experienced serious crises. The reverse is true. Most of the older companies include one or several life-threatening disasters in their history. But they usually emerged stronger; 69.6% rate their ability to survive as above average. Even most of the younger companies seem to be well prepared for their future competitive battles.

Comparing their long-term performance with that of large corporations, the hidden champions seem to be doing very well. Only two years after Peters and Waterman (1982) identified 43 excellent companies, *Business Week* uncovered at least 14 companies that were experiencing declining profits or facing more severe problems ("Who's Excellent Now?" 1984). From 1955 to 1980, 238 large companies disappeared from the Fortune 500 list, followed from 1985 to 1990 by 143 more. Of the top 100 German companies in 1960, only 38 made the 1990 list. Of the original Dow-Jones companies chosen in 1897, only one, General Electric, is still on the list. While it is impossible to draw a direct comparison between large corporations and hidden champions, since I do not have an earlier list of the latter, their long-term staying power seems at least as strong, if not stronger than that of large corporations.

The ability to flourish under tough conditions was also proved in the early-1990s recession. Like other companies, the hidden champions are not immune to the general business cycle. But overwhelmingly they fared well in the crisis; fully 68.1% believe that they coped with it better than their competitors did. The following headlines from 1992 to 1994 support this judgment:

- Märklin, world market leader in model railways: Märklin Customers Continue to Spend Money.
- Krones, 80% world market share in bottle labeling machines: Hardly Affected by Recession.
- CeWe, European market leader in photo services: Not Dependent on Business Downturn.
- Brückner, world-leading manufacturer of biaxial film stretching systems: A Winner in the Recession. Gained Advantage Due to Competitors' Mistakes.
- Stihl, world market leader in chain saws: Stihl Is Recession-Proof.

- Dürr, world market leader in paint-finishing systems: Almost All Industries Were Affected—Dürr Was Nevertheless Able to Maintain the Positive Trends of Previous Years.

- Prominent, world leader in metering pumps: In 35 Years We Never Had a Recession, Only Variations in Growth.

There is no doubt that companies like the hidden champions profit from tough conditions. In the sample, 76.2% report that they increased their market share in the five years from 1989 to 1994. This was evidently not achieved by complacency but through rigorous cost cutting, restructuring, and transplanting jobs from high-wage Germany to foreign locations, mainly the United States and Central and Eastern Europe. It is often contended that the recession has wrought havoc on German companies. Indeed, quite a few medium-size ones, particularly in the machine tool sector, for example, Deckel and Maho, have fallen victim to the recession, but they did not belong to the elite considered here. The crisis made the strong stronger and eliminated weaker competitors. It can definitely be concluded that the hidden champions are extremely successful survivors.

Market share is another criterion of success, particularly popular with Japanese corporations. The excellence of the sample companies in that regard is clear. If a company attains a world market share of 30, 50, or 70%, or a relative world market share of 1.5, 2, or 5, it must be doing something right and can assuredly be considered successful.

As to profitability, the success rate is good but less impressive. Only a small percentage of the hidden champions are public companies obliged to publish profit figures. Not surprisingly, only a small minority, 22.7% in the sample, were willing to reveal their return on investment (ROI). The mean ROI before taxes was 13.6%. If we assume a debt-to-equity ratio of 60:40, the figure is almost identical to the return on equity found in a McKinsey study of successful German companies (Rommel et al. 1995). While this profitability may not appear high relative to international standards, it compares very well with the average ROI of the large industrial companies in Germany. In the five-year period 1989–1993, their pretax ROI was about 2.6% (Institut der deutschen Wirtschaft 1994, 3). In a relative assessment reported by 99.1% of my respondents, 56% estimated their profitability as above or well above average. In conclusion, the hidden champions are clearly more profitable than an average company operating in the same environment, but their profitability may not be spectacular. Short-term profit does not seem to be their most important concern.

Are the hidden champions satisfied with their performance? The question "How satisfied are you overall with the success of your business activities in the last five years?" should be rated on a seven-point scale ranging from 1 (not at all satisfied) to 7 (fully satisfied). Figure 1.2 shows the distribution of the answers.

A clear majority, 63.9%, lies above the average, but only a few rate themselves at the highest level of satisfaction. The picture can be interpreted as a mixture of moderate pride and awareness that success is never guaranteed but has to be fought for.

The various indicators of success show that the hidden champions are successful organizations, but not as extraordinary in this regard as one might expect. I am highly skeptical of all publications that describe spectacular successes and recommend the underlying behavior as formulas for other companies. Such successes, rarely attributable to hard work and diligence alone, almost always involve a substantial element of luck. An entrepreneur has hit a fashion wave, a new, protected technology meets an expanding demand, or a currency exchange rate develops favorably. But such windfalls are usually short-lived. Once the recipes for success are broadly disseminated, they lose their value, because others

Figure 1.2 Hidden Champions' Overall Satisfaction with Success

Percentage of Hidden Champions

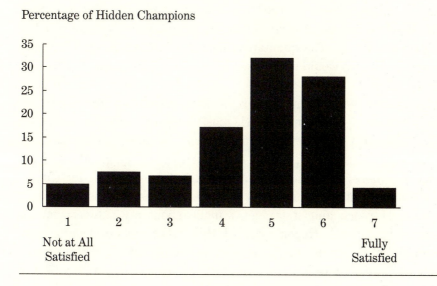

adopt and imitate them. The hidden champions do not offer us magic formulas for success. Most would certainly agree with the following statement of Ted Levitt (1988): "Sustained success is largely a matter of focusing regularly on the right things and making a lot of uncelebrated little improvements every day."

Certainly the majority of hidden champion leaders with whom I spoke subscribe to this philosophy. Time and again they said that their competitors are good, some even excellent, that they owe their success not to one specific factor but rather to the sum of their implementing many small moves slowly and consistently to improve their performance. They believe they are exposed to the same difficulties and challenges that every company faces and do not consider themselves extraordinary managers.

I would like to emphasize that in judging corporate excellence, one should remain, above all, realistic and sober. The hidden champions are not miracle firms; they are exposed to the same threats of competition, market turbulence, and management errors as other companies. And some of them will fail in the future.

These observations led me to refrain from the usual approach to research on success factors in which two samples of more and less successful companies are compared. Statistically significant differences are then interpreted as pointing to success factors. While this technique is scientific in spirit, I have learned very little from the dozens of such studies, most of whose findings are trivial. In my research, the problem is aggravated by the choice of a control group. With whom should the hidden champions be compared? The second best? Average companies? From the same industry? Considering all these aspects, I decided not to use a control group. The qualitative aspects of the research, which are the most revealing, would in any case have escaped comparison with such a group.

I have learned during my numerous visits to and assignments for the hidden champions that some of their most essential characteristics, such as the personality of the leader and the corporate culture, let alone their level of sophistication, can hardly be defined by purely quantitative approaches. I therefore consciously take the liberty of injecting my subjective evaluation into the discussion of some of these aspects. Not every conclusion I reach and statement I make about my subjects can be scientifically verified. Nevertheless, I think that my observations are essentially true. But it should be kept in mind that often there is no simple black and white truth. I assure the readers that I did my best to understand the hidden champions and to convey what they do and how they do it.

I would like to warn my audience not to interpret the subsequent findings as simplistic recipes for success. Instead, readers should critically evaluate which lessons and comments apply to their particular situation and which do not. Take everything with a grain of salt and remain skeptical!

WHO CAN LEARN FROM THE HIDDEN CHAMPIONS?

This book is targeted primarily at practitioners and managers of both small and large companies. Academics and researchers may also gain new insights. Many of my findings run counter to current accepted management teaching.

Each firm should be ready to learn from other successful companies. In the past, this type of instruction seems to have been a one-way street running from large to small companies, a route I wish to reverse. As readers will gather from subsequent chapters, large companies can learn a great deal from the hidden champions. In many seminars with sizable companies, I have discovered that the lessons of the hidden champions stimulated self-reflection, stirred discussion, and led to concrete action. In *Built to Last*, Collins and Porras (1994) call the large firms they investigate visionary companies and the best of the best. I think these authors would have been more circumspect in applying this superlative had they been aware of the hidden champions.

While many of the two groups' qualities are remarkably similar, the hidden champions are superior in most of them. Take continuity as measured by CEO tenure. At seventeen years, the visionary companies are excellent in this regard, but the hidden champions older than fifty years outdo them with twenty-four years' average tenure. Compared with the typical large firm, the hidden champions are much more effective and efficient. Adopting only some of their practices could translate into a huge improvement for large companies. Applying the lessons to large firms, however, requires radical changes in organization, corporate culture, and leadership. To illustrate this, I compare attributes of the hidden champions with those of large corporations. These contrasts suggest envisioning the big company of the future either as a highly focused big champion, say, Boeing, or as a group of hidden champions. I discuss these aspects more thoroughly in Chapter 11.

Smaller and less successful firms can also learn from comparing their strategies with those of the hidden champions to determine where the differences lie. They undoubtedly involve such essential elements of hidden champion strategy as goal setting, focus, and concentration. Chapter 11 provides a checklist for a hidden champion audit.

Perhaps non-German companies can profit most. While the management styles and strategies of American and some Japanese firms are well known internationally, Germany has remained an enigma in spite of its enormous successes in exports and international competition, of which few people outside the country are aware. As will become apparent, the hidden champion strategy, based on a few simple principles applied with common sense and immune to the latest in management fashions, may lead back to the core of good management. In Chapter 11, I also discuss implications for companies throughout the world.

SUMMARY

This chapter has shown that beyond the obvious success stories of large corporations widely recognized in the business world and reported in the business press, a different kind of success is hidden under a layer of inconspicuousness and secrecy. Among the least known are some of the best companies in the world, the hidden champions.

- They are small and medium in size;
- dominate their markets worldwide, often with market shares of more than 50%;
- often trade in "invisible" or low-profile products;
- have a remarkable record of survival;
- earn a large part of their revenue from exports, enabling them to contribute heavily to a country's trade balance;
- are truly global competitors;
- are largely family owned; and
- are successful but not miracle companies.

The policies and practices of the hidden champions contain potential for emulation by firms both large and small, regardless of industry and nationality.

2
The Goal

Our goal is to become number one.

T HE PRIMARY GOAL of the hidden champions is market leadership—nothing else. But what is market leadership? How do hidden champions view this concept? How do they attain and defend their leading position? What role do goals and visions play toward their success and how are they implemented? These are some of the questions I address in this chapter.

MARKET LEADERSHIP

Interest in market leadership has been increasing rapidly in the recent past (see, e.g., Biallo 1993, Adamer and Kaindl 1994, Treacy and Wiersema 1995). Market leadership is usually defined in terms of market share, and the company with the largest share is market leader. As previously noted, the hidden champions are definitely leaders in this sense. They have an average world market share of 30.2% and a relative world market share of 1.56; that is, in quantitative terms they are 56% larger than their strongest competitors. Indeed, one-quarter surpass their largest competing firm by more than 150% and have a relative market share greater than 2.5.

Table 2.1 lists the world market positions of selected hidden champions. It provides for each company its primary product, sales revenue, number

Table 2.1 **World Market Positions of Selected Hidden Champions**

Company	Primary Product	Sales in Millions of U.S. $	Employees	World Market Position		
				Rank	Absolute Share in Percentage	Relative Share
Aesculap	Surgical instruments	350	4,500	1–2	15	1.5
Hensoldt & Söhne	Binoculars and telescopic sights	60	957	1	>50	2.5
Brähler	Rental of conference/ translation systems	45	390	1–2	30	1
Hille & Müller	Cold rolled steel stripes	330	1,500	1	>50	2
Matth. Hohner	Mouth organs and accordions	127	1,050	1	85	42.5
Carl Jäger	Incense cones, incense sticks	3	10	1	70	2.3
Arnold & Richter	35mm film cameras	130	700	1	60	3

Company	Description					
Deutsche Messe	Organization of trade fairs for capital goods	267	600	1	12.5	2
Ex-Cell-O	Track-mining and grinding machines for constant velocity universal joints	300	1,300	1	70	3.5
Söring	Ultrasonic dissectors	3	20	1	36	1.2
Physik Instrumente	Piezoelectric actuators	66	440	1	50	3.3
Grenzebach	Computer-controlled cutting, handling, and stacking lines for the production of float glass	67	450	1	50	5
Märklin	Model railways	147	1,700	1	55	3
SAP	Standard client/server applications	1,800	5,000	1	40	1.5
ASB Grünland	Potting soil	191	465	1	40	4
Carl Walther	Sports guns	17	200	1	50	2

of employees, market rank, absolute market share in percentage, and relative market share, namely its own share divided by the share of its largest competitor. The table illustrates that in market share terms these companies lead the pack and are mostly well ahead of their competitors.

Market leadership is not necessarily synonymous with largest market share. Asked why they consider themselves market leaders, the hidden champions replied as follows. (Multiple answers were permitted, making the sum of the percentages greater than 100.) Sales revenue and unit sales, with 72.6% and 46.6%, respectively, are seen as the two most important criteria of market leadership; 36.2% think that their market leadership is also defined by technology; 6.9% believe they are product-line leaders, and 14.7% think that some other qualitative criterion, such as quality, service, worldwide presence, defines their leadership (see Table 2.2). Our interviews clearly support the finding that for the hidden champions, market leadership transcends the quantitative dimension of market share. Leadership in a market includes aspects like superiority in innovation, technology, core competencies, trend setting, influence on the market, and power. True market leadership means more than having the largest market share.

The hidden champions consider market leadership as a long-term rather than short-term concept. On average (median) they have been market leaders for ten and a half years, with roughly one-quarter having held their position for more than twenty-five years. Glyco is almost one hundred years old, and Horst Müller, its CEO, says that technological leadership has always been its strength. Scheuerle, founded in 1869, has been the leader in heavy transport technology (up to 10,000 tons) since its inception.

Table 2.2 **Hidden Champions' Criteria of Market Leadership**

What Makes a Company a Market Leader?	
Largest in Sales Revenue	72.6%
Largest in Sales Units	46.6%
Technological Leader	36.2%
Product Line Leader	6.9%
Other Criteria (e.g., quality, service, worldwide presence)	14.7%

Past leadership is the foundation for current and future strength. The responses to the question "How dominant are you as a market leader?"— on a scale ranging from 1 (not at all dominant) to 7 (very dominant)—are shown in Figure 2.1.

Almost three-quarters, 74.4%, perceive their dominance above the average score of 4; only 13.7% fall below 4. Consistent with this picture is their evaluation of their influence on future developments in their markets: 66.4% think it will be strong or very strong, with only 16.4% rating it below average. The dominance and influence patterns from the quantitative survey were confirmed by and reflected in our interviews. These observations led me to suggest the concept of psychological market leadership, which is meant to include such parameters of a leading role as technology, market coverage, and quality. The interviewees adopted this concept enthusiastically and considered it much more meaningful than simple market share leadership.

Dr. Hans-Michael Müller of Eppendorf-Netheler-Hinz, world leader in pipettes, said, "I like the term 'psychological market leader.' That is what we are. Nobody can ignore us. When it comes to comparisons we are always a benchmark. We set the standards, definitely. Competitors say,

Figure 2.1   **Hidden Champions' Perception of Dominance as Market Leader**

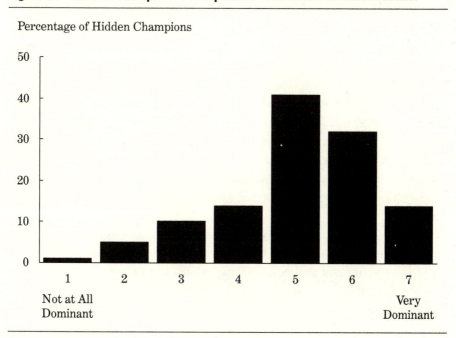

Percentage of Hidden Champions

'We are as good as Eppendorf.'" E. C. H. Will, whose machines are used to produce half of all the school exercise books in the world, stated: "Our business is not to copy the state of the art but to initiate it. We have set the trade standard." Alfred K. Klein, chief executive officer of Stabilus, the world market leader in gas-pressurized springs, thinks in terms of psychological market leadership:

> After a while, we find our ideas reflected in the products and habits of the industry. We once changed the technical sign for "force" from p to f. Shortly thereafter, the whole world switched from p to f. We even see some of our past mistakes repeated in our competitors' behavior. Isn't that psychological leadership?

And Günter Fielmann, founder and CEO of the largest retailer of eyeglasses in Europe and number two in the world, added,

> We have taken the lead and totally redefined the rules in our industry. Our market share is unmatched in the Western world. But long before we became the largest in sales, we were the psychological market leader. Psychological leadership is the cause and market share leadership is the effect.

In *Competing for the Future*, Hamel and Prahalad (1994, 47) speak of "intellectual leadership" as the first of three phases of future competition. The concept sounds similar, but "psychological market leadership" is explicitly meant to include power and will, not only intellectual elements. It is clearly associated with the claim to leadership, resulting in a combination of intellectual and "implementation" leadership.

The hidden champions excel not only in building market share but also in defending their leading market positions. Behind the directly observable success in market share lies the more profound psychological leadership that lays claim to setting standards in an industry, to defining and redefining the rules. It is built on both superior competencies and the will to determine rather than accept market trends. Psychological market leadership often precedes market share leadership, the former causing the latter.

Market leaders, particularly large corporations in large markets, seem prone to cement the rules of the game to retain their position. This attitude induces inertia and complacency and ultimately results in the loss of a leading position. Foster (1986) calls this phenomenon the leaders-lose-syndrome. The market-leading hidden champions seem less likely than market-leading large corporations to fall victim to this syndrome. The long-term retention of their leadership positions provides evidence that they remain flexible and cautious enough never to feel comfortable in their role. They continue to innovate and to redefine the rules in their industry.

THE ROLE OF MARKET LEADERSHIP

The evidence that the market leader fares better than the average competitor is so overwhelming that the issue requires no detailed elaboration. The profit impact of market strategy (PIMS) findings provide the most conclusive support that higher market share, whether in rank or in absolute or relative share, is related to higher return on investment (ROI). Figure 2.2 depicts the well-known findings of Buzzell and Gale (1987) for market share percentage and rank.

The PIMS findings, which have been contested (see, e.g., Jacobson and Aaker 1985), are probably not a fully valid measurement of the degree of causality between market share and ROI. Nevertheless, it is beyond doubt that market share tends to have a positive causal effect on profitability. Market leaders typically enjoy both cost advantages—economies of scale and experience curve effects—and marketing advantages. The simple fact that a firm is a market leader signals trust and confidence to customers. The leader has the ability to set or influence standards,

Figure 2.2 **The ROI Advantage of Market Leadership According to PIMS**

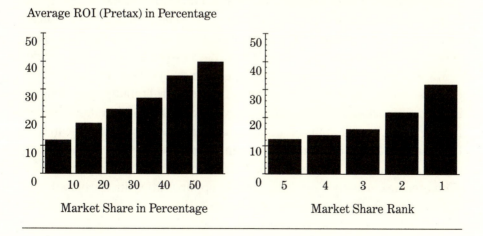

Average ROI (Pretax) in Percentage

Market Share in Percentage

Market Share Rank

better utilize sales and service organizations, and command a goodwill advantage.

Slogans that emphasize market leadership serve as strong advertising messages. Boeing introduced its 767 model with the slogan "Fly the leader." A message like "Hearne Brothers manufacture and sell more than all their competitors put together . . . There must be a reason" contains an extremely strong connotation of superiority. Similarly, many hidden champions employ their leading position in marketing communications.

In my sample, however, the PIMS findings on the correlation between market share and ROI were not confirmed. I couldn't find a significant correlation between these two variables. This is not too astonishing since all these firms have high absolute or relative market shares, most of them in the highest market share or rank category considered in the PIMS sample. I found, however, that the change in market share showed a highly significant correlation with the ROI. The 67.4% of companies that increased their market share in the last five years achieved an average pretax ROI of 16%. On the other hand, the 19.6% that lost market share in the same period had an average ROI of only 3%. Thus market share changes in this sample had a very strong positive effect on profitability. Figure 2.3 illustrates this finding.

It is also interesting to note how much the market shares changed. The winners gained eight percentage points and the losers lost ten percentage points. Contrary to prevalent opinion, my finding suggests that building a market position may be less costly than defending one. I attribute this to psychological market leadership. Market share gains follow superior performance in innovation, technology, quality, and similar factors. The successful hidden champions were almost always clear psychological leaders operating in an active, aggressive, and optimistic mode.

Market share defense, on the other hand, typically requires price concessions that directly and negatively affect profitability. The defense is often supported by an increase in advertising and sales budgets, which further erodes profitability. The drive to increase market share can also be related to the discussion on core competencies and renewed focus (see, e.g., Prahalad and Hamel 1990). Concentrating on a company's core competencies usually restricts growth opportunities in unrelated and diversified noncore businesses. A company that wants to keep growing

Figure 2.3 **The ROI of Market Share Winners and Losers**

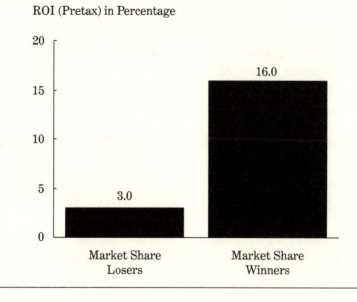

ROI (Pretax) in Percentage

under these circumstances has to grow in its core markets, which is equivalent to striving for higher market share and an ever stronger market leader position.

Focusing on core competencies and the pronounced striving for market leadership, essentially two sides of the same coin, have become popular for large and small companies. Among large firms, Jack Welch of General Electric (see Slater 1993) is the paragon of this strategy. He wants all GE divisions to strive for the number one or number two position in their world markets. United Airlines announced that it wants to become global market leader; Lufthansa sets a goal of becoming number one in Europe. Gillette, according to its former CEO Alfred M. Zeien will "only introduce products for which we are or can become the worldwide leader" ("Gillette hat ehrgeizige Ziele und eigenwillige Grundsätze" 1994, 3). Braun AG, a Gillette subsidiary, seems to be the firm's vanguard in implementing this goal, since it holds world leadership positions in almost all its small appliances. A company brochure declares that Motorola is "striving for a worldwide leadership position." Schering announces that it "wants to dominate specialty markets worldwide" ("Schering will weltweit Spezialmärkte beherrschen" 1994). And since mid-1994 my company has experienced a strong increase in consulting assignments to develop strategies for market leadership and dominance.

This trend may be new to many Western corporations, but there are two kinds of companies to which this sounds very familiar, the first being Japanese. Professor Horst Albach of Humboldt University in Berlin carried out an extensive study on innovation in Germany, the United States, and Japan (Albach 1994). With regard to global market leadership he reports from Japan: "We have not found a single company that was not committed to the goal of becoming number one in the world in its market." He adds, "We have not found a single Japanese company—large or small—that did not know all its international competitors higher in the rank of competitiveness in the global markets" (21). These words send a clear message!

The second category of companies for which the goal of world market leadership is an old story is that of the hidden champions.

THE GOAL

How do you become a market leader? First and foremost by wanting the position, by determining the goal, by having the will to attain the number one spot. For most of the hidden champions the goal of becoming market leader—ideally, world market leader—marks just the beginning, the very foundation of their success. Their market positions have not been reached without a clear goal, a long-term vision, an extremely strong determination, and the will to pursue this goal over decades.

An unnamed world leader in several subfields of special chemistry, an ideal type of hidden champion, states: "The entrepreneurial goal is the worldwide technology and market leadership in profitable niches of special chemistry." And Winterhalter Gastronom, world leader in hotel and restaurant dishwashers, is hardly less specific and ambitious: "Our goal is the absolute market leadership in our precisely defined market throughout Europe and Asia." From Villeroy & Boch: "We have never been after quick successes, but after long-term results. We always wanted to belong to the biggest companies in our market, ideally to be the biggest." The 150-year-old company is the world market leader in tiles and also one of the world's three largest manufacturers of ceramic dishes. Dräger, world leader in incubators, has as one of four company principles: "Top Position: We want to stay ahead! We have always striven for and occupied the top position in our market. This applies both to technology and market leadership." The governing principle of Braun, the affiliate of Gillette, is world market leadership. It has declared that it wants to be first in all its divisions, not only those for which it already holds the distinction, clearly outdistancing its competitors in electric toothbrushes, hand blenders, and hair care appliances. It is fighting for number one in electric shavers against Philips and in coffee machines against Mr. Coffee. Its strengths in design, technology, and market presence make Braun the likely eventual winner.

These are marked statements, but not isolated observations. The journalist Horst Biallo (1993, 17) writes about Jörg Siebert, the CEO of DGF Stoess AG, the world market leader in gelatin: "Although he officially denies it, Siebert wants nothing less than world dominance in the gelatin market." By the way, Siebert was a gold medal winner at the 1968 Olympics in Mexico, in rowing, certainly a discipline that demands the same stamina necessary to conquering a world market. And in an interview Fritz Mayer, one of three sons of the founder Karl Mayer, the world market leader in rashel machines (machines used for the production of silk), said: "Our motto is to sell our machines in all parts of the world at the most acceptable price possible and to beat any competition occurring in our niche markets" ("Geht Karl Mayer nun auch den Weg nach China?" 1993).

The clarity and firmness of these stated goals leave no room for ambiguity and doubt. Viktor Dulger, the founder of Prominent Dosiertechnik, world market leader in metering pumps, even linked the name of his firm to his goal of being number one: "At the beginning, I set the goal to surpass all the *prominent* manufacturers of pumps with my invention. That's why I named my pump Prominent!" (Hoffmann 1995, 16). The following, elicited from interviews, are various hidden champions' statements of the goal to become number one.

- From the very beginning, the declared goal was to become the international leader.

- When I had two employees I wanted to become number one in the world. Now I have thousands of employees and we are number one.

- We strive to be supplier to the global top thirty customers.

- The identity of our company is defined by our leading position in the world market.

- We want to be big in small markets.

- Defending the leading position in our area of competence—one of three company goals.

- I want my company still to be market leader in a hundred years. We made this market, and we want to dominate it now and in the future.

- Our boss sees us as the world market leader, so we have no choice but to become the world market leader.

The wording of some of these goals may sound a bit too strong and overstated. Of course I cannot guarantee that some may have been coined after the fact or in the process. But having talked to so many of these firms' CEOs and employees, I know that most are deadly serious about these goals. Maybe the goal was being pursued before it was explicitly verbalized. Behavior is what counts.

Consciously or intuitively, these people have grasped the extreme importance of goals and visions. They often reminded me of the Spanish philosopher José Ortega y Gasset, who defines man as "a being that consists not so much in what it is as in what it is going to be" (Ortega y Gasset 1960). These leaders, who control the present from the future, would probably subscribe to the following observation from this work: "Man is not where he stands now but he is ahead of himself, far ahead at the horizon of his self, and from there he controls and leads the actual, the current life. We live from our illusions, as if they were already reality." The goals and visions of the hidden champion leaders may frequently look like illusions but in the course of time the thoughts, visions, words, and mental images turn into reality because they are supported by deeds.

Peter Drucker (1988, 76) defines the critical role of such goals and visions succinctly:

Every enterprise requires simple, clear, and unifying objectives. Its mission has to be clear enough and big enough to provide a common vision. The goals that embody it have to be clear, public, and often reaffirmed. We hear a great deal of talk these days about the culture of an organization. But what we really mean by this is the commitment throughout an enterprise to some common objectives and common values. Without such commitment there is no enterprise, there is only a mob. Management's job is to think through, set, and exemplify those objectives, values, and goals.

Many hidden champions are exemplary in setting goals and visions and planning their long-term strategies. In 1979, Würth, the world market leader in assembly products, had a turnover of $286 million. At that time, Reinhold Würth, then its CEO, set a new sales goal of $667 million for 1986 and $1.33 billion for 1990. Würth comments: "It is amazing how quickly such goals develop a life of their own and become part of the corporate culture. The employees identify with these forecasts and do everything to realize them." In 1989, when the $1.33 billion turnover goal was achieved, Würth didn't hesitate to set a new goal, $7 billion for the year 2000. With well over $2.67 billion in 1995, the company is on target. Again Würth evaluates the new goal:

> This new vision was accepted by the employees in a very short time. Nobody any longer thinks twice about this enormously high figure and nobody has problems adjusting his activities to it. I do not exaggerate the fact that this new vision created an almost magnetic attraction.

Klaus Hendrikson, general manager of Würth do Brazil, comments: "This is no longer a vision. It is a clear attainable goal. The optimistic view that we can attain this turnover is based on sober analyses." The last aspect is critical. Würth concedes that you cannot just throw such a vision into the discussion.

> You must be able to substantiate it. You have to check all the limitations and your resources, the market, financing, human resources, managerial capacity, and so forth. Only after you have done your homework very carefully should you announce such ambitious visions and goals. But if the foundation is solid, the vision will take care of itself.

A second example is Kärcher, world market leader in high pressure cleaners. After the death of the founder in the mid-1970s, a young man, Roland Kamm, came into management. In 1978, when the company had a turnover of about $20 million, Kamm wrote his goals in "Report 1995," in which he envisioned sales of $667 million for 1995. "Report 1995" contained explicit strategies for new products, including a section titled "yet unknown," and international expansion. In 1993, Kärcher reported worldwide sales of $691 million. In the meantime new explicit goals have been set for the next decade, and they are hardly less audacious. After having met Kärcher's international management team, I have no doubt that they will be achieved. I have never seen a long-term vision carried out as meticulously as that of Kärcher.

In the mid-1970s, Webasto had about the same sales revenue as Kärcher. Werner Baier, who became CEO at that time, considered this a good starting position for world market leadership in sunroofs for cars. "This was the groundwork on which we built our long-term vision of world market leadership," he says. Webasto, now with $1 billion in sales, is world market leader in sunroofs and auxiliary heating systems. Its new management team, with Dr. Rudi Noppen as CEO and Franz-Josef Kortüm, has set similarly ambitious goals for the next decade.

Many hidden champion chiefs and employees are forward looking. Winterhalter Gastronom, world market leader in hotel and restaurant dishwashing systems, has an explicit company principle: "We devote a substantial part of our time to the future." At the end of interviews I usually asked: "Where do you see your company ten years from now?" Most of the answers were spontaneous and clear. Their future goals seem to be as definite as their past goals were for the present.

This may sound as if all hidden champions apply the planned strategy approach as defined by Mintzberg and Waters (1985, 270), where

> planning suggests clear and articulated intentions backed up by formal control to ensure their pursuit, in an environment that is acquiescent. In other words, this is where the classic distinction between "formulation and implementation" holds up. Leaders formulate their precise intentions and strive for implementation with a minimum of distortion, surprise free.

While the strategies of Würth, Kärcher, and Webasto resemble this planned pattern, the implementation of all three was certainly not free of distortion and surprise.

The goal and vision of typical hidden champions are clear, but they rarely elaborate. They are qualitative rather than quantitative. This seems different from the typical approach of large corporations in which a great deal of attention is given to details, precise numbers, and analytical foundation.

A second difference between large and small companies lies in the unity of planning and implementation. In hidden champion firms, the same person is usually both planner and implementor. He is unlikely to fool himself with pseudoprecise numbers or shaky long-term forecasts.

If plans don't materialize as anticipated, he is willing to adjust the strategy. This approach, which Mintzberg and Waters call "emerging strategy," is quite prevalent among the hidden champions. Mintzberg and Waters describe this approach as "a pattern in a stream of decisions." Emerging strategy "evolves through a process whereby the results of many individual actions come together to form a consistent pattern" (1985, 257).

Emerging strategy does not imply that the overall goals are less clear than in planned strategy. Although the goal of becoming market leader can be equally clear and explicit in both approaches, the market may be less well defined or more dynamic, alternative ways may lead to the leadership position, and the problem of procuring resources may still have to be solved.

A typical example of emerging strategy among the sample firms is JK Ergoline, the world market leader in "sunbeds" purchased by suntanning studios. The market for suntanning services is volatile, depending on tastes and changing fashions, and thus difficult to predict. To my question as to where he sees the company in ten years, CEO Josef Kratz responded:

> That is difficult to say in such a volatile market. But I can assure you of one thing. Wherever the opportunities lie, we shall be fast enough and flexible enough to grasp them. And we will strive for market leadership, there's no question about that. We have proven our flexibility. Saunas were our first product, and we had a leading position there. But the barriers to entry in this market were low and everybody could participate. Therefore we gave up on saunas and entered the market for professional sunbeds determined to become number one in the world. That was our goal, and here we are.

Kurt Held, whose company is the world's second largest manufacturer of double-belt presses, is a further example of emerging strategy. Held, located in the Black Forest, started out as a supplier of mechanical components to local watchmakers. Discerning the decline of the watch industry early on, Held, seeking new opportunities, invented a new process for double-belt pressing in 1974. This discovery led him into completely new markets. "Today I am not dependent on a specific type of customer but I continuously search for new applications of my technology. This leads my company into ever new directions," Held says.

A third type of strategy is entrepreneurial. Mintzberg and Waters describe it as follows:

> One individual in control of an organization is able to impose his vision of direction on the company. Those strategies most often appear in young or small organizations. The vision only provides a general sense of direction. There is room for adaptation. Since here the formulator is the implementor, step by step, that person can react quickly to feedback on past actions or to new opportunities or threats in the environment. It is the adaptability that distinguishes the entrepreneurial strategy from the planned one. It provides flexibility at the expense of the specificity and articulation of intentions.

This strategy is not typical for the hidden champions. A company does not become a world market leader by changing directions frequently. However, exceptions are to be found in some very young companies in our sample. They often create new markets, search for better understanding of customer needs, take advantage of opportunities, and have to remain flexible until they find their long-term goal and direction. Then they typically stop wavering and head single-mindedly in the direction of their goal.

Clean Concept is an example. Based on the perception that hygiene is a serious problem in public rest rooms (e.g., more people die from infections in sanitary installations in hospitals than from traffic accidents), Clean Concept developed a totally new toilet system, Cleanomat. But then the company recognized that developing such a system was not enough. Annett Kurz, spokeswoman for Clean Concept, explains: "The Cleanomat was great, but insufficient for new hygienic standards. Our goal was to find a totally new solution to a common quality of life problem—to assure that users of public rest rooms are provided with completely touch-free equipment."

Then Clean Concept had to extend the concept to make it feasible for people with handicaps. The company developed a clean-help program that it presented at the Rehabilitation Fair 1993 but subsequently realized that the product was not enough. It started to provide the service and such nondurables as liquid soap, cleansers, and paper and founded Clean Out, a subsidiary that provides those services. All rest rooms in a building can be reached by remote control, with everything programmed into a computer network. Sensors in each restroom measure certain parameters of hygiene and report them back to a central control unit.

This comprehensive solution emerged over the past six years. In the meantime, Clean Concept has acquired some prestigious customers. Its products are found in the Casino Monte Carlo, in the Majestic, the largest hotel in Cannes, and in the KLM building at Schiphol Airport in Amsterdam. They are also being tested in seventeen highway rest stops in Germany. Clean Concept is convinced that this idea will mark the beginning of a new hygienic culture on the brink of the next century because everyone in the world hates unhygienic toilets. But it will take time to develop this market, since a cultural change has to take place. Clean Concept, with a clear mission, has remained entrepreneurial and flexible enough to adjust to circumstances.

Interface is a second case of entrepreneurial strategy. Rainer Wieshoff is one of many personal computer entrepreneurs, but he has a very special product. After studying computer science, he worked three years for IBM in Germany. In 1983, he successfully started his own computer company, Interface, with standard applications. By 1989, when this market experienced increasing competitive pressure, he began to differentiate his product line. In a collaboration project with the University of Frankfurt, he determined that computer security was becoming increasingly important, but not easily affordable. Wieshoff recounts: "At that time, people were looking for a software security solution at around $133 per PC, but nobody could deliver one at this price. Suddenly, I had the inspiration to secure a personal computer with an affordable hardware solution, simply by locking the floppy disk drive." At the beginning, he produced 1,000 disk locks, which represented a large financial risk for the small firm. Today, Wieshoff sells 40,000 of his Floppy Lox every year and is a world leader in personal computer security.

Pursuit of the Goal

The substance and clarity of the goal to become world market leader are one side, the implementation of the goal the other. In pursuing their goals, the hidden champions are extremely persistent. They pursue their targets over decades and rarely ever lose sight of them. A motto of Ted Turner, the founder of CNN, describes this attitude adequately: "Never get discouraged and never quit. Because if you never quit you are never beaten" (Landrum 1993, 213). Michelangelo, the famous sixteenth-century Italian artist, said: "Genius is eternal patience." Patience and persistence can flourish only under long-term orientation. The short-term profit pressures typically faced by large public corporations would render many of the strategies and goals pursued by the sample companies unfeasible. Public companies often lack patience, but patience is the parent of long-term success.

The following example of a manufacturer of consumer nondurables illustrates such patience and persistence. The CEO, who prefers to remain anonymous, explains his long-term advertising strategy:

> Advertising is important in our business. We start to advertise many years before our products actually enter a market. I have done this since 1969 and everybody thinks I am mad. But I know how long it takes to build up awareness. And we want to be in a market mentally and image-wise before we appear physically. We have been extremely successful; we have climbed from seventh to second place in our market. Today we are seen as the paragon of patience and continuity in our industry.

Würth and Kärcher, described earlier in this chapter, further illustrate perseverance in pursuing goals over decades. Or think of SAP, the world leader in client-server applications, founded in 1972. In 1995, Hasso Plattner, vice chairman and cofounder, says, "We had a vision and we stuck to it." In these companies, success resulted not only from the clarity of the goals but equally important was the incessant drive to take them seriously and to turn them into reality. The realization of the goal hardly ever comes smoothly but these companies never lost sight of it, and the energy to pursue it never burned out.

High continuity in leadership usually underlies such patience and perseverance. As detailed in Chapter 10, the leaders of the hidden champions remain at the helm of their companies for decades. Dr. Werner Pankoke, CEO of Hymmen, world leader in continuous pressing and heating systems, comments on the effect of such continuity: "This company is 102 years old and I am the fourth CEO. You can imagine that we are patient and focus on the long term." Most hidden champion CEOs would agree with him.

Communication of the Goal

An important aspect of the implementation is communication of the goal and the vision. Better than almost any other objective, the goal to become leader or number one is ideally suited to communication. Almost everyone identifies with the goal to be the best, and number one is a simple, easy-to-understand concept. Simplicity of the goal is a prerequisite for effective communication. Dr. Wigand Grosse-Oetringhaus of Siemens comments in a letter:

> Whether to use the simplified number one formula for goal-setting is more than a semantic question. I believe that the number one formula has an extremely strong communicative power. Often the communication of goals is ineffective. Simplicity and clarity are so important for the effective communication of goals that I prefer the number one formula over more differentiated formulations.

Whether a goal is written or not is less important than whether it is lived. Though many hidden champions have no written formulations, each employee knows where the ship is heading because the goal is continually communicated and lived. Some chiefs are masters in using the power of metaphors. One always speaks of his company as a tree to instill the goal of growing in his employees. He says: "Our company is like a tree. A tree which grows is healthy. The day a tree stops growing it starts dying. Therefore we have to grow." Nobody in this firm wants to be part of a dying tree.

In the early years of his company, which is the leading European retailer of eyeglasses, Günter Fielmann used the metaphor of Robin Hood. He portrayed himself as the guy who fought for the people and brought them high-fashion eyeglasses at low prices. "I have been fighting against the discrimination of millions of people. I want to change society through my company. This can be achieved only if we are the market leader," he says. Metaphors such as Robin Hood are popular with the media and consumers. Many hidden champion leaders have taken advantage of such pictures, examples, and metaphors to communicate their goals effectively.

Quite a few use their exceptional market position and unique products and technologies for fairly spectacular publicity. Often, only a leader is in a position to recognize the existence of newsworthy accomplishments, which receive media attention that develops into cost-free advertising. Such spectacular actions signal to employees, customers, and the public at large that a company is number one in the most prestigious or demanding applications. Table 2.3 provides several examples.

Whether these communications are addressed to a specific clientele or the public at large depends on the products. They are definitely perceived by and have an effect on relevant customers. Their motivational effect

Table 2.3 **Accomplishments That Signal Market Leadership**

Company	Primary Product	Newsworthy Accomplishment
Glasbau Hahn	Glass showcases for museums	Installed in all famous museums in the world
Sport-Berg	Discuses, hammers, for athletes	Supplies Olympic Games, World Championships, and so forth
Gerriets	Neutral lighting cloths for stages	For Metropolitan Opera, New York; Opéra Bastille, Paris; opera houses in Istanbul, Taipeh, Wang Center, Boston, for example
Kärcher	High-pressure cleaners	Spectacular cleaning services for Christus statue, Rio de Janeiro, Statue of Liberty, New York, Alaskan coast after *Exxon Valdez* oil spill
Von Ehren	Large living trees	Trafalgar Square, London, National Gallery, Washington, D.C., Euro-Disneyland, France, Munich Airport, Kurfürstendamm, Berlin
Röder	Rental of tent systems	Olympic Games, World Expos
Louis Renner	Premium piano mechanics	Steinway & Sons, Schimmel, Bechstein, Grotian-Steinweg, Sauter, and others
Wige Group	Time measurement for major sports events all over the world	Olympic Games at Barcelona, Formula One Races
Trasco	Secured sedans	Cars for Frank Sinatra and Pope John Paul II "on tour," as well as for numerous governments—even six for the People's Republic of China
Germina	Cross-country skis	Four gold and five silver medals won on Germina Skis at Olympic Winter Games, Albertville, France
Biotest	Hygiene test devices	Test devices used in many manned spaceships

Table 2.3   *continued*

Company	Primary Product	Newsworthy Accomplishment
Sachtler	Camera tripods	In 1992 the Motion Picture Academy awarded Sachtler's chief designer a technical Oscar for his patented invention
Brähler	Rental of conference/ translation systems	Supplier to the White House and the Kremlin at press conferences; equipped United Nations Summit on Environment and Development in Rio de Janeiro, G7 Summit in Munich, the World Bank, and the International Monetary Fund
Putzmeister	Concrete pumps	Many "world records" in pumping concrete: distance (1,600 m), height (530 m), pressure (170 bar). Participated in spectacular projects like covering the Chernobyl reactor with concrete, building the Eurotunnel, and building Storebelt Bridge in Scandinavia

on employees can be enormous. For all groups, these spectacular accomplishments function as effective signals of world market leadership, instilling in employees pride in and identification with their company. Such opportunities are open only to market leaders.

Tradition can serve a similar purpose: Faber-Castell, world leader in pencils founded in 1761, can present a long list of prominent users. Otto von Bismarck wrote with Faber-Castell pencils, Vincent van Gogh praised their "famous black," and Max Liebermann called them the best. No advertising money can buy such tradition.

SUMMARY

Hidden champions pursue and attain the goal of market leadership. Market leadership means more to them than market share.

- Market leadership involves psychological market leadership, namely the claim to being the best or number one.
- The leadership position brings advantages in terms of cost, marketing, communication, and motivation.
- The goal to become market leader is the very foundation of the current leadership positions of the hidden champions.
- In setting a goal and determining strategy, planned, emerging, and entrepreneurial modes are observed among these firms. There is more than one road to leadership and success.
- The implementation of goals is governed by long-term orientation and persistence. The determination to become and remain number one is never lost.
- The simplicity and clarity of a goal support its effective communication. The goal is the primary interest of the leaders.

These are simple and commonsense guidelines. There are no miracles and nothing revolutionary. The message is that a clear and ambitious goal is the foundation of each success. If communicated effectively, the goal leads the conduct of all employees. Long-term orientation, persistence, and never-ending energy are necessary to pursue it. The hidden champions exemplify its accomplishment.

3

The Market

A big splash in a small pond!

Speaking of market share, we frequently forget that "share" must always be related to a "market." And because it is difficult to define "market," it easily lends itself to self-deception and illusions. Lufthansa's market share between Frankfurt and Munich is more than 80% if the market is defined as "air passenger traffic." If the railway is included, and the market is redefined as "public passenger traffic," Lufthansa's market share falls to less than 10%. And if we include all means of transportation, particularly cars, and consider "total passenger traffic" as the market, Lufthansa's share is less than 2%. This simple illustration proves that market definitions must be handled with great care.

Definitions of "market" and "market share" are essential to the assessment of strategy, competition, and market leadership. Defining "business" and "market" is, in the words of Derek Abell (1980), "the starting point of strategic planning." It should be observed that the boundaries of a market are not solely determined by external forces like customers and competitors but depend to a larger or smaller degree on the behavior of a company. Accepting a given definition or redefining a market can play a critical role in formulating strategy.

NARROW MARKETS

The hidden champions define their markets narrowly. Consequently, their markets are relatively small. The size of the world markets as defined by the sample companies is represented in Figure 3.1. Roughly one-quarter of the markets fall into each of the four categories: 23.6%, with less than $67 million, are extreme niche markets, but 29.2%, with more than $1.67 billion, are sizable. The median world market is $467 million.

In the context of Michael Porter's (1985) generic strategies, the hidden champions' competitive scope definitely falls into the narrow-target category. In many cases the target is extremely narrow and pointed. About three-quarters of the markets (77.7%) have been expanding over the last ten years, with only 13.2% shrinking. On a scale of 1 to 7, growth potentials rated at 5.1 signal generally positive but not dramatic growth. The average prices in these markets have, however, been stagnating over those years, with 42.1% of the respondents reporting a decrease and 47.1% an increase in price levels. In spite of their small size, these markets generally face what leaders consider to be tough competition.

The hidden champions are amazingly well informed about their markets—82.7% of the respondents provided estimates on their size. Half were based on subjective knowledge while the other half came from objective sources like surveys or statistics. The overall reliability of the

Figure 3.1 **World Markets Served by the Hidden Champions**

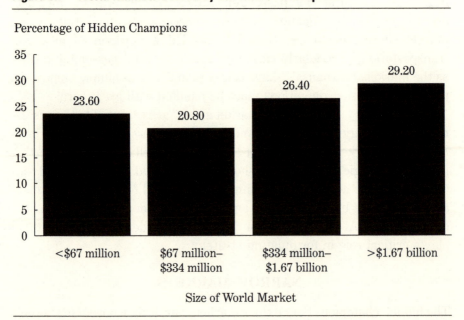

Percentage of Hidden Champions

Size of World Market

information was rated 4.9 on a scale of 1 to 7. Only 16.1% considered the reliability of the market information below average. With a score of 5.9, the hidden champions see market knowledge as the third most important strength after customer relations (6.1) and image (6.0) and equal to technological know-how (5.9). Of course, not all companies are that well informed. Some operate in such highly fragmented markets that it is impossible to ascertain the exact size of the world market. Examples are potting soil (ASB Grünland is world market leader), submersible pumps (ABS is number two in the world), and radio-controlled wristwatches (Junghans is number one). Many of the sample companies' markets are not well-defined, are highly fragmented, or have fuzzy boundaries. Such firms have only two choices: either refraining from establishing a quantitative estimate of market size or making a subjective estimate. Most hidden champions prefer the second option but are aware that the resulting numbers are imprecise. This situation implies that they often know their absolute market share measured in percentage of the total market less well than their relative share measured relative to the largest competitor, on which they can usually obtain valid information. In their world, market size and market share can be relatively vague concepts.

This fuzziness is not necessarily a disadvantage. Many hidden champions view it as a barrier to entry. As Albert Blum, the former CEO of ABS Pumps commented, "If you don't know your market share, you don't have to be afraid of the Japanese." Indeed, the Japanese seem to prefer large, well-structured, and researchable markets over the fragmented and fuzzy niches in which the hidden champions operate.

A further reason for the difficulty some respondents encounter in providing exact market-size figures is that markets don't exist as such but are created by companies. Quite a few of the interviewees contended that they created a completely new market and that the creation process continues from year to year and from country to country. Brita, the leader in point-of-use water filters, SAT, the on-site road recycling company, and Lobo Elektronik, a champion in computer-controlled laser display systems, fall into this category. There is no way to provide precise data on the size and the boundaries of such markets. This doesn't mean that there aren't big opportunities. Often the reverse is true. Availability of market statistics should not be mistaken for high market attractiveness. Despite offering scant information, some obscure markets are highly appealing.

CRITERIA FOR MARKET DEFINITION

There are many different ways to define a market, the traditional one being based on product: "We are in the dishwasher market." This approach has been under attack since Ted Levitt's seminal article "Marketing Myopia" (1960). But according to the hidden champions, the product-based market definition should not be dismissed too quickly. Closely related market definitions are based on technology and, in a wider sense, on competencies. More recent approaches derive a market (or business) definition from customers' needs or applications: "We are in the market of cleaning dishes." The hidden champions like this approach too. A further closely related approach looks at the market from a competitive perspective and asks which competing products customers see as substitutes. This approach is less popular with the hidden champions, because they try to make their products as dissimilar as possible from those of their competitors, often objecting to their competitors' market definitions and instead redefining their markets. Markets, in their opinion, are not necessarily defined by given and accepted criteria. The market definition itself is part of strategy.

The importance the hidden champions attribute to certain criteria of market definition is illustrated in Figure 3.2. With multiple criteria permitted, most respondents rated several. The figure shows that the company leaders approach the problem of market definition both from the application and customer group perspective and from the product/technology, price level, and quality perspective. Both aspects have importance scores of similar magnitude. The product, backed by the core competencies of a company, must not be ignored in defining a market. In the same vein, customers' needs and application problems have to be observed. Leadership in a market can be attained only if both sides are taken into account.

This is also evident from a theoretical point of view. A priori, there are no markets. At most, potential markets may exist before an exchange. But until an exchange takes place, one cannot know what the market is. A company always competes for different customers' needs, and competitors may offer different types of products that could substitute for each other. The hidden champions understand this relationship, depicted in Figure 3.3, and try to influence the degree of substitutability in their own favor. They do not confine themselves to one criterion of market definition

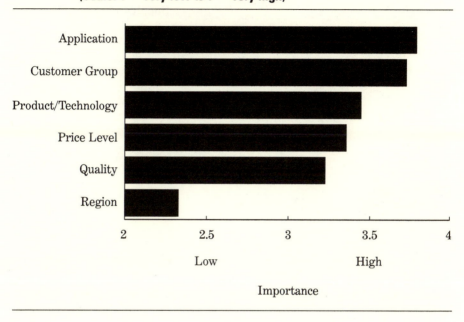

Figure 3.2 **Importance of Market Definition Criteria**
(Scale: 1 = very low to 7 = very high)

but observe both the aspects of external opportunities and internal resources.

The hidden champions assign an inferior role to region as a market definition criterion. In this regard they are distinct from more ordinary firms, which typically include regional boundaries as a factor. The champions' attitude is in stark contrast to my experience with many companies, for which "country" seems to be the main determinant of market definition. This applies particularly to companies with strong country subsidiaries. Their region-oriented organizational structure may well lead to a wrong approach to the markets.

It is interesting to note that once the sample companies have selected a target market, they stick with it. Their last major decision to focus on a specific market was made, on average, about ten years ago. And that decision was made only slightly later than the last major decision on their basic technology. Their perseverance in sticking with a market sheds light on important aspects of their continuity. To customers, it signals a strong commitment.

Figure 3.3   **Interacting Hierarchies That Define a Market**

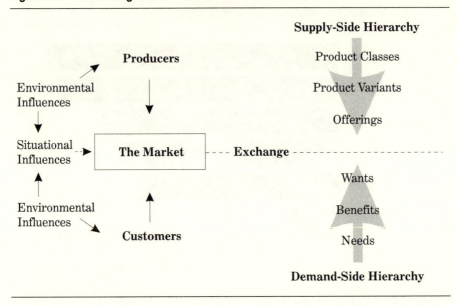

Source: Adapted from Miguel A. Arrufat and George H. Haines, "Market Definition for Application Development Software Packages," Carleton University School of Business, working paper 93-02, 1992.

FOCUS AND CONCENTRATION

Going beyond the statistical aspects of market definition, a look at concrete cases provides a deeper and more substantial understanding of the high degree of focus, specialization, and concentration involved. It also illustrates the astonishing variety and range of markets served by the hidden champions.

The fundamental and typical attitude of their CEOs is reflected in statements like the following:

- We are highly specialized.
- We concentrate on what we can.
- Niche! (very frequent)
- We are deep, not wide.
- We stick to our knitting.
- No diversification.

Clean Concept, maker of the new touch-free toilet system, formulates its focus as follows: "The age of hygiene has just begun. We have specialized in hygiene. We have invested all our capabilities and competencies in this area. We don't want to be an organization that does a little bit of everything, we want to do one thing really well. We don't improve hygiene among other things, we deal purely with hygiene."

Most, but not all the hidden champions have resisted the temptation to diversify, and the ones that have stuck to their knitting have almost always fared better. Their commitment to a special field of competence is usually very strong. Often developed over decades or generations, it is as much an emotional as a rational concept. Quite a few of their chiefs are monomaniacs who have the ability to focus on their market for their lifetime. Table 3.1 illustrates the variety and specificity of market definitions applied by twenty-four of the hidden champions. The first sixteen are primarily product oriented, the last eight need oriented.

These examples of market definitions may appear quite specific to readers, but they are typical for the hidden champions. They clearly support the observation that the markets are narrowly defined and the companies highly focused. The deliberate focus is a pillar of their strength.

Beyond the "typical" hidden champions reflected in Table 3.1 I found two additional categories that drive market focus and specialization even further. The first consists of ultraspecialists that try to build very strong positions in very small markets. I call them super nichists. The second category create their own markets, having no competition in the usual sense. I call them market owners because they are virtually alone in those markets. Among them are some of the most secretive of the hidden champions.

SUPER NICHISTS

First look at some super nichists. Their strategies contain important lessons concerning the depth and breadth of product lines. Table 3.2 lists a selection of super nichists.

These super nichists are stars among the hidden champions in market leadership and competitive strength. Most of the ones for which a relative market share is available are three times larger in market share than their strongest competitor. Sometimes they have no real competition,

Table 3.1 Selected Hidden Champions' Market Definitions (P = product oriented; N = need oriented)

Company	Market Definition	Product or Need Oriented	World Market Position		
			Rank	Absolute Share in Percentage	Relative Share
Suwelack	Face cosmetics, collagen masks	P	1	70	2.3
G. W. Barth	Roasters of cocoa beans	P	1	70	>3
Erhardt & Leimer	Web-handling technology	P	1	80	8
Krones	Labeling machines for bottles	P	1	70	4
Weinig	Automatic molders	P	1	50	4
Heidenhain	Measuring instruments for length and angles	P	1	40	4
Stihl	Gasoline chain saws	P	1	30	1.9
Rofin-Sinar	Industrial CO_2 lasers	P	1	21	1.6
Trasco	Secured sedans	P	1	50	2.4
Gartenbau Dümmen	Poinsettia plants	P	1	16	2.6
Schwank	Gas-infrared heaters	P	1	30	2

Company	Product/market				
Neumann	Green coffee	P	1–2	13	1
Joh. Barth	Hops and hops products	P	1	15	2
ASB Grünland	Potting soil	P	1	40	4
Automatik Apparate Maschinenbau	Underwater pelletizers	P	1	70	>4
Smithers Oasis	Floral foam	P	1	75	7.5
Clean Concept	Hygienic use of toilets	N	1	Self-defined market	
Dürr	Painting systems for cars	N	1	30	1.3
Institut Förster	Destruction-free material testing	N	1	35	3.5
Kärcher	Cleaning of buildings and cars	N	1	35	1.6
Leybold	Generation of vacuums	N	1	30	1.7
Webasto	Climate comfort for cars	N	1	50	2.5
Suspa	Damping/control of washing machine vibration	N	1	40	2.3
SAP	Client-server applications	N	1	40	1.5

Table 3.2 **Selected Super Nichists**

Company	Market Definition	World Market Position		
		Rank	Absolute Share in Percentage	Relative Share
Hahn	Glass showcases for museums	1	40	4
Paul Binhold	Anatomical teaching aids	1	34	3.4
König & Bauer	Money-printing presses	1	90	10
Weckerle	Lipstick foundering machines	1	70	3.5
DMI	Air-cooled diesels	1	80	10
Tente Rollen	Casters for hospital beds	1	50	3
Winterhalter Gastronom	Restaurant dishwashers	1	15–20	4
Gerriets	Scrims	1	100	10
Steiner Optik	Military field glasses	1	80	>4
Tetra	Tropical fish food	1	80	5
Märklin	Model railways	1	55	3
Union Knopf	Buttons	1	3	1.5
Grohmann Engineering	The 30 top electronics companies in the world	One of the best	Fuzzy market	
Scheuerle	Heavy transport technology	1	Fuzzy market	
Aeroxon	Nonchemical insect traps/ fly strips	1	50	>2
Becher	Large umbrellas	1	50	>3

since they are the only suppliers for certain applications. Jürgen H. Schulze, head of Deutz Motor Industriemotoren (DMI), comments on his air-cooled diesels:

> They are a real marvel. A few years ago we wanted to abandon them due to environmental restrictions. But in the meantime we have learned that these engines are irreplaceable in certain applications and locations, in extremely hot or cold climates, in deserts, in out-of-the-way places where maintenance is difficult. And we are virtually the only manufacturer in the world that can make these motors in substantial quantities.

Union Knopf, the world leader in buttons, produces only buttons, but buttons in all conceivable varieties—250,000 altogether. Whatever kind of button one needs, it can be found at Union Knopf. Or take Aeroxon, a specialist in nonchemical devices to fight household insects. Its main product, the fly strip, has not changed in ninety years, and it holds 50% of the world market. Klaus Grohmann is a special kind of super nichist, defining his niche by his customers. His company, Grohmann Engineering, which makes machines and systems for the assembly of electronic products, is one of the top guns in this field. He explains his market definition:

> We focus on the thirty top companies in the world, the most aggressive and leading ones and define them as our market. In working for these globally most demanding customers, we ourselves become world class. This strategy may limit our growth, but it guarantees that we stay at the top.

He then showed me some ongoing projects, which were for Intel, Motorola, L. M. Ericsson, Nokia, Bosch, and Alcatel—real world-class customers.

Super nichists can be found around the world. A U.S. company that certainly qualifies as a super nichist is St. Jude Medical. With a world market share of 60% in artificial heart valves, it is about ten times larger than its strongest competitor, the Swiss company Sulzermedica (Carbomedics). St. Jude is extremely profitable, enjoying a gross return on sales of 75.7% and a net return of 43.4%. Or take Gallagher, a company from New Zealand, which has 45% of the world market in electric fences.

The super nichists exemplify a principle that applies to a certain degree to all the hidden champions. They don't accept markets as defined by competitive or external forces but they see the definition of a market as a parameter they can control. They don't accept the structure of their industry as implied in most of Porter's (1980, 1985) work but redefine and change this structure if necessary. Hamel and Prahalad (1994) see this attitude as an important part of a future-oriented strategy. And what I said about psychological market leadership in Chapter 1 is largely aimed at this task.

Winterhalter, discussed in the following section, illustrates how such a redefinition of a market can work. BBA, an English company in the textile sector, includes such a statement in its corporate philosophy: "Our tactic is to become market dominant in our market niches by transforming general markets where we are nobody to market niches where we are somebody." It clearly shows that a company that pursues leadership should not accept existing market definitions and boundaries. The possibility of redefining a market varies from company to company, but the firm decision not to accept but to determine a market definition is a first precondition of leadership.

BREADTH VERSUS DEPTH

The super nichists direct attention to a most important strategic trait, which applies to a considerable degree to many hidden champions, namely, the issue of breadth versus depth of a product line or a business in general. Breadth of a product line means the number of products a company carries. A company that makes dishwashers, washing machines, and refrigerators has a broader product line than one which manufactures only dishwashers. The concept of breadth can also be related to markets. A company that serves both the commercial and the consumer market for dishwashers is broader than one which serves only the commercial market.

Depth, on the other hand, refers to the number of variants of a single product or to the complete solution of a problem within a narrowly defined market. Thus a maker of dishwashers can sell many different variants for varying applications. It can also add products related to dishwashing, such as detergents, to its line. The number of articles may be similar for a "broad" and a "deep" supplier, but the structure of the line would be totally different.

A further way to look at this distinction is along the value chain suggested by Porter (1985). For a broad manufacturer, the value chain would be wide—many different products or markets—but the section served in the chain would be short. A deep supplier would have a narrow value chain—few products or markets—but cut out a long section of the chain. This difference is illustrated in Figure 3.4. The hidden champions generally prefer the narrow and deep approach, and the super nichists are exemplary in this regard.

An excellent example is provided by Winterhalter Gastronom, which makes dishwashers for commercial use. There are many different markets for such a product—hospitals, schools, companies, public organizations, hotels, restaurants, military installations, and so on. Therefore the market potential is large, but the customers' requirements vary from segment to segment. Many different products are available on the market for the various segments.

Manfred Bobeck, director of Winterhalter, recounts:

> We analyzed the total market for commercial dishwashers and found that our world market share was about 2 percent. We were an also-ran. This led

Figure 3.4 **"Broad" versus "Deep" Approach to Strategy**

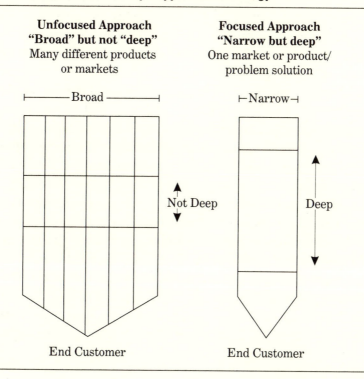

us to totally redirect our strategy. We began to focus solely on hotels and restaurants; we even renamed the company Winterhalter Gastronom. We now define our business as supplier of clean glasses and dishes for hotels and restaurants and take full responsibility. We include water-conditioning devices and our own brand of detergent in our product line. We offer excellent service around the clock. Our world market share in the hotel/restaurant segment is now 15 to 20 percent and climbing. Nobody can match us any longer.

And Jürgen Winterhalter, Bobeck's colleague in management, adds: "This narrowing of our market definition was the most important strategic decision we ever made. It is the very foundation of our success in the past decade." Winterhalter's strategy is illustrated in Figure 3.5.

The focus on depth as opposed to breadth is typical of the hidden champions. Clean Concept makes only touch-free toilets, but supplies everything their use requires. Dürr focuses on the auto industry, but achieves depth through supplying complete painting systems including paint application, paint storage, logistics, software, technical support, and buildings. St. Jude Medical, the American world market leader in artificial heart valves, focuses on the human heart; to build depth, it created a value-added chain in buying the heart pacemaker business from Siemens in 1994. Future market synergies are likely to result from the coordination of valves and pacemakers.

Tetra Pak, the Swedish world market leader in cardboard packaging systems for beverages, traditionally confined itself to packaging, which is a small part of the value chain. But in 1993 it deepened its involvement in the value chain of beverage manufacturing by acquiring Alfa Laval, a company that produces beverage-processing equipment. Tetra Laval, the merged company, is narrow and deep. It takes full responsibility for both processing and packaging beverages. In the same manner, Germina, in number of units the second largest producer of cross-country skis in the world, is building on its past, when East Germany's top athletes dominated cross-country competition. Shunning the much larger alpine ski market, it confines itself to the high-performance segment of the smaller cross-country market.

Time and again, focused strategy proves its superiority. Heinz Hankammer, the founder of Brita water filters, explains his thoughts:

Leifheit, one of our competitors, has a thousand products, one of which is a water filter. That's no match for us, because we have only water filters.

Figure 3.5 **Depth Rather Than Breadth: Winterhalter's Focused Strategy**

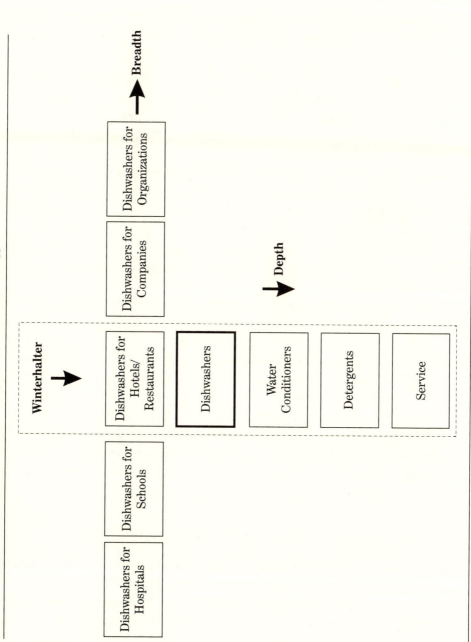

Five years ago, Melitta, itself a hidden champion in coffee filters, tried to attack us and failed. In America, Mr. Coffee, the largest producer of coffee makers, lost against us. The guys who do many different things are no threat for us because we direct all our energy and concentration toward one product.

Gerhard M. Bauer, marketing director of Brähler International Congress Service, concurs: "We are focused. Compare us to Siemens or Philips. For them this market is of minor concern. That's our advantage, and we can live comfortably in the niche. Siemens and Philips can't!" Peter Barth of the world leader in hops reflects: "Some of our competitors have diversified into other agricultural brewing ingredients like malt and barley. We refrained from doing the same and stayed with hops, nothing but hops. Through this focus we have achieved a perfection which hardly anybody can match."

An important aspect of strategy is knowing what one doesn't want to do. This aspect may be as critical as knowing what one wants to do. In a stimulating interview in *Fortune* (Schlender 1995), Bill Gates formulated Microsoft's strategy in both these terms. Most of the hidden champions know pretty well what they want and what they don't want, which is one of their safeguards against distraction.

Depth rather than breadth is a foundation of their success. Implementing this strategy requires both a clear vision and a strong-willed strategic focus. The most difficult part is resisting the temptation to engage in a side business here and there. Super nichists could often profit from additional business in complementary fields, particularly in a favorable business climate. But the true champions withstand this temptation and remain focused having learned that this is the only way to attain world-class status.

MARKET OWNERS

Another category of hidden champions consists of a select few companies that virtually dominate their field. I call them market owners. Of course, in a strict sense, nobody owns a market. Usually these companies have created their niche market. Through sustained superiority, unbeatable barriers to entry, and luck, they have managed to defend their quasi-monopolistic positions. Normal considerations of market size and share do not apply to them. Their markets and products are unique. Without them the self-defined market wouldn't exist. The market owners tend to be the most secretive of all hidden champions.

A case in point is Hummel, famous for its figurines. Collectors throughout the world, particularly in the United States, pay fantastic prices for these little objets d'art. Though I wasn't able to learn many details about Hummel, I have every reason to assume that it is a hugely successful organization. Nothing can replace Hummel figurines for devout collectors, who form the entire market. There is no substitute for the Hummel product, which creates a self-sustaining market, the ultimate barrier to entry.

Margarete Steiff has built a similar position. Its first product, a little felt elephant, appeared in 1880. In 1902, the famous teddy bear followed. It was named for U.S. president Theodore ("Teddy") Roosevelt after a cartoon depicted the president sparing the life of a bear cub while hunting. All Steiff animals have a button in the ear. Tradition and continuity characterize the firm's strategy. A collector's movement similar to Hummel's has been developing. The United States is the most important market. Some new teddies cost as much as $2,000. Many times in its history Steiff had waiting lists of customers who couldn't be supplied owing to lack of capacity. Keeping its products scarce and consciously staying small can be a critical strategic aspect for a market owner.

Hein is a tiny market owner with $7 million in revenue. The company makes Pustefix, a liquid soap product that children can blow into bubbles. According to Gerold Hein, the CEO, "Pustefix does not compete against other products of its kind; it competes for kids' money against chocolate bars, sweets, and anything else they can buy." The product is exported to fifty countries with the United States and Japan the main markets. Not only does its small niche make it unattractive for larger competitors, but the product is protected by six patents.

Fischertechnik, whose founder Artur Fischer was probably the most prolific inventor in the postwar period, is another market owner protected by a fortress of 5,500 patents (see also Chapter 6). Fischertechnik is a toy consisting of parts that can be assembled into all kinds of end products. Popular not only with older children, it is also used to build models of factories and industrial processes. Fischertechnik is sold in more than one hundred countries. Because its solid patent protection ensures it against comparable competitors, Fischertechnik defines and owns its market.

There are many similar market owners in the toy sector. Lego, the Danish company, certainly qualifies, as does Playmobil, a plastic toy from hidden champion geobra Brandstätter. Ferrero, a company headquartered in Italy, has been successful in many countries with its "Surprise Eggs," chocolate eggs which contain a little figurine or plastic pieces that have to be assembled. A collector's market has developed for them as well.

Marsberger Glaswerke Ritzenhoff, a glass manufacturer, started creating an owned market in 1992. The company has been a leader in beer glasses and glasses for special applications in cars and industrial installations. Realizing that while there are glasses for all kinds of beverages, like beer, wine, liquor, but none for milk, Ritzenhoff conceived a special milk glass and invited artists to submit color designs for it. This international project, "Milk, Lait, Leche, Milch, Latte . . . ," became an instant success. In the first year, the company sold 600,000 glasses at the very high price of $11.67. This "global product" can already be found in U.S. and Asian galleries and museums. Glasses from the first series are traded at $533. The company, which has initiated the Ritzenhoff Milk Club of Collectors, produces limited editions of new designs every year, some exclusively for club members. With this concept Ritzenhoff sells more than just glasses. Their glasses are the carriers of something unique and therefore don't compete with other glasses.

On whom do you call on if you need money? Imagine coming to power in one of the new states in Central or Eastern Europe and your country needs its own money. Giesecke & Devrient, the second largest nongovernmental money printer in the world, is a company that can help you. A fairly sizable market for money printing exists, because only larger countries can afford their own operations. In addition, Giesecke & Devrient prints about 50% of German bills. The company was founded in 1852. It's no surprise that this company is very secretive. With the emergence of many new states, Giesecke & Devrient's business has been booming. Theodor Gräbener is in a similar position. This company is the world's leading manufacturer of coin presses. And coins are needed everywhere.

In a totally different market, Paul Schockemöhle, a former world-class rider, and Ullrich Kasselmann have a position of which normal horse breeders can only dream. While excellent horses sell at auctions for $20,000, their horses bring in $200,000 to $500,000. Schockemöhle is not a small player: according to a customer who knows the market well, he has 3,000 horses, although not all are in this price class. Obviously, the superior ability to select and train the horses is the foundation for this unmatched hidden championship.

Karl Mayer, the world leader in rashel machines, has systematically built a position as a market owner over the years. As a result of a successful implementation of this strategy, the company can say that "only for 10% of our revenues do we have any competition at all." Many customers consider Mayer's products irreplaceable. Convac, maker of coating systems for disks and fotomask processing equipment, with 100% of the world market for its products, is in an even stronger position.

It may be difficult or impossible for a normal company to replicate these market owners' strategies. Nevertheless, these strategies hold interesting lessons that can benefit any enterprise.

The best way to appropriate a market is to create it. Ideally, it is a market that, like Hummel, becomes defined by its product. Its uniqueness must be sustainable and, if necessary, defended over time. Achieving uniqueness can depend on artistic quality (e.g., Ritzenhoff), a strong logo or trademark (e.g., Steiff), patent protection (e.g., Fischertechnik), or customer relations and confidentiality (e.g., Giesecke & Devrient). The products must be kept scarce, like money and Hummel figurines, and difficult to obtain. Peter Schutz, the former CEO of Porsche, once said, "Two Porsches in the same street are a disaster." Scarcity creates value in the eye of a devout customer. It also requires that these companies consciously refrain from exploiting their full growth potential. The biggest enemy of exclusivity is rapid expansion.

Market owners also teach us lessons in relationship marketing. This concept, which originated in the literature of the early 1990s, is old and familiar stuff to them. They have been spoiling their loyal customers for decades. They initiated clubs and collectors' movements long before these ideas were detected by marketing researchers and strategists. In this way they built a loyal following of customers who are fanatic about their products and willing to pay very high prices. The market owners described here have been wise enough to stay focused and secretive and to keep their markets small.

Again, market owners can be found in all industries and throughout the world. Rolls-Royce cars definitely fall into this category, as do the cameras of Sweden's Hasselblad and France's Mouton Rothschild vines. There are many theme parks, but only one Disneyland, and no watch compares to a Rolex. Further examples prevail in the service sector, for instance, in private banking and the hotel business. Market owners' strategies can succeed everywhere.

RISKS OF OVERSPECIALIZATION

Because hidden champions are highly focused on narrow markets and competencies, one may question whether they are overspecialized and thus exposed to extremely high risks. Don't they depend to an unacceptable degree on their narrow markets, on few customers, on uncertain business cycles and technological changes?

Indeed, their dependence on one market is very high—67.1% of their sales revenue comes from one main market and, on a scale of 1 (unimportant) to 7 (very important), they rate the importance of their main market, as shown in Figure 3.6, at an average of 6.21. The respondents expect this importance to further increase in the future, 60% predicting an increase and only 8.7% a decrease. The focus is becoming more rather than less pronounced.

The high importance of markets for suppliers is matched, to a large extent, by customers' strong dependence on the hidden champions. The

Figure 3.6 **Hidden Champions' Ratings of Importance of Primary Market (Scale: 1 = unimportant to 7 = very important)**

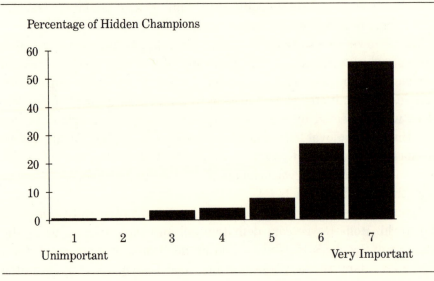

Percentage of Hidden Champions

average score on the question of whether customers could find substitutes for the hidden champions' products was 5.9, a rating of 7 showing that a product is irreplaceable. So there is mutual dependence between suppliers and customers. This situation induces a strong commitment by both sides. The hidden champions are strongly committed to their narrow markets, and their customers, for the most part, have little choice. Whether some of the companies are overspecialized and overfocused cannot be judged conclusively. Clifford and Cavanagh (1985) reported in their investigation of fast-growing American companies that small niche markets were associated with higher returns on investment. In my sample, market size was positively correlated with overall success. This result should be interpreted with caution, for it can best be seen as a weak indication that profitability suffers if markets become too tiny. The overspecialization has frequently been criticized in the German trade press. It may well be that some hidden champions have withdrawn into niches that are too small for long-term profitable survival.

Essentially, the risks from overspecialization and overfocus have three possible causes:

- Dependence on one market ("putting all one's eggs in one basket");
- A niche may be attacked by standard products, causing the loss of a premium or unique position;
- A small niche may incur high production costs in economies of scale and experience curve effects that cannot be exploited.

Dependence on one market is an obvious risk. If a market turns down, experiences problems, or disappears, a company with a share of typical hidden champion magnitude is apt to go under. A company that can build the best steam locomotive in the world cannot survive because nobody any longer buys steam locomotives.

Early in this century, Welte & Söhne was a company with a unique product. The playing of famous piano soloists was mechanically recorded on a cylinder, which, when placed in a player piano, reproduced the original performance. This product was a favorite of many wealthy people worldwide. But with the invention of the phonograph, it disappeared, and so did hidden champion Welte & Söhne.

In the mid-1950s, NSU of Heilbronn, Germany, then the major motorcycle manufacturer in the world, was highly focused on the motorbike

market. But about that time, the use of motorbikes for primary transportation began to decline in Europe. As soon as people could afford to,
they switched to cars. In spite of several attempts, NSU was unsuccessful
in following this trend. Neither did it understand that increased leisure
time was developing a secondary market for motorcycles. Riding this new
wave, Japanese competitors like Honda, Yamaha, and Kawasaki became
the new world champions. Unable to survive on its own, NSU merged
with Audi and eventually Volkswagen. Its once-famous brand name disappeared. These illustrations show that the risk of being confined to a
single market which disappears is high, and the narrower the focus, the
higher the risk.

But market risk is only one side; the other is the risk of being beaten
by a competitor superior in the same or a closely related technology. This
risk can probably be reduced by employing a clearer focus. Both types
of risk are graphically compared in Figure 3.7, which clearly shows that
the choice is not between higher or lower overall risk but between higher
market and lower competitive risk, and vice versa.

There is no simple answer to the question of whether a focused or a

Figure 3.7   **Comparative Risk with Regard to Focus**

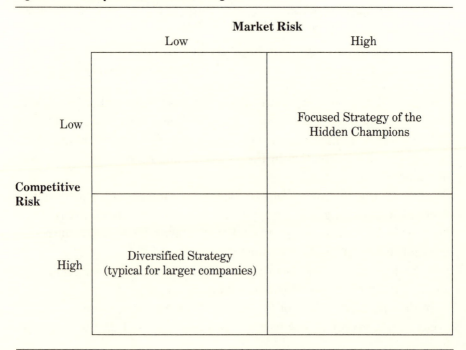

diversified strategy is better. The hidden champion CEOs favor that of focus. Hans Riegel of Haribo, the world market leader in Gummi bears, says, "Risk is actually reduced if you focus on what you really master." Another respondent commented, "Isn't it less risky to be a big fish in a small pond than a small fish in a large pond with many sharks?" Michael Steinbeis, CEO of Steinbeis Holding, a world leader in battery labels and special paper products like linters, explains his philosophy: "We want to be big in small markets. We may even pull out if a market becomes too large and, due to our size and resources, we can be only a small player." The emphasis on the role of core competencies (Prahalad and Hamel 1990, Hamel and Prahalad 1994) and the findings on failures of diversification moves suggest that the overall risk of a focused strategy may be less than the risk of a diversified strategy. Evidence from a McKinsey study (Rommel et al. 1995) supports this conclusion. Companies that focus on fewer products and customers were found to be more successful. Figure 3.8 compares successful and less successful machinery manufacturers in this study. The number of products per $67 million of sales is

Figure 3.8   Comparison of Successful and Less Successful Machinery Manufacturers

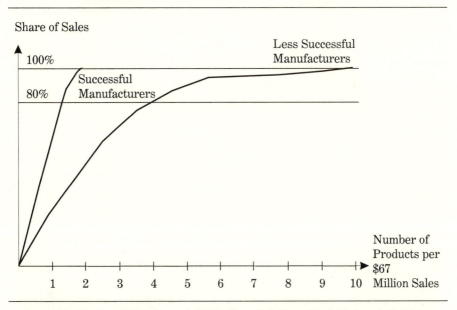

Source: Modified from Günter Rommel, Jürgen Kluge, Rolf-Dieter Kempis, Raimund Diederichs, and Felix Brück, *Simplicity Wins: How Germany's Mid-Sized Industrial Companies Succeed* (Boston: Harvard Business School Press, 1995), 44. Reprinted by permission.

much smaller for the successful companies. A similar relation was observed for numbers of customers. Companies with fewer products face less complexity. The "simplicity approach" suggested by the McKinsey study is one of the foundations of success.

The risk of a too narrow focus and overspecialization has to be judged against that of too little focus and spreading one's interests through overdiversification. A one-sided view of these risks is inadequate. Diversified companies frequently sell off and add businesses to their portfolios. But that philosophy does not apply to the hidden champions. They have to hang on to their markets. Perhaps one of the riskiest situations in this regard results from a technological change. The same need, or market, is satisfied by a different technology, as in the mechanical versus electronic recording of piano music. Though evidence is limited, it seems that some hidden champions have fared quite well under this most serious threat. The fact that, come what may, they depend on only one market makes them ferocious defenders and great innovators. They simply have no choice.

Trumpf, world leader in machines for precision sheet metal cutting, is a case in point. Traditionally, sheet metal cutting was done mechanically. In the early 1980s, however, laser technology began to invade this field, a very serious threat for Trumpf. But under the leadership of Berthold Leibinger, a paragon hidden champion CEO, the company stayed focused and developed its own laser. It not only defended its leading position in sheet metal cutting but became one of the top companies in industrial lasers. Dr. Werner Sterzenbach, CEO of Kiekert, world leader in locking systems for cars, describes a similar development for his company: "In the seventies we left the world of purely mechanical locks and developed a systems approach with our electronic central locking system. By 1979, we developed our first electronic chip. This has decisively contributed to our world leader position." In the same vein, when in the 1980s some hidden champions were threatened with falling seriously behind their Japanese competitors in the integration of electronics and mechanical parts, those which were focused coped relatively well with this challenge.

When I visited the training facility of a company in northern Germany in 1981, I found it to be much the same as a 1960s operation. There was a real risk that the company had missed the boat to the electronics age. But when I returned to the facility about ten years later, it resembled an electronics laboratory. That company, like many others, not only added electronics to mechanical parts but integrated the two technologies. The engineers came up with completely new solutions to problems and fundamentally redesigned machines and instruments. Like Trumpf, this hidden champion has stayed focused and retained the lead in its market.

This discussion has revealed that the strong focus involves two risk aspects. It certainly makes a company highly dependent on one market, with all the eggs in one basket. If this market experiences problems, the champion is negatively affected. The market risk is somewhat moderated by the geographical spread of the activities, an aspect addressed in the following chapter. On the other hand, the focus reduces competitive risks. The hidden champions are strongly committed to their narrow markets. Their focused competencies lay the best foundation for superior competitive performance and their dependence induces a strong will to defend their markets. They have no option but to hang on.

SUMMARY

The hidden champions define their markets narrowly and serve them in a highly focused way. Their market definitions are characterized by the following properties:

- Both customer needs and product/technology perspectives are taken into account.

- In spite of the fragmentation and fuzziness of many of these markets, the hidden champions are relatively well informed about them, owing to their focus and closeness to their markets.

- Market definitions and boundaries are not accepted as givens but are considered as part of strategy and actively controlled. Many hidden champions carve out super niches, some market owners creating unique products that self-define the markets in which they are dominant.

- Market definitions and product lines are deep rather than broad. The value chain served is accordingly narrow but long. This induces a degree of specialization and perfection difficult to match.

- Once the hidden champions have selected a market, they stick with and are highly committed to it. Redefinitions occur about as seldom for markets as for basic technology.

- The hidden champions accept the risk of staking their success on a single product, a result of narrow market definition and focus. They believe that this market risk is outweighed by an increase in competitive strength. Some that exaggerate their specialization may, however, be driven into niches that eventually become too small for survival. Large corporations, on the other hand, are often characterized by lack of focus. The optimum probably lies neither at the extremes nor in the middle but toward a rather strong focus. This is exactly the point at which most of the hidden champions have arrived.

Finding the right market definition and focus is a difficult task. The success of the hidden champions suggests an approach based on concentration, specialization, and core competencies. While this may not be the right answer for all markets, each company should seriously consider the focused strategy and reassess its position from time to time. The danger of overfocusing seems less serious than that of spreading one's talents and resources around. The specialist frequently beats the generalist.

4

The World

The customer's language is the best language.
—Anton Fugger

HOW DID THE HIDDEN CHAMPIONS become world market leaders? Definitely not by staying home and waiting for customers to call on them. Rather they went out into the world to make their products and services available wherever their customers were. Their presence in target markets throughout the world is all encompassing and highly impressive. Most are true global competitors. Predominantly they establish direct contacts with customers through their own subsidiaries in the target market countries. They don't like to delegate customer relations to middlemen, importers, or distributors. They are close to their customers when it comes to languages. Their knowledge of foreign languages and their internationalization are necessary prerequisites of their business success.

GLOBAL SCOPE

On average, the hidden champions realize more than half their sales (exactly 51.2%) outside their home markets. If they include indirect exports (i.e., exports through finished products), this figure probably rises to more than 70%. The share of sales to distant, non-European markets amounts to almost one-third (exactly 30.4%). Their main target markets outside Europe are the United States and the industrialized countries in Asia. Table 4.1 illustrates the importance of foreign sales for selected hidden champions; 80 to 90% represents a normal share.

It is evident that companies with foreign shares of this magnitude must be international and global in scope and thinking. With the majority of their customers foreign, company personnel deal primarily in foreign languages, and many have to travel excessively. Most firms run a global network of subsidiaries in many different countries.

Table 4.1   Foreign Sales as Share of Sales Revenue for Selected Hidden Champions

Company	Primary Product	Foreign Sales in Percentage of Sales Revenue
Koenig & Bauer	Money-printing presses	95
Schlafhorst	Rotor spinning machines	95
SMS	Rolling mills for flat products	90
Fischer	Laboratory equipment for the oil industry	90
Binhold	Anatomical teaching aids	87
Würth	Assembly products	85
Dürr	Paint-finishing systems	84
Aixtron	Equipment for thin film fabrication	80
Götz	Dolls	80
Sachtler	Camera tripods	80
Förster	Nondestructive testing	75
Leybold	Vacuum thin film coating technology and vacuum components	75
Tigra	Cutting inserts for woodworking tools	75
Krones	Bottle labeling machines	75

It is interesting to consider the role the hidden champions play for Germany's long-term export performance. Germany's position is reflected by a comparison of the cumulative exports of the six largest exporting countries for the ten-year period 1985–1994. These are shown in Figure 4.1, both in absolute terms and on a per capita base. The ten-year perspective neutralizes short-term fluctuations and measures the long-term export performance of these countries validly and reliably.

The comparison of absolute exports reveals that the United States and Germany lie close together. Both are well ahead of Japan and even further ahead of the other large European countries. A per capita comparison between the larger United States and Japan and the smaller European countries is not too meaningful, because larger countries tend to have lower per capita exports. Among the European countries, however, the per capita comparison makes sense, because all four countries are similar in population and geoeconomic location. The comparison reveals that Germany is well ahead of its European neighbors. The strong export performance of its economy is largely attributable to its medium-size and small companies, among which the hidden champions shine as export stars. The average hidden champion in my sample contributed $66.5 million to German exports in 1993. Multiplied by 500 firms, this amounts to a total export figure of $33.3 billion, which is more than 12% of total German exports. The enormous strength of the hidden champions and other medium-size companies explains Germany's excellent export standing to a substantial degree.

Each country seems well advised to foster strong small and medium-size companies and to encourage them to conduct business internationally. Many countries have difficulties in this area, Spain being a case in point. According to a *Wall Street Journal Europe* article, the vast majority of small Spanish firms export barely, if at all. The article says that "Spanish politicians and business leaders worry that not enough is being done to help small and midsized firms to enter new foreign markets" (Vitzthum 1994a, 8). This serious problem is difficult to cure. It will become evident that the internationalization of small companies depends on a whole framework of culture, mentality, and history. The role of the government has limits in this regard.

As discussed in Chapter 3, the definition and perception of a market can have several dimensions: the product, the technology, and the customer's needs. A further dimension concerns the regional scope. Inter-

Figure 4.1 Cumulative Exports, 1985–1994, for Six Largest Exporting Countries

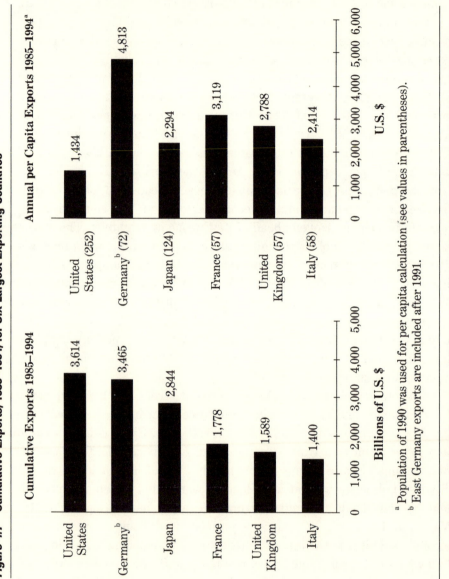

Cumulative Exports 1985–1994

Annual per Capita Exports 1985–1994[a]

Billions of U.S. $

U.S. $

[a] Population of 1990 was used for per capita calculation (see values in parentheses).
[b] East Germany exports are included after 1991.

Source: Statische Jahrbücher der Bundesrepublik Deutschland (Statistical Yearbooks of the Federal Republic of Germany) (Stuttgart: Schäffer-Poeschel, 1986–1995).

nationalization starts with the realization that this regional scope goes beyond one country. Globalization is largely equivalent to seeing the whole world as one's market, which is exactly what the hidden champions do. Whenever I asked, "What is the mental map of your market?" the reply was almost always: "The world." Alfred K. Klein, CEO of Stabilus, world market leader in gas pressurized springs, states: "The regional definition of our market is very simple, it's the world." Rittal, the world market leader in enclosure systems, has myriads of local small competitors. But Friedhelm Loh, CEO of Rittal, says: "We are the only producer of enclosure systems that truly operates worldwide. This gives us the power to set global standards in our business." Being a presence all over the world is an integral part of the hidden champions' market leadership.

World maps are the favorite wall decorations in hidden champion offices—I saw them almost everywhere. The global orientation is also reflected in numerous company principles and brochures. Dragoco, a world leader in fragrances, says: "Our market is the world market for fragrances, aromas, and cosmetic ingredients. And we are present wherever our customers need us." Stihl, world leader in chain saws, lists, as one of twelve principles of its company philosophy, "International Thinking"; it includes "worldwide distribution of our products, strategically located manufacturing facilities, and quality foreign suppliers." Brähler International Congress Service declares, "We are at home in the whole world." And Hillebrand, the world's leading wine shipper, says in its brochure: "Close to our customers wherever they are!" Herion, a world leader in pneumatic valves (e.g., for nuclear power stations), similarly posits worldwide marketing as a company principle. The same is true for Wandel & Goltermann, world leader in measuring analog electronic signals. Webasto, global market leader in sunroofs, says: "The internationalism of our automotive customers as well as the will of Webasto to deal with the world market means crossing national boundaries." Worldwide ambitions are frequently not confined to selling and marketing. DGF-Stoess, world leader in gelatin, has goals to secure a global raw material base and to build a global sales network. For Neumann Group, number one in raw green coffee, securing global access to raw material sources is a most critical factor.

While many other companies may declare similar grand slogans on globalization, the hidden champions "walk the talk." They usually establish their presence in foreign countries through their own subsidiaries.

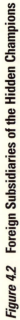

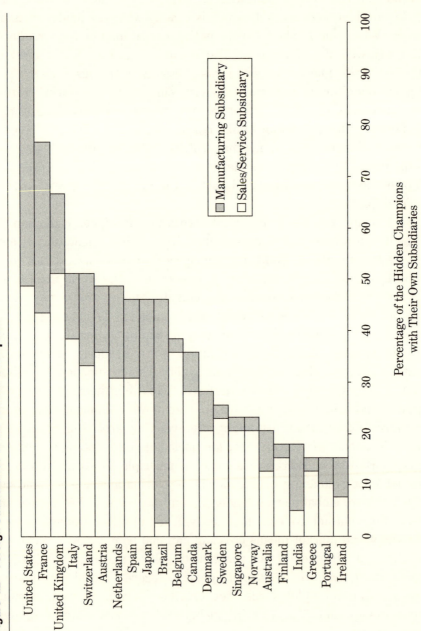

Figure 4.2 Foreign Subsidiaries of the Hidden Champions

Percentage of the Hidden Champions
with Their Own Subsidiaries

Figure 4.2 shows the results of my detailed investigation of foreign subsidiaries for a subsample of thirty-nine hidden champions. The graphic distinguishes between sales/service subsidiaries and manufacturing subsidiaries. Virtually 97.4% of the companies are represented in the United States by their own affiliates. Their presence in the United Kingdom and France, the next most important markets, is also extremely high. Even in Japan, the most difficult foreign market, almost half the companies are represented by their own firms or offices. In the larger countries, a high percentage have manufacturing subsidiaries and thus can act like local competitors. Almost all Brazilian subsidiaries are manufacturers, owing to restrictions on imports of finished goods. It should be observed that the figures in Figure 4.2 do not include agents, importers, or other nonowned forms of company representation. The thirty-nine hidden champions fully or partially own a total of 354 foreign subsidiaries. This corresponds to 9.6 foreign subsidiaries per hidden champion—an extraordinarily high number for companies their size.

A look at individual companies is even more impressive. A small one like Brähler International Congress Service, with $40 million in sales revenue and 390 employees worldwide is represented in 89 cities in 60 countries. Hillebrand, a firm with 600 employees, has offices in 30 countries. According to Christof Hillebrand, its chief executive, these offices form a global network which creates unique business opportunities in trading and forwarding wine from many production to many consumption markets.

The larger hidden champions have their own subsidiaries in many countries, as the examples in Table 4.2 illustrate.

The hidden champions express a strong preference for direct access to foreign markets and customers—they do not want third parties to come between themselves and their customers. Dr. Wolfgang Pinegger, president of Brückner, the world-leading manufacturer of biaxial film stretching systems, expresses this view candidly:

> We know all our customers in the world. Some of our people have been in China a hundred times. We do everything ourselves. Sometimes I am asked how we can manage all this with only 280 employees and whether we shouldn't have sales agents. We categorically reject agents. We have our own offices and some of our best guys spend 80 percent of their time traveling. That's how we cover the world.

Table 4.2 **Foreign Subsidiaries of Selected Hidden Champions**

Company	Primary Product	Number of Foreign Subsidiaries
Fresenius	Dialysis instruments	50
Würth	Assembly products	44
Al-Ko Kober	Trailer components	37
TÜV Rheinland	Technical inspection and certification	32
SEW Eurodrive	Power transmission	31
Villeroy & Boch	Ceramic products	27
Prominent	Metering pumps	26
Knauf	Plaster products	26
Dragoco	Fragrances	24

It must be true: whenever we tried to call, Dr. Pinegger was on his way to distant destinations. Only after months were we able to set up an appointment with him in Germany. This illustrates how the hidden champions run their global systems. Besides the narrow market focus, these global selling and marketing networks constitute the second pillar of the hidden champions' strategy. Thus, their strategy is seemingly contradictory, being narrow, focused, and deep as far as product, technology, and customer needs are concerned, and wide, broad, and global with respect to the regional dimension of business activities. This ambivalence is portrayed in Figure 4.3.

The narrow-global combination has a number of most interesting and relevant implications. First and foremost, small, even tiny, niche markets can become amazingly large when extended to the whole world. Thus, a globally expanded market with a narrow focus does not necessarily preclude economies of scale and experience curve effects. It may very well allow for an attractive combination of market specialization, and cost efficiency.

The hidden champions seem to teach us that this is the right way to

Figure 4.3 Two Pillars of Hidden Champion Strategy

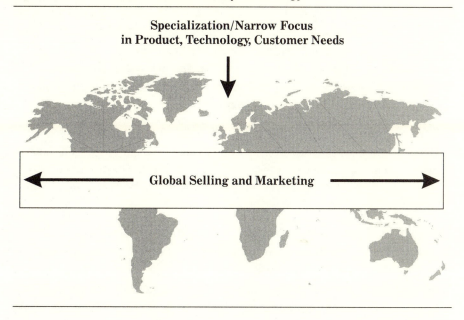

Specialization/Narrow Focus
in Product, Technology, Customer Needs

Global Selling and Marketing

operate, and that the reverse is wrong. For example, a friend of mine runs a very successful supermarket in a small town. When the problem of where to reinvest his profits arose, he decided to open a hotel in the same town. According to the hidden champions, this is not the way to go. Instead of remaining in the one place and establishing a new business—about which he knew little—he should have stuck to his retail business and opened new supermarkets in other towns. Similarly, one of our consulting clients had exclusively focused on the German market and attained a share of 80% in its high-tech, very competitive market. When I asked why the company shouldn't be equally successful in foreign markets, its managers were stunned. They admitted that they had simply been constrained by their mental boundaries. Now this "local" hidden champion has set sail for the world, and it will succeed because most markets are less difficult and demanding than Germany. But in the past, the company had sacrificed huge opportunities due to its regional limitations.

The similarities of a business across countries and regions are usually more pronounced than those between different businesses in one region. As Peter Drucker pointed out, all hospitals in the world have essentially the same problems (Drucker 1993). Somebody who can provide solutions for a problem to a hospital in Los Angeles can probably do the same for hospitals in Tokyo and Paris without even having to speak Japanese or French. Hospital people speak the same technical language everywhere, and the same holds true for hotels and restaurants.

As noted in Chapter 3, this is exactly the basis for the strategy of Winterhalter Gastronom, the dishwashing specialist for the latter industry. Manfred Bobeck, its director, explains:

> It's easier for us to adjust our systems to the needs of hotels in different countries because they are similar everywhere. It would be difficult, however, to adapt our systems to the needs of different customer groups because those are much different. Hotels in Asia and Europe are more similar than hospitals and hotels in Germany. It's that simple!

This is in the best tradition of Levitt's globalization theory (Levitt 1983). These insights contain an important lesson for every company, even one that operates on a local level: it seems advisable to focus on a narrow competence or product area and to expand regionally to increase the market. Many companies do exactly the opposite. Because they are afraid to internationalize, they stay within one region or country and attempt to expand by initiating activities in unfamiliar fields. Consequently, they lose their focus and eventually their competitiveness.

THE ROAD TO GLOBALIZATION

A few of the older hidden champions have been global firms for an impressive number of years. Heidenhain, founded in 1889, the world market leader in measuring systems for lengths and angles, exported more than 50% of its products before 1960. So did Koenig & Bauer, founded in 1817, which holds a 90% world market share for money-printing presses.

However, only in the past twenty to forty years have the younger companies become engaged in internationalization. There is an extensive literature on the subject (e.g., Cavusgil 1980, Andersen 1993, Miesenbock 1988). The first aspect generally explored is motives for export. These can be classified according to source, internal or external, and according to mode of activity, proactive or reactive. Table 4.3 defines a classification by combining the two dimensions.

The initial export motives of the hidden champions fall predominantly into the internal-proactive category. The most important factors are the

Table 4.3   **Classification of Export Motives**

Mode/ Motive of Activity \ Source of Activity	Internal	External
Proactive	• Goal driven • Managerial urge • Marketing advantages • Economies of scale • Unique products/technology competencies	• Foreign markets • Change agents
Reactive	• Risk diversification • Extend sales of a seasonal product • Excess capacity of resources	• Unsolicited orders • Small home market • Stagnant or declining home market

Source: Adapted from G. Albaum, *International Marketing and Export Management* (Boston: Addison-Wesley, 1989).

goal to become an international market leader (as discussed in Chapter 2) and the managerial urge to expand the market. The external-reactive category is the second most important. Quite a few interviewees reported that people from foreign countries had seen their products in stores, in factories, and at fairs and wanted to purchase them. Heinz Hankammer, the founder of Brita water filters, recounts how internationalization began:

> Visitors, mainly distributors, from abroad found our products in the stores in Germany. They became interested in them and called us. That's how it started in London in 1980. We found an excellent man there who sold the product to department stores, health food shops, and other outlets. People from all over the globe saw the product in those stores and approached us. London became the springboard for the world. In this initial stage we didn't call on any foreign customers but they called on us, wanting to distribute the product in their country. That's how it began, and today we are in sixty countries.

I should add that the reactive mode didn't last very long. Once Hankammer realized the international potential of his product, he initiated a highly proactive globalization campaign.

Typical patterns or paradigms of internationalization may be found in the literature. One such is indirect exporting → direct exporting → licensing → joint venture → sales and service subsidiary → assembly → local production (e.g., Root 1987). It has also been suggested that there are ideal patterns of the internationalization process. Ayal and Zif (1979) define "concentration" and "diversification" as alternative options. In concentration, a company starts by selling to few, carefully selected countries, while diversification signifies simultaneous market entry in several countries. Concentration is more time consuming but less demanding on capital and human resources. Attiyeh and Wenner (1981) extended the concept to "sequential concentration," in which at any given point resources are focused on one country; once the "critical mass" has been reached there, that is, the business has become self-sustaining, internationalization proceeds to the next country. This option also consumes a great deal of time since it ordinarily takes four to six years per country to reach critical mass (Simon 1982).

The hidden champions rarely follow such ideal patterns. Rather they started to internationalize very early, very rapidly, and often chaotically. The question: "How early, relative to the start of the company, did you begin to export?" should be answered on a scale of 1 (from the very beginning) to 7 (very late). Figure 4.4 presents the distribution of the replies.

These indicate that 82.4% scored below 4, which means that they began exporting early or very early. The mean score was 2.4. Viktor Dulger, founder-CEO of Prominent, world leader in metering pumps, exemplifies this spirit: "I was always first in the market." He attributes his success to three factors: "Product quality, high R&D intensity, and early presence in the market." These findings demonstrate that typical hidden champions had an international perspective of their business very early on. Even if internationalization occurred reactively, they were receptive to the opportunities offered by foreign markets. Without this attitude, rapid internationalization would not have been possible.

This result is consistent with a study conducted in Australia on emerging exporters (Australian Manufacturing Council and McKinsey & Company 1993). So-called born-global firms—a label coined for companies

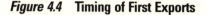

Figure 4.4 **Timing of First Exports**

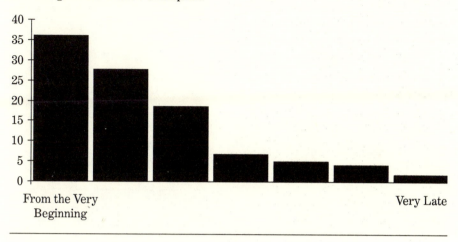

Percentage of the Hidden Champions

From the Very Beginning

Very Late

that from the outset view the world as their marketplace—play an increasingly important role in Australia's export performance. Rather than viewing foreign markets as useful adjuncts to domestic ones, these firms see their domestic activities as supporting their exports. The average born-global Australian firm started its foreign activities in its second year of existence, and has an export share of 75%. Many hidden champions can lay claim to the born-global designation.

This is true in spite of the fact that many do not operate in industries that are global by nature. Modern industries like computers, mobile phones, and hi-fi equipment are in this category. These are generally new industries without historical restrictions and national standards, so their products become global at birth. Many hidden champions are found in fragmented and mature markets that are not global by nature, and they must overcome national barriers.

The characteristic process of globalization for a hidden champion is best illustrated by a concrete example. Figure 4.5 shows the international expansion of Kärcher, the world market leader in high-pressure cleaning systems.

Kärcher, which was founded in 1935, did not establish its first subsidiary until 1962, when it became a presence in France. Its internationalization through subsidiaries proceeded relatively slowly for the next dec-

Figure 4.5 **The Internationalization Process of Kärcher**

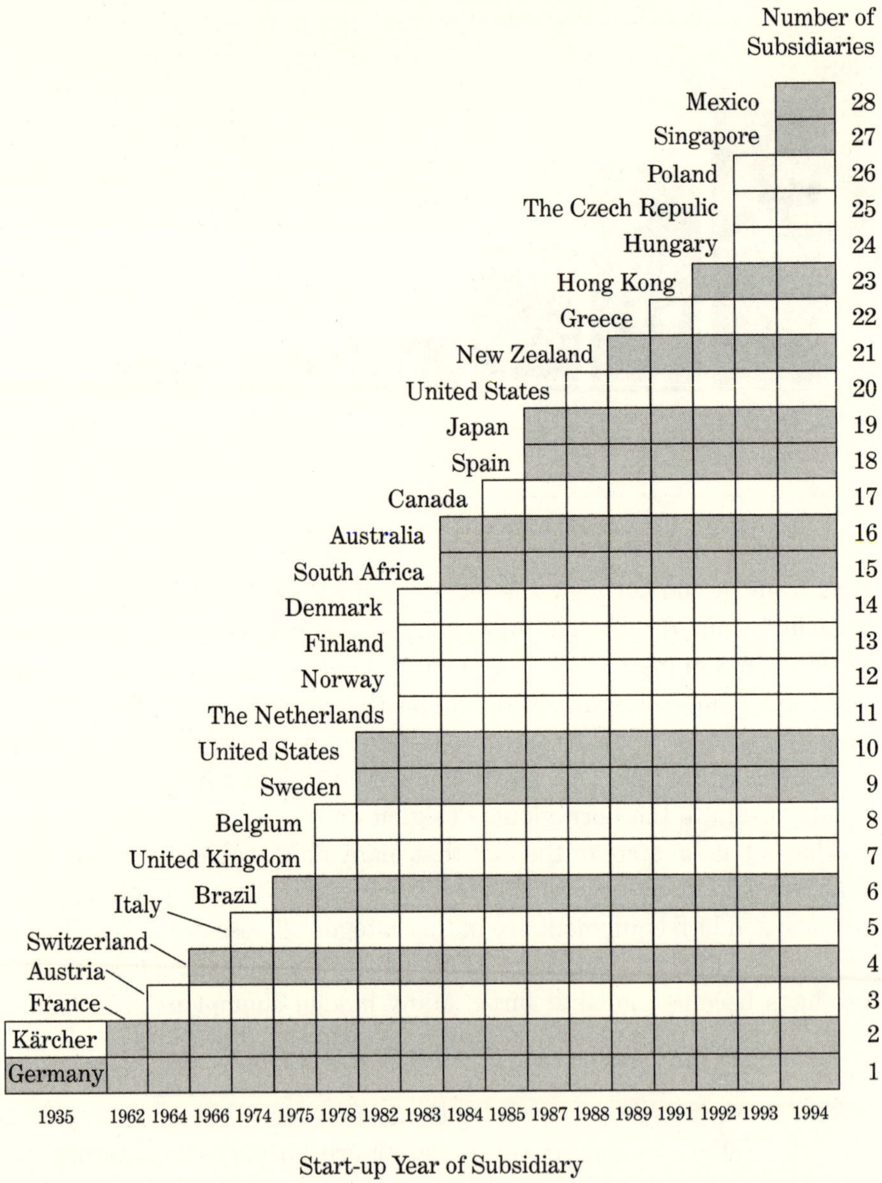

Number of
Subsidiaries

	Number of Subsidiaries
Mexico	28
Singapore	27
Poland	26
The Czech Repulic	25
Hungary	24
Hong Kong	23
Greece	22
New Zealand	21
United States	20
Japan	19
Spain	18
Canada	17
Australia	16
South Africa	15
Denmark	14
Finland	13
Norway	12
The Netherlands	11
United States	10
Sweden	9
Belgium	8
United Kingdom	7
Brazil	6
Italy	5
Switzerland	
Austria	4
France	3
Kärcher	2
Germany	1

1935   1962 1964 1966 1974 1975 1978 1982 1983 1984 1985 1987 1988 1989 1991 1992 1993 1994

Start-up Year of Subsidiary

ade—by 1974, only three more had been formed, in Austria, Switzerland, and Italy. The next decade saw rapid acceleration with the appearance of eleven new subsidiaries. In the most recent ten-year period another twelve were added to the group. This number will most likely climb even higher in the next decade, particularly with Kärcher's pending entry into Asian and East European countries.

Market entry as such is often prepared and executed by a hands-on method rather than with a highly planned or systematic approach. Hermann Kronseder, the founder of Krones, world leader in bottle labeling machines, describes his entry into the U.S. market:

> In 1966, an American businessman called me. Four weeks later I flew to the United States, accompanied by my cousin who spoke English and functioned as interpreter. It was my first visit to the States and I was overwhelmed. We visited New York, Chicago, Detroit, and eventually Milwaukee. I came to the conclusion that we needed our own subsidiary in the United States. Two days later we founded Krones Inc. in a room at the Knickerbockers Hotel in Milwaukee. Another two days later we had our first order from a Milwaukee brewery.

It took a couple of years for this operation to go smoothly, and over time several people had to be replaced.

The entry of Brita to the U.S. market is another example. Heinz Hankammer recounts:

> Somebody in Salt Lake City expressed interest in our products. I flew over to see whether Brita water filters could be sold in the United States. I went to a drugstore and asked whether I could install a table. I started to make tea with Brita-filtered water and talked to the customers passing by, and I sold my filters. After three days I knew what works in America and what does not. That was ten years ago, and today our U.S. sales are more than $150 million. Four weeks ago I was in Shanghai and did the same. And last week I was in Tiranë, the capital of Albania. I want to get hands-on experience.

Many international opportunities develop by chance, as for Brita in Russia. Hankammer again:

> I sponsor a soccer club, which was being visited by a Russian team, and I got to know the mother of one of the Russian players. It turned out that she spoke English and was a business-minded person. She started our

business in Russia in 1993, and the company now has twenty-five employees and produced sales of $1.33 million in 1994. A good start!

The most critical aspect in international market entry according to the CEOs is to find the right personnel. The multiplication of the hidden champions from country to country relies on key people rather than on systems. This explains why, as for Kärcher, the process may take many years. In its initial phase, the international experience of a hidden champion is quite limited. A company has few people whom it can deploy to set up foreign ventures. But over time, as more people become familiar with these activities, the internationalization process can be rapidly accelerated. It should be evident that such complex processes do not always run smoothly and without difficulties. Serious problems arise frequently, and crises are encountered in individual countries, particularly in markets like the United States or Japan, which are difficult to enter.

So the origin of the impulse to internationalize doesn't matter much. The process is primarily goal- and will-driven. What really matters is that once the hidden champions have smelled blood, they pursue globalization with determination and relentless energy. Initially, the effort proceeds slowly, since management bottlenecks and available capital set limits to the speed of internationalization. But with learning and capital accumulation, the process accelerates and international expansion is carried out with maximum possible speed.

THE RISKS OF GLOBALIZATION

Chapter 3 examined the risk of focusing on a narrow market defined by product technology or customer needs. In this mode, the hidden champions, by depending on a single market, incur a relatively high degree of risk. However, the narrow-market hazard is considerably moderated by the geographical spread of their activities. Business climates and cycles differ from country to country. A company's presence in many markets can provide a hedge against such fluctuations and thus protect it against risks.

Dürr, the world leader in car painting systems, characterizes 1993 as "a successful year, thanks to our presence worldwide" (Annual Report 1993). Sixteen of its nineteen foreign subsidiaries are fully owned, which allowed Dürr to cope well with the post-1992 currency crisis and business cycles. Work could be reallocated from countries with high-value currencies, thus lowering the high costs that would have been incurred owing to the devaluation of their currencies. At about the same time, the European auto industry experienced a major downturn and halted the building of new plants. Nevertheless, with its strong position in the U.S. market, Dürr could compensate for this negative trend through larger orders from American automotive companies, which were experiencing an upswing and starting to invest in new equipment. Its global presence allowed Dürr to continue its positive development in the past couple of years, which is rather unusual for such a cyclical industry.

But the globalization process itself holds considerable risks. Doing business and having subsidiaries in many countries can be a major addition to the complexity of a company. It is difficult to judge the potential of risk in new areas. Markets in emerging or culturally alien countries carry objectively higher risks. Krones, with nineteen foreign subsidiaries, suffered serious learning experiences in 1994. In 1993, it had won a hotly contested contract of $113 million—the largest contract ever awarded in the industry—to build twenty bottling lines for Baesa, an Argentinean company licensed to bottle Pepsi-Cola. Krones SA, the Brazilian subsidiary slated to handle this project was concurrently building forty-two labeling machines for a Brazilian customer. Therefore, some of the Baesa production had to be shifted to the German factories, where costs are much higher. According to the *Wall Street Journal Europe,* this screwup may have cost Krones $13.4 million to $20 million in pretax earnings (Ascarelli 1994). But the article, adding that these were not Krones's only international problems, listed the following information:

- In Algeria, Krones decided that the political situation is too unstable to risk sending employees to install equipment ordered by a multinational company. It has decided to swallow the costs rather than risk damaging business relations with a major customer.

- In Yemen, Krones had begun installing equipment for a customer when civil war broke out. The project was scrapped.

- In Poland, a customer of several years with a perfect payment record suddenly didn't make his October monthly installment on his order. Krones is writing off the rest of the amount owed but will continue trying to collect the money.

- A complicated barter deal involving one of the former Soviet republics fell through when the customer there couldn't deliver on his end of the deal. The transaction still could be resuscitated sometime next year.

- Even in Brazil, Krones admits, it has been unable to properly manage its subsidiary. It installed a new finance director earlier this year [1994] in an effort to improve reporting to group head-quarters. But he was let go after only three months, and the company has ended up trying to manage its Brazilian operations from its German headquarters.

Krones, an exemplary hidden champion in the past, illustrates the potential complexity of globalization and the difficulty involved in controlling it. Rapid international expansion, management bottlenecks, and unlucky coincidences can combine to create serious risks. But by 1995, Krones had these problems under control and was back on its successful track (see "Nach dem Schock über den Kursrutsch zeight der Vorstand Einsight" 1995). Of course, large corporations face the same problems in international markets and experience failures as well. But the hidden champions have fewer people and resources for coping with these difficulties.

Some of these firms apply one of two specific strategies in limiting competitive international risks. They first avoid world regions with strong local competitors. Some therefore have consciously not entered U.S. markets whose market leaders reciprocate by refraining from attacking European or other markets. JK Ergoline or Claas, for example, although they are active in other foreign markets, do little business in the United States. Other barriers to entry, such as distribution channels and differences in technology, may add to their self-restriction. A second strategy involves consciously and aggressively entering the competitor's home turf to keep it at bay there.

In *Triad Power*, Ohmae (1985) suggested that global companies place a "leg" in each of the three economic centers of the industrialized world: the United States, Europe, and Japan/Asia. Many hidden champions share this view. Some distinguish between "profit markets" and "learning markets." In a profit market, a company sells enough to show a gain. In a learning market, its main purpose is to learn about the competitive environment, innovative developments, and so forth, and to that end accepts losses or low profits. Quite a few of these companies assign their international engagements to the latter category. So learning early on about foreign competitors, keeping them at bay, and preventing their becoming global can be an excellent strategy against competitive risks in international business. Christian Brühe of Uniplan, a world-leading exhibition contractor, recounts:

> We were the first company in our business to internationalize. After having gained several years of experience in Hong Kong, we feel strong enough to enter other Asian markets. Our competitors, with no experience in this region, just do not have a comparable opportunity.

The hidden champions are firm about not yielding international markets to their competitors.

Japan

The Japanese market presents a formidable challenge to all foreign companies, including the hidden champions. In a separate study I investigated factors that lead to success or to failure in Japan, where I interviewed sixty-six managers by means of a questionnaire. Table 4.4 ranks the factors' importance.

Looking at the success factors, one realizes that some of the most important, like perseverance, commitment, uniqueness of product, are congruent with particular strengths of the hidden champions. In the same vein, the champions avoid many important failure factors, such as short-term orientation and lack of flexibility and commitment. The requirements of the Japanese market and the capabilities of the hidden champions match pretty well. It is therefore no surprise that they have greater success there than typical Western companies. Almost half the companies covered in Figure 4.2 (46.2%) have a subsidiary in Japan. Their satisfaction with business in Japan shows a highly significant correlation with their overall success, indicating that the better the company, the better its success there; some achieve extraordinary success. The latter include Karl Mayer, Heidelberger Druckmaschinen, Weinig, and Trumpf.

Karl Mayer, the world market leader in rashel machines, was, in 1968, the first foreign company to establish a majority position in a Japanese firm, namely Toyo Menka. Within four years after its entry, Karl Mayer and its CEO in Japan, Kotaro Ono, had pushed all Japanese competitors out of the market. In the meantime the Japanese subsidiary, Nippon Mayer, has been fully acquired and is the leading contender in the product's Asian markets. The parent and the subsidiary have been planning a foray into the huge Chinese market. The service of Nippon Mayer in Japan matches that of Karl Mayer in Germany.

Table 4.4 **Factors Affecting Success and Failure in Japanese Markets**

Rank According to Importance	Factors Contributing to Success	Factors Contributing to Failure
1	Perseverance, patience	Short-term orientation
2	Commitment of parent company	Lack of flexibility
3	Distribution strategy	Wrong products
4	Uniqueness of product	Lack of commitment of parent company
5	Image/positioning	Insufficient market research
6	Personality of management/individuals	Lack of understanding of Japanese consumers
7	Product support/service	Wrong local management
8	Careful market research and analysis	Lack of professionalism
9	Advertising/communication	Lack of understanding of Japanese competitors
10	Early market entry	Market entry investment too low
11	Personal connections	Wrong positioning
12		High prices
13		Market entry too late

The same is true for Heidelberger Druckmaschinen, the world leader in offset-printing presses. Even a good product has been known to break down occasionally and need repair, and the hidden champions do not compromise their service standards in any market. Heidelberg's Japanese service network is as comprehensive as that of its German home market. The head of Heidelberg's Tokyo subsidiary noted, "How could we afford to offer an inferior service here?"

For Weinig, world leader in automatic molders—special woodworking machines—one could argue that it is closer to its customers in Japan than to those in Germany. Weinig Japan maintains a service branch on each of the four main Japanese islands and plans to open three additional offices in the near future, while the German service operation is centralized at headquarters in Tauberbischofsheim. All of Weinig's Japanese service engineers are trained in Germany for up to a year and receive additional training at the German headquarters each ensuing year. The sales manager for Japan says, "We offer German products and Japanese service. That's our secret." Weinig's Japanese sales exceed those in Germany.

Berthold Leibinger, CEO of Trumpf, world leader in sheet metal cutting devices, shares these views:

> Our numerically controlled machines are serviced solely through employees of Trumpf Japan. The importance of training our Japanese employees cannot be overemphasized. Continuous contacts between the parent company and Trumpf Japan guarantee that each service technician in Japan is always up to date and has access to the most recent information. Our own manufacturing operation in Japan allows us to make spare parts available within forty-eight hours. This wouldn't be possible if they had to be shipped from Germany.

The success stories of foreign companies in Japan are not confined to industrial products. Braun, a world leader in several fields of small appliances, sells twice as many electrical shavers in Japan as in Germany, in spite of extremely strong Japanese competitors, for example, Matsushita. Braun's image, its design, its brand franchise, and its strategy of commitment have led to this firm's success in the lion's den. Wella, world leader in professional hair care products, is another success story. Under the leadership of Dieter Schneidewind, it became hugely successful in the Japanese market. Wella targeted its strategy at hairdressers and elevated the role of women in society, which was most unusual in Japan. Wella was the first company to use only a female speaker in its TV advertisements, a real innovation in Japan during the early seventies. Its ad for "Dancin," which showed young women dancing without males, sent the message that women are self-sustained and independent and made Wella's products extremely popular with young women.

To be successful in a foreign market as demanding as Japan, a company has to deploy its full competitive arsenal. The hidden champions have cracked foreign markets as difficult as Japan partly because they were willing to make a strong commitment, for example, in capital investment and in people. Although a high initial investment may not be justified by short-term returns, they consider it necessary for other reasons, but mostly to show potential customers and other constituencies that they are serious and determined to stay.

BMW, although too large to be a hidden champion, exemplified this approach. When it entered the Japanese market in the 1980s, its initial investment was several times higher than the amount required to run what was then a very small operation. Lüder Paysen, at the time head of BMW Japan, commented: "In Japan a high initial investment of a foreign company signals to suppliers, customers, banks, the public at large, and to the employees how serious the company is with regard to the Japanese market." If these aspects are not observed, Japanese competitors can easily take advantage of a lack of perceived commitment by foreign companies. During my stays in Japan I have heard that competitors exploit the Japanese stereotype that foreign companies which have entered the Japanese market don't have the will to persevere there. BMW used the heavy investment as a selling point to dealers, banks, and potential customers. Today BMW has its own highly visible and prestigious building in Tokyo, a symbol of its continued commitment. Its sales in Japan are ten times higher than they were in the early 1980s.

The commitment of people means, more specifically, continuity of people. Many of the executives who run hidden champions' foreign operations have been in charge of their units for more than ten years. The revolving door that often characterizes foreign subsidiaries of large multinational corporations is rare among the hidden champions. As a result, managers know that they will probably be working with the same customers ten or more years down the road and are therefore highly committed to them. Commitment and the will to persevere are certainly keystones of the successful hidden champions in Japan.

Emerging Markets

While Japan constitutes one extreme of difficulty in entering a foreign market, emerging markets pose a different challenge to the hidden champions. As is evident in Figure 4.2, many of them are represented in larger emerging markets like Brazil and India. Since the late 1980s, such third world countries have been joined by an ever increasing number of new states in Central and Eastern Europe. Both because of their proximity and their state of development, these countries are of primary interest to many hidden champions, which prove that they act quickly and grasp new opportunities. A case in point is Würth, world leader in assembly products. By early 1995, it had established subsidiaries in the following Central and East European countries: Bulgaria, Croatia, Poland, Romania, Russia, Slovakia, Slovenia, Chechnya, Ukraine, and Hungary.

It would probably be difficult to uncover a company of similar size with equal coverage in this part of the world. Other hidden champions, well aware of the importance of being first in emerging markets, have entered or are considering entering them. Many accord a high priority to building a market position before the competition shows up. One of the fastest and most determined is undoubtedly Baader, a company that dominates the world market for fish-dissection devices with a whopping 90% share. Until 1992, the closed city of Vladivostok, one of the main ports of the Soviet-Russian navy in the far east of Russia, about 9,200 kilometers (about 5,700 miles) and seven time zones from Moscow, was forbidden to foreigners. Almost immediately after its opening, in 1993, Baader set up shop in this remote and harsh place. Two engineers, Hartmut Fischer and Thomas Schrader, renovated, by themselves, the building into which they then moved. Now they equip and service ships with Baader products, most assuredly transferring Baader's wide-ranging dominant position to this location as well. To a certain degree, the firm is simply continuing a tradition begun in 1906, when two merchants from Hamburg built a huge department store in Vladivostok. It conducted business under their names, Kunst & Albers, until it was nationalized in 1930 and became GUM, which has remained the most important department store in Vladivostok and become the most famous retail emporium in Moscow. Hidden championship is not a new phenomenon!

Deutsche Messe AG/Hanover Fairs, the world leader in industrial fairs and exhibitions, is another interesting case. Although its international business is still in its infancy, it is supposed to contribute one-third to total sales in ten years. In the past, fairs have been, almost by definition, locally organized businesses, a situation Hanover Fairs intends to change. Since industrial countries are well covered by national companies, Hanover Fairs focuses on emerging markets in Asia, founding Hanover Fairs Asia in Singapore, Hanover Fairs Middle East in Istanbul, and opening two offices in China.

For many hidden champions, China is a primary target market. Eff-eff

Fritz Fuss, one of the world's leading companies in security systems, invests heavily in China and received the "China Business Award" from Cathay Pacific Airlines and the business magazine *Impulse*. Eff-eff's CEO, Dr. Willi Merkel, comments: "For a mid-size company, it is easier to conquer a new market like China than to make inroads into established markets with strong incumbents like the United States or Japan." Another company that builds its success in China and other emerging Asian markets such as Vietnam is Windhorst. Its founder, Lars Windhorst (born in 1976!), has already acquired fame (Rohwedder 1996)—and the nickname "Xiao Lao Ban" (The Little Boss)—in China and Hong Kong.

These examples show that the hidden champions are persistently building positions in the markets of the future, an indispensable activity in attaining and defending world market leadership.

INTELLECTUAL FOUNDATIONS OF GLOBALIZATION

While, from a superficial viewpoint, achieving global business scope may appear to be easy, it was anything but easy for the hidden champions. Not a short-term result, it must be built on cognitive and behavioral foundations that transcend the narrow boundaries of business. Corporate culture and societal factors play an important role in overcoming barriers to globalization.

The most obvious barrier is language. The advice of Anton Fugger, "The customer's language is the best language," is taken seriously by the hidden champions, for they don't accept language as a barrier to internationalization. Some have an exceptionally proactive approach to the language problem. Peter Barth, managing director of Joh. Barth, the leader in hops, says:

> Our philosophy is that each manager should speak at least three foreign languages in addition to his native tongue. This is important because of its psychological effects. In learning a foreign language, one gains an understanding of the foreign culture. This is the very base for our superior relationship with our customers throughout the world and no doubt our main competitive advantage. We happen to be located in Germany. Mentally, however, we are not German but international.

Willingness to adopt foreign languages must not be confined to management levels. At many hidden champions, the customary language is English, and during my numerous visits I frequently had the impression that I was outside Germany because phone conversations and meetings were being held in a foreign language.

These are the seeds and the soil from which true globalization grows. In my own company, we demand that even the secretaries speak three languages, German, English, and one more. I believe that such demands are largely a matter of corporate culture. Languages are an indispensable prerequisite for international business, and one of the biggest mistakes companies make is not to be demanding. The hidden champions have no natural advantages in this regard. Many of their founders received only the traditional eight years of German schooling, without foreign languages, and three years of vocational training. But everyone I met had learned English, either self-taught or on the job, and could conduct business in this language. Lars Windhorst speaks Chinese.

Quite a few had acquired knowledge of other foreign languages. Lars Windhorst speaks Chinese. Some, like Dieter Schneidewind, formerly of Wella, even learned Japanese, as did Otto Gies, sales director of Paul Binhold, world leader in anatomical teaching aids (skeletons etc.), which cracked the Japanese market. Binhold's market share in Japan is about 50%. Binhold's catalog is available in fifteen languages—the catalog of the next best competitor is printed in only three languages. The CEO of a technical company who prefers to remain anonymous recounts:

> In the 1960s, as a young man, I worked for a couple of years in Japan and I learned Japanese intensively. Today I can still understand seventy to eighty percent of a Japanese conversation. This is a tremendous advantage in my frequent negotiations with Japanese business partners.

Lars Windhorst, whose company was founded in 1993 and has sales revenues of about $140 million mainly from markets such as China and Vietnam, learned Chinese and even Vietnamese to come closer to his customers there.

I think that the importance of language is grossly underrated by many people. The appreciation of foreign language ability varies between companies and countries. Some companies require, as a matter of course, that a local language be learned. Royal Dutch Shell is among them, and consequently each foreigner in the management team of Deutsche Shell AG, its German subsidiary, has learned and speaks German. The same cannot be said of most American multinationals. The American managers they deploy to Europe rarely bother to learn the local language. They take it as a given that everyone can deal with them in English, which is

Table 4.5 **Understanding Spoken English**

	Self-assessment	Actual Understanding
Belgium	41%	17%
France	20	3
Germany	32	15
Italy	9	1
Netherlands	51	28
Spain	9	3

Source: Adapted from C. Drewes, "Euro-Kommunikation," in *Euro-Dimensionen des Marketing,* ed. H. G. Meissner (Dortmund: Fachverlag Arnold, 1992), 82.

indeed mostly true. There are also differences between the hidden champions and large German corporations. The latter's employees often find it hard to switch to foreign languages at meetings, seminars, and conferences, but hidden champions, whose international management meetings are almost always in English, do it more easily.

Behind an individual company's ability to adopt foreign languages stands a country's overall language competence. Major differences exist. Table 4.5 shows the self-assessment and actual understanding of English for various European countries.

Today, children in most countries receive at least some instruction in English. However, the effectiveness of the training differs markedly from country to country. The more valid and interesting figures in Table 4.5 are the percentages of actual understanding. Here it is clear that smaller countries like Belgium and Netherlands are the leaders. Among the larger countries, Germany is well ahead. In the Romance language countries of France, Italy, and Spain, only a small portion of the population really understands English. Although England, naturally enough, is not represented, a survey of British business directors found that "half make no effort to study local business etiquette and three in ten do not bother to learn a few foreign phrases" (Burke 1994, 1). A company that works in an environment unconducive to foreign languages must undertake major efforts to overcome these deficiencies in order to globalize successfully.

A concrete case illustrates this problem. Cecilia Simon is managing director of Lingua Video Media GmbH, a small German company that imports video films from many different countries and sells them in Germany. The Spanish wholesaler from which Lingua Video Media buys employs no one who speaks sufficient English or any other foreign language to take orders by telephone. This is an extremely annoying impediment, so Simon has begun to learn Spanish, her fourth language, to facilitate purchasing in Spain. If a company is serious about its international business it must overcome the language barrier.

Internationalization also involves the clever use of symbols. People often feel insecure when they visit foreign countries, and small symbols can offer them comfort. Tracto-Technik, a leading company which makes machines that dig horizontal subterranean holes like a mole without an open trench, welcomes foreign customers by flying their country's flag. Many other hidden champions practice this and similar symbolic actions. One CEO, who offers a choice between a Japanese and a German restaurant to his Japanese guests, finds that they frequently prefer the first alternative. During a business negotiation in a foreign country, they feel more comfortable in a familiar environment. In the same vein, products have to be adjusted to a country's preferences. Paul Binhold offers torsos with Japanese features in Japan and with African features in Africa. Such simple amenities are often neglected in international business.

Beyond language and symbols the overall internationalization of society affects the ability of companies to globalize. While it is difficult to measure the degree of internationalization for an individual society, a possible single indicator is the number of international telephone calls made in selected countries. These are shown in Figure 4.6 for 1989, the most recent year for which data were available.

This indicator confirms that relative to countries of similar size, Germany seems to be strongly internationalized. Its per capita international telephone intensity is 3.7 times higher than that of Italy and almost ten times higher than that of Japan. Since 1989, international telephone traffic has more than doubled but there is no reason to assume that the relative positions of countries have changed.

A further trend from which international business can profit is cross-border travel, but it is difficult to come by meaningful statistics. Table 4.6 provides the numbers of overnight stays according to country of origin. It shows that French visitors spent two million bed-nights in Germany, while German visitors spent 26.9 million bed-nights in France, a difference corresponding to a factor of 13.5. The situation is similar if Germany is compared with Italy and Spain. On a per capita

Figure 4.6 International Telephone Calls in Selected Countries, 1989

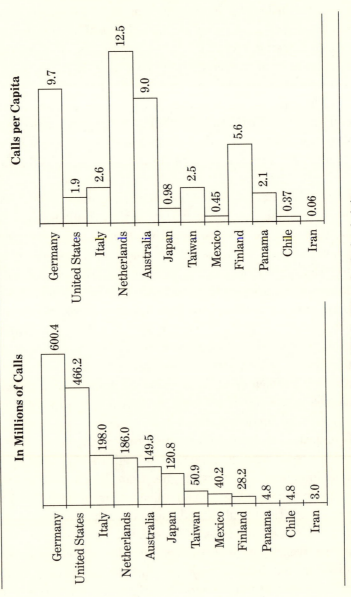

In Millions of Calls

Germany	600.4
United States	466.2
Italy	198.0
Netherlands	186.0
Australia	149.5
Japan	120.8
Taiwan	50.9
Mexico	40.2
Finland	28.2
Panama	4.8
Chile	4.8
Iran	3.0

Calls per Capita

Germany	9.7
United States	1.9
Italy	2.6
Netherlands	12.5
Australia	9.0
Japan	0.98
Taiwan	2.5
Mexico	0.45
Finland	5.6
Panama	2.1
Chile	0.37
Iran	0.06

Sources: Wall Street Journal Europe, October 10, 1991, for 1989, and author's calculations.

Table 4.6 **International Travel, 1992, Measured by Bed-Nights (in millions of bed-nights)**

Country of Origin of Customer	Country of Overnight Stay						
	France	Germany	Italy	Spain	United Kingdom	Total Bed-Nights	Bed-Nights per Capita
France	—	2.0	7.0	13.5	16.3	38.8	0.68
Germany	26.9	—	45.2	39.0	17.6	128.7	2.04
Italy	17.3	2.0	—	8.3	8.2	35.8	0.62
Spain	8.3	0.7	1.8	—	8.3	19.1	0.49
United Kingdom	25.6	3.5	6.2	44.1	—	79.4	1.38

Sources: Jordi Montaña, ed., *Marketing in Europe* (London: 1994) and author's calculations.

basis, the Germans spend about three times as many nights abroad as the French or the Italians, and about four times as many as the Spaniards.

The asymmetry is similar if one compares spending in the United States and Germany. While American visitors spend $1.09 billion in Germany, Germans spend $2.34 billion in the United States (Statistisches Bundesamt 1993, 135). The factor of this difference is 2.15.

Since tourists are included, one may rightly object that these figures compare apples and pears. But this is only partially true, because foreign experience as a tourist widens one's international horizon and makes it much easier to send somebody abroad to execute a job. Hidden champions have an urgent need for people who are willing to accept foreign assignments. Reinhard Wirtgen, CEO of Wirtgen, world leader in road recycling machines, comments: "I frequently need a team which can be deployed anywhere in the world on short notice. With enough people who have been abroad, we are able to assemble such a group in a few days, be it for Alaska, Siberia, or the Sahara. This capability is a huge advantage." Only employees who feel at home everywhere in the world, who have traveled in several countries, are ready for such challenges. In general, the hidden champions do not consider employee mobility a major barrier to globalization.

I observed further asymmetries between countries from my university work. In two student exchange programs, one with an American, the other with a French university, we never had any difficulty filling the slots available for Germans. Demand was typically three to four times higher than the number of available places. Both the American and the French partners, however, had trouble finding enough students who wanted to go to Germany. Either their language capabilities were insufficient or there was simply not enough interest in studying abroad. Such an attitude among young people is not a good foundation for the globalization of a country and its businesses.

With telephones and fax machines, almost every place on the earth is only a minute away, given that one can overcome language and mental barriers. And the maximum time for the delivery of people and goods is about twenty hours. Only a century ago, it took that amount of time to cover a distance of 100 kilometers (62 miles). In this historical perspective, the world has shrunk to a radius of 100 kilometers. Costs of travel present no obstacles either, amounting on average to only 1% of the sales revenues of the hidden champions. The most costly exception is Japan, where for every dollar earned, two cents have to be spent on travel. Considering all these facts there is really no reason not to view the world as one market. The barriers exist only in the mind, and the hidden champions have shed them. These companies do not accept their small size as a limiting factor. Each company should, however, realize that the environment can favor or disfavor globalization. Germany seems to provide an environment that strongly supports it, which may explain the prevalence of so many hidden champions within its borders. But as examples from other countries show, hidden champions can flourish everywhere (see Table 11.1 for a selection). They may only have to work a little harder to overcome societal impediments in order to create the corporate culture and the intellectual foundations that foster globalization.

SUMMARY

The discussion in this chapter has shown that the hidden champions are true global firms. They view the whole world as their market and act accordingly. Their global success contains important lessons for any company.

- A narrow focus on product, technology, and customer need is combined with a global perspective in marketing and selling. This two-pillar strategy is based on the perception that customers in the same industry tend to be more similar across countries than customers across industries within the same country.

- A global scope can make niche markets large enough to allow for sufficient economies of scale and experience curve effects.

- Successful globalization can originate from different motives, but it should start as early as possible and proceed rapidly.

- It seems preferable to establish direct customer contacts through owned subsidiaries in target markets; customer relationships should, ideally, not be delegated to third parties.

- Globalization can moderate the risk associated with a narrow market focus because a company can sell in many countries. But at the same time, globalization introduces new risks owing to an increase in complexity.

- A company that globalizes should closely observe competitive aspects both with regard to avoiding head-on collisions with strong local competitors and with regard to keeping competitors at bay in their local strongholds.

- The Japanese market can be cracked, but accomplishing it requires excellent performance, including high commitment and superb service.

- In emerging markets, companies should recognize the importance of arriving first.

- Language ability, travel, educational exchange, and international experience form the intellectual and psychological foundations for global business success. Companies can create these foundations, but they depend to a certain degree on the international orientation of their societies.

The hidden champions prove that small companies can surmount barriers, which are mainly mental, to becoming global competitors. The world, having shrunk in size, is accessible. For many companies, ignorance of their opportunities is their only boundary. The hidden champions have overcome these mental barriers and successfully negotiated the difficult road to globalization. They can serve as role models for the many firms about to set sail on the same course.

5

The Customer

I know and have visited each of our customers in the world.

T HE HIDDEN CHAMPIONS maintain close relationships characterized by mutual dependence with their customers. Companies with a narrow focus, on the other hand, usually have to rely strongly on a small number of customers that would find it extremely difficult to replace the unique products they require. This situation creates commitment on both sides and forms the basis for a long-term relationship built on trust and respect, but does not necessarily include friendship. While the hidden champions are close to their customers, they are not the marketing professionals of textbook fame. Less apt than large corporations to offer lip service, the hidden champions pay a great deal of attention to customer orientation. Their deeds, not their words, say a lot about the effects of closeness to customers. But take these precepts with a grain of salt— the sample firms' generally customer-specific actions should not naively be mimicked.

THE NATURE OF CUSTOMER RELATIONS

Many of the hidden champions do not deal in simple products but in complex problem solutions and systems. This has a direct impact on their relations to and involvement with the customers. In the hidden champion sample, 69.7% of the respondents rated the importance of customers' evaluation of transactions as high or very high. And 68% gave an above-average rating to the statement that their customers expect to receive a great deal of information. A clear majority of the companies think that purchasing their product is not a routine matter for customers. Three-quarters of the firms agreed with the statement that it would be difficult for their customers to replace their products.

But customers are not unilaterally dependent; 77.7% of the firms believe that they depend just as strongly on their customers. About half agreed that customers can put pressure on them and that a loss of important customers would threaten their existence. As a consequence of their narrow focus, many hidden champion firms derive a large percentage of their sales from few customers. One-seventh said that more than 50% of their sales come from only five customers, and for another quarter their five largest customers contribute between 20% and 50% to total sales.

All these findings confirm the strong mutual dependence of the two parties. Both the products and the purchasing of them tend to be complex and associated with substantial transaction costs and high uncertainty. Significant barriers to switching exist for both sides, a situation that typically leads to a long-term relationship.

Given sixteen factors to consider, the hidden champions scored long-established customer relations as their major strength—6.1 on a 7-point scale. Two-thirds view a sale to a new customer as the starting point for a long-term business relation. And 82.5% classified their customers as loyal or highly loyal, occasional buyers playing a minor role. The respondents, by 85.8%, expect to retain their current customers. Less successful companies can only dream of such figures. And these findings from the quantitative survey were consistently reenforced in the interviews. Time and again the persons with whom we spoke emphasized the long-term nature of the business relation, which has to be based on a win-win situation.

With their market power, hidden champions occasionally attain short-term positions of strength relative to their customers, for example, when a supply bottleneck occurs. But they are careful not to abuse such a situation, sometimes explicitly refraining from imposing higher prices under the given circumstances. Most customers show their appreciation of this sort of behavior when the business tide turns. I have heard many customers praise the dependability of such suppliers.

The long-term customer orientation of the hidden champions is in line with recent research findings. The customary wisdom that it costs five times as much to replace a customer as it does to keep one is old wine for them. They are also well aware that the contribution per customer is higher the longer a customer has been with a company (Heskett et al. 1990). Hidden champions like Hauni, Barth, Heidenhain, and many others have done business with customers uninterruptedly for decades, even for generations. When in conversation I referred to recently published findings of this nature, I received a sympathetic, sometimes contemptuous smile. One CEO commented: "What's new about it? Isn't it common sense? These obvious principles have always governed our policy. If you keep your customers satisfied through excellent quality and service, they stay with you forever—and pay you a good price." Indeed, it is common sense! But it is often difficult to implement.

The hidden champions build customer relations on economics and rationality, not emotion and friendship. They are well aware that the relation between supplier and customer involves a substantial element of power and try mightily to shift the power balance in their favor. One company systematically shields its customers from its suppliers by relabeling and repainting components to prevent the customers from recognizing their origin and buying directly from the original manufacturers. Another firm makes a deliberate attempt to increase its supply shares to increase customer dependence. A third company deepens its product line through vertical integration and creates incompatibility with component suppliers to decrease customer choice. But while such actions are primarily undertaken to strengthen a firm's position, they may also work to the benefit of customers. They are relieved of the burden of dealing with multiple suppliers when one manufacturer assumes responsibility for a whole system, for example. Again, customers pay with growing dependence, and as long as suppliers refrain from taking undue advantage of it, both parties may benefit. Many hidden champions secure their leadership positions through skillful employment of such tactics. However, these tactics are rarely primary building stones; leading positions are achieved only by overall superior performance.

The hidden champions do not think highly of modern buzzwords like "customer enthusiasm" or "customer delight." They have a more sober view of the customer relation, namely that performance, value, and price play central roles. When they speak of customer relations, they mean economic substance rather than fads. While friendship, emotion, and delight may not be foundations of their customer relations, trust and mutual respect definitely are. And these attitudes produce highly tangible advantages in reducing legal work and in saving time and resources.

Excor, a pseudonym, a supplier of turnkey processing systems for the food industry, illustrates some of these advantages. A long-standing customer, a large multinational company, which I'll call Confood, was under extreme time pressure to build a new processing plant in an East European country to preempt a competitor. Excor started to build the plant without a contract from Confood, in whose large organization the process of collecting necessary approval from various committees and numerous signatures took much longer than the company could afford. The project went so well that Excor received a further large order from Confood. In this second project, which was completed by late 1994, Confood delegated only one project controller. Excor's CEO comments, "Although this signaled great trust in our work, it put extreme pressure on us because we had to carry the full responsibility. I know that in a similar project, another customer might have deployed fifteen project controllers, which in the past was a normal number." In return for its trust, Confood spared the efforts of fourteen controllers, and hidden champion Excor was definitely ready to do its utmost to satisfy and retain this important customer.

In the next project, begun in 1995, Confood went a step further. Setting a budget of $63 million, it asked Excor to build a factory of a specified capacity for this amount. There was no competitive bidding, no written contract, only trust and a long-term business relation. The savings in time, cost, and human resources through this new type of supplier-customer relationship are enormous, as is the pressure on Excor to perform. While this is not yet a typical business relation, it illustrates the direction in which many hidden champions are heading. The tendency toward closer and ever more demanding business relations is particularly characteristic of industrial suppliers.

These observations offer several important lessons. The hidden champions and their customers are mutually dependent. One who wishes to establish a strong position vis-à-vis a customer must focus on, in turn becoming more dependent on, the customer. To a certain extent, market strength and dependence are two sides of a coin: on one side the customer demands superior performance; on the other, the supplier demands loyalty. This situation creates commitment and leads to a long-term relation that fosters trust and saves transaction costs, a profitable outcome for both.

CLOSENESS WITH THE CUSTOMER

In Peters and Waterman's *In Search of Excellence* (1982) the authors hold, in their "Close to the Customer" chapter, that "the excellent companies *really are* close to their customers. Other companies talk about it, the excellent companies do it" (156). From my current perspective, I have to question whether the excellent companies were really that close or if the book reproduced the lip service these large corporations paid to words or spectacular actions. I do think that the hidden champions are much closer to their customers than a typical large corporation can ever be.

What creates closeness with the customer? Obviously, every business person has a theory about it, but hardly anyone bothers to define it precisely. Christian Homburg (1995) recently developed a scientific conceptualization for it. Based on a sound theoretic concept and a questionnaire survey of 327 customers of industrial corporations and using a technique called causal analysis, Homburg found that closeness with a customer consists of two dimensions, "performance" and "interaction." The first comprises what the customer receives in terms of product, service, and quality of process, while the second relates to the interactions of the supplier with the customer representatives, whether they are open, responsive, and so forth. The two dimensions are in turn defined by seven factors, which reflect their different facets and are measured by twenty-eight single indicators. Figure 5.1 represents the closeness-to-customer concept developed by Homburg (1995).

Performance and interaction are roughly equal in importance to a business relationship. The hidden champions tend to exhibit the same degree of closeness to their customers on both dimensions. They perform excellently and show strength in interaction, particularly in openly offering information, in receptiveness, and in contacts with nonsales personnel. In this regard they differ substantially from typical large corporations. The sample companies are also more flexible in dealing with their customers (Factor 3). One can further simplify the concept by considering only the two dimensions, performance and interaction, as in Figure 5.2.

Figure 5.1   Closeness to Customer: Homburg's Concept

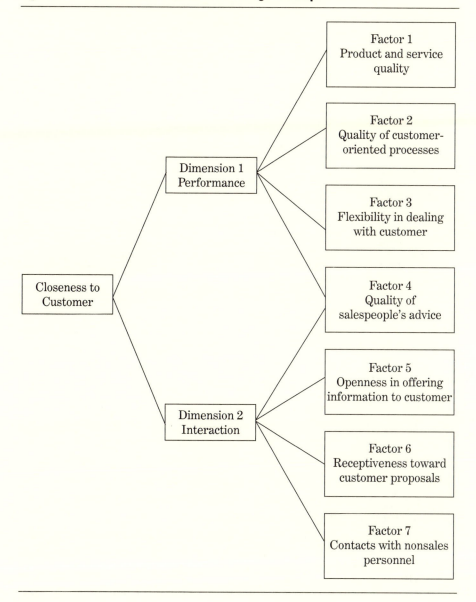

Figure 5.2 **Hidden Champions' Rates of Performance and Interaction**

	Performance	
	Low	High
Low		Large Firms
High	(Average) Small Firms	Hidden Champions

(Interaction is labeled along the left vertical axis, with Low and High rows)

The hidden champions are high on both dimensions. Large firms are often rated high on performance, but low on interaction. Average small firms display the opposite, sometimes with low rates of performance, but high scores on interaction.

The hidden champions are superior to large (high-performance) corporations in interaction and to (average) small companies in performance. They are high on both dimensions of the closeness-to-customer system, a combination definitely worth striving for.

While they are very close to their customers, these companies are not marketing professionals, at least not in the textbook sense. If the marketing professionalism of a company is measured by the percentage of its employees who work in a marketing function—planning, analysis, market research, and the like—the hidden champions fare poorly relative to large companies, rating their marketing professionalism as the third lowest among nineteen factors. Many don't have a staff member with a marketing title or a market research function or even employees with a marketing education. But almost every member of a hidden champion firm has some contact with customers.

The percentage of employees who see customers more or less regularly is two to three times that of large companies. I estimate that figure to be about 20 to 25% in the typical hidden champion versus just below 10% in large corporations. This important difference is illustrated in Figure 5.3. The distinction between closeness to customer and marketing professionalism may sound artificial. Isn't true marketing the same as being close to one's customers? Ideally this should indeed be the case, but as my comparative study has revealed, the reality is different. The hidden champions are not marketing professionals but they are closeness-to-customer professionals. The reverse is true for the typical large firm.

Of course, it is desirable to be high on both dimensions—close to customers with a market approach based on solid analyses and a professionally planned marketing mix; the hidden champions have to improve in the latter category. With increasing size, complexity, and number of countries served, the reliance of an entrepreneur on subjective feelings

Figure 5.3 **Closeness to Customer versus Marketing Professionalism of Hidden Champions and Large Firms**

| | Marketing Professionalism[a] | |
	Low	High
Closeness to Customer[b] — Low		Large Firms
Closeness to Customer[b] — High	Hidden Champions	Ideal

[a] Percentage of marketing experts.

[b] Percentage of employees with regular customer contact.

becomes less and less tenable. The larger sample companies, for example, Kärcher, Würth, and Wella, show a clear trend toward more marketing professionalism. Such a change often accompanies the transition from a founder-entrepreneur to a professional management. In the course of this development, the hidden champions should pay attention to preserving their closeness with customers. Increasing size and professionalism tend to be natural enemies of closeness to customers because, as illustrated in Figure 5.1, they negatively affect important factors like flexibility, openness, receptiveness, and personal contact. Some hidden champions are well aware of, and take precautions against, these looming dangers. A case in point is Putzmeister, a rapidly growing company, which is world market leader in concrete pumps. Karl Schlecht, its owner-CEO, has initiated decentralization by creating independently operating units. He aims explicitly at preserving the old strength of closeness to customer while the company continues on its path of fast expansion.

Figure 5.3 contains an important lesson for large firms, namely that they must improve in closeness to customers. While these firms usually have well-thought-out marketing plans and organizations, they are deficient in closeness to customer as defined in Figure 5.1. They are particularly lacking in flexibility, openness, receptiveness, and contact intensity. They usually have a multilayered hierarchy vis-à-vis the customer through a pronounced division of labor that results in keeping most employees distant from customers. The hidden champions display less division of labor and much more multifunctional deployment, which brings employees into direct contact with customers. These differences are illustrated in Figure 5.4. While the portrayal may be somewhat idealized, it points to important aspects. Large companies clearly define the lines between those who have direct customer contact and those who don't. In the hidden champions, however, the borderline between external—customer contact—and internal functions is fuzzy.

A typical employee of a sample company has a holistic view of the process of value creation in his firm and a clear understanding of his contribution to the ultimate value of the product the customer purchases. This attitude makes it easier for those in charge of external functions to assure that the customer's wishes are adhered to throughout the firm.

Small size necessitates multifunctional deployment, for instance, when people in production and R&D frequently are called on to assist in technical services. Codevelopment with customers is a popular activity

Figure 5.4   Hierarchies vis-à-vis the Customer in Large Companies and the Hidden Champions

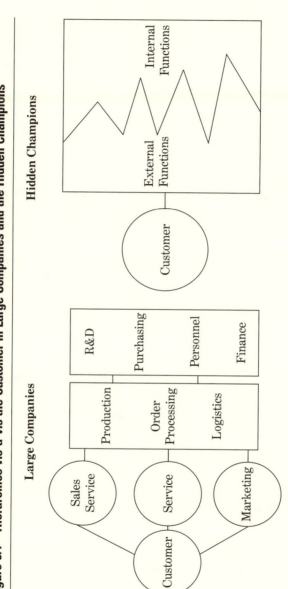

among the hidden champions (see Chapter 6). Top managers generally have intensive direct customer contact, a statement that was highly rated (5.70 on a 7-point scale).

Modest size and such attitudes help an organization create a flat and lean hierarchy vis-à-vis the customer. Interestingly, many of these problem areas are addressed by business reengineering (Hammer and Champy 1993, Davenport 1993). Instituting the "business revolution" proclaimed by Hammer and Champy is not a necessity for many of the hidden champions. With their narrow focus on the customer they have been observing most of the reengineering postulates for years. Seemingly new concepts like "case worker" or the "case team" have long been familiar to them.

Klaus Grohmann, founder-CEO of Grohmann Engineering, top supplier to the electronics industry, explains his system:

> We consciously employ no salespeople. Our managers have total responsibility for their projects: they sell, make the offer, develop the solution, and execute the project. These project leaders have all the competencies of general managers for their projects. We assign a team to each project, and the team acts like a small company. Everyone adopts a holistic view of the project. This approach guarantees an incredible closeness with the customer.

A world leader in several specialty chemicals uses a similar system in which its sales engineers have full technical and business responsibility and competence in dealing with the customer. While this is nothing new, the vigor with which these concepts are implemented by the hidden champions is exemplary.

I also have the impression that the foreign subsidiaries of the hidden champions have considerably more freedom and autonomy than those of large corporations. The main reason is that there is simply no large control hierarchy at headquarters. The main criticism I hear when visiting large corporations' foreign subsidiaries concerns too much intervention from the head office, a complaint I rarely hear from hidden champion subsidiaries. A further cause may be that the disapproving subsidiaries are led by entrepreneurial types who defend their autonomy. The same conditions that foster closeness to the customer in the parent company prevail in foreign markets. While it may not be possible to transfer fully the insights on better customer orientation to large firms, the hidden champions' practices point to enormous potential for improvement.

DIRECT CONTACT

The hidden champions are convinced that they know their markets well; market knowledge ranked third in strength among nineteen factors. This seems to contrast with their weakness in marketing professionalism and formal research, yet the statement "Our most frequently used information source on the market is the customer" garnered the highest approval rating among twelve items (5.82 on the 7-point scale). This results partially from the hidden champions' preference for direct customer relations, but it also reflects the reality that the sometimes fragmented markets served do not lend themselves well to structured market research.

In a study on information gathering by small and medium-size companies, Staudt et al. (1992) confirmed these patterns, finding that directly contacted customers are the most important source. The results appear in Figure 5.5. The preference for direct contact pervades the whole strategy of the hidden champions. In my survey, 69.4% said that they deal directly with their customers. As noted in Chapter 4, they avoid middlemen when entering foreign markets and establish their own subsidiaries. Of course, hidden champions that sell to consumers like Tetra (fish food), Haribo (Gummi bears), and Wella (hair care products) have to operate through retailers. But even they push directness as far as possible. Thus, Wella has its own subsidiaries in almost all Asian countries and in its professional hair care business tries to establish direct contacts with hairdressers throughout the world. Tetra offers seminars for fish owners, creating an opportunity to receive feedback from its customers.

Another outstanding trait of the hidden champions is the heavy involvement of management in direct customer contacts. Many top managers consider that as one of their primary responsibilities, even when it requires incessant travel. Dr. Wolfgang Pinegger, president of Brückner, the world-leading manufacturer of biaxial film stretching systems, says: "I know and have visited each of our customers in the world. The direct relations I build through these visits are invaluable." Once I read an article in a daily newspaper somewhere in the United States that difficulties arose in the paint shop of a large auto plant because the workers in the region used hair sprays with metallic particles that settled on painted surfaces. I cut out the article and sent it to Reinhard Schmidt, then CEO of Dürr, in Stuttgart, Germany, world leader in car painting systems. Schmidt wrote back to me: "I know about this problem because I have been in that plant. The current equipment is from a competitor

Figure 5.5 Importance of Sources of Information

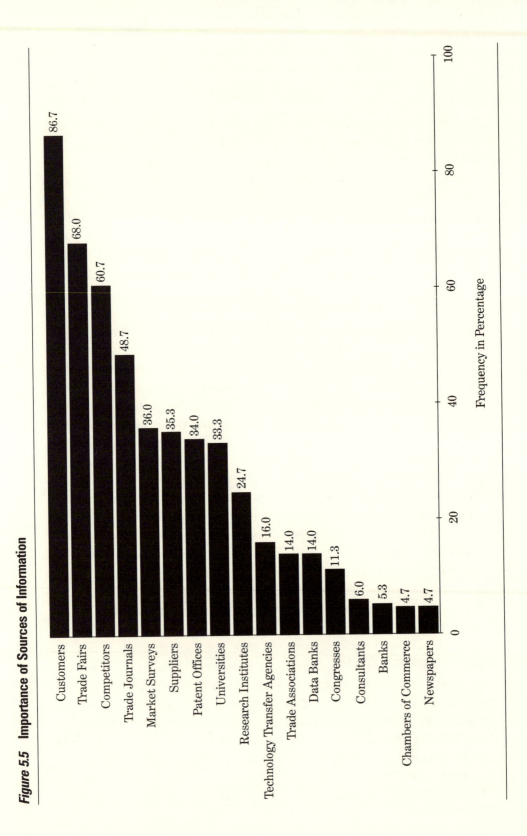

Frequency in Percentage

Customers — 86.7
Trade Fairs — 68.0
Competitors — 60.7
Trade Journals — 48.7
Market Surveys — 36.0
Suppliers — 35.3
Patent Offices — 34.0
Universities — 33.3
Research Institutes — 24.7
Technology Transfer Agencies — 16.0
Trade Associations — 14.0
Data Banks — 14.0
Congresses — 11.3
Consultants — 6.0
Banks — 5.3
Chambers of Commerce — 4.7
Newspapers — 4.7

who can't handle the problem. We have a solution and next time it will probably be our turn." That's closeness to customer: a CEO of an $800 million company in Stuttgart not only knows about a specific local U.S. problem, but he has been there and experienced the problem and has a solution for it.

Würth requires that all managers visit a customer at its site at least once a month. Reinhold Würth, now chairman of the company, has himself adhered to this principle during his forty years at its helm. When a problem whose cause was unclear turned up in Holland, Würth spent a whole week there with his salespeople, talking to customers. He has visited auto repair shops in Istanbul, Turkey, for a full day to see the conditions there for himself. He cannot be deceived of customers' problems anywhere in the world. He doesn't develop his strategies from his desk in Künzelsau, Germany, but wants on-the-spot experience of a market before entering it. The same is true for Heinz Hankammer of Brita water filters. The week before I talked to him he had been in Shanghai and in Albania to inspect drugstores there for himself.

Executives who visit customers are not mere figureheads. They are competent technical representatives (many hidden champion managers have engineering degrees) who don't hesitate to roll up their sleeves to immerse themselves in a customer's work. When Günter Sieker, an engineer by training and director of Lenze, a world leader in small gears for photocopiers, wheelchairs, and so on, visited a customer in Singapore, he discovered that local technicians had been unable to repair a machine his company had sold them. Removing his jacket, he worked for two hours to solve the problem. Needless to say, the customer was impressed by his knowledge of the equipment.

One of the most important effects of direct experience is that it has a much stronger impact on behavior than any kind of printed market research. This observation is confirmed by the findings on the effects of customer visits by McQuarrie (1993). But unlike large companies, hidden champions have no need to schedule special customer visits. In their philosophy of doing business, periodic visits to customer sites are the normal way of doing business.

CUSTOMER LOCATION

The country of location is another specific aspect pertaining to closeness to customers. Figure 5.6 shows the local distribution of the hidden cham-

Figure 5.6 **Location of Hidden Champions' Most Demanding Customers**

Percentage of Hidden Champions

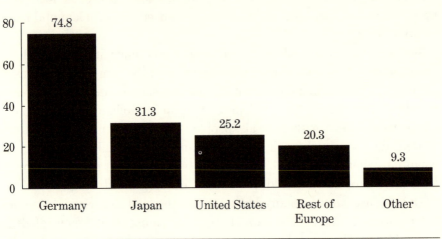

pions' most demanding customers. Because multiple answers were possible, percentages add up to more than 100. Roughly three-quarters (74.8%) say that their most demanding customers are in Germany. This is well in line with Porter's (1990) finding, in which "firms gain competitive advantage . . . because their home environment is the most challenging" (71). The spatial closeness to the most demanding and challenging customers adds to the attainment of global leadership.

Of the foreign highly demanding customers, the Japanese play the most important role. This is not congruent with the share of sales to Japan, but, as discussed in Chapter 4, it explains why Japan has such a high priority on the agenda of many hidden champions.

Future global leadership probably has to be separated from spatial closeness to customer. Some hidden champions are already practicing this lesson. Klaus Grohmann wants to be a prime supplier to the thirty top electronics companies in the world regardless of their location. Fischer Labor- und Verfahrenstechnik, exporter of 90% of its sales, whose main customers are in the oil industry, regards itself as being close to its customers although they are spread all over the globe.

Porter's paradigm of spatial closeness to the most challenging customers while still valid for most of the hidden champions is losing significance for the most outstanding ones. The latter pay great attention to maintaining direct contact with their leading customers no matter where in the world they are located. Closeness to customer for them ceases to be primarily a matter of space or nationality.

PRICE, VALUE, SERVICE

While the hidden champions adjust performance to customer requirements (an aspect more thoroughly considered in the context of competitive advantage in Chapter 7), their main selling point is superior value, not price. Service also plays an important role in the value they deliver. The strategies of a number of them are set forth in the following statements:

- Our sales are not based on price.
- Our message is the value, not the price.
- Quality remains, long after price is forgotten.
- Our strategy is value-, not price-driven.
- Our products, though expensive, are economical.
- Customers return 100 percent loyalty for value received.
- We don't exploit our position because customer loyalty is more important than short-term profit.

In the framework of generic strategies suggested by Porter (1985), the hidden champions lean toward differentiation, not price/cost leadership. This doesn't mean that they are immune to competitive pressures, but their primary emphasis is not on price. Within a certain range, their sales' sensitivity to raising prices is relatively low, an observation substantiated by Figure 5.7. It shows how the market share of the hidden champions would decline if they raised their prices from current levels by 10 or 20%. The price curve is rather flat for a 10% price increase, indicating that only about 8% of current market share would be lost. Even for a 20% price increase, the relative change in share would be around 20%. Only if price increases exceed 20% would the loss in market share become substantial. The companies would lose half their current customers should prices increase by 28%. From a short-term profit perspective this response suggests that increasing price by up to 20% would be acceptable. But the hidden champions consciously refrain from exploiting

Figure 5.7 **Effect of Price Increase on Hidden Champions' Market Share**

Market Share in Percentage

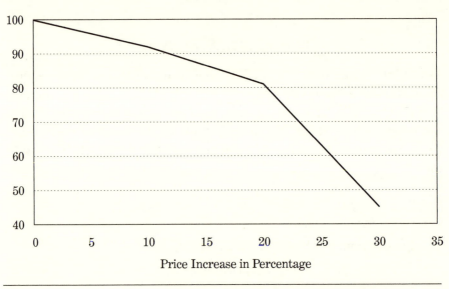

Price Increase in Percentage

such short-term opportunities because long-term profitability is more important to them. In this respect they are similar to Japanese companies. Defending market position and market share has a higher priority than exploitation of short-term price potential.

There are some exceptions to my statement that the hidden champions don't set price aggressively, but those constitute a small minority. Suspa, a leader in vibration damping, offers "German quality at Taiwanese prices." Paul Binhold, world leader in anatomical teaching aids, has a worldwide price guarantee: if a product of comparable quality at a lower price is available, Binhold absorbs the difference. And Fielmann, the European leader in eyeglasses, has built its strategy on aggressive pricing and heavy advertising of its price advantages. But even these atypical hidden champions offer good quality; their sales don't depend solely on price.

Superb, quick service is an important part of many hidden champions' strategy. Most see service as a clear competitive advantage (see Chapter 7), and their services are usually very comprehensive and customized.

This observation is consistent with Homburg's (1995) finding that companies which are very close to their customers differentiate themselves through service rather than product features. Their reasoning is that competitors can imitate special product features more easily than service. Superior service, which usually results from superior competencies of employees, is exceedingly difficult to reproduce.

Brähler International Congress Service offers its clients totally individualized designs frequently developed jointly with the interior designers of buildings. Gerhard M. Bauer, Brähler's director of marketing, comments:

> We create any design the customer wants, be it round or oval or quadratic. In the new German parliament building we used high-grade steel; in McDonald's Euro-Center, we integrated voting, discussion, and simultaneous translation systems into quarter-circle desks. These customized services are our specialty.

Training is an extremely important aspect of service. Hidden champions run hundreds of training centers throughout the world. The French training center of Stihl, the chain saw leader, for instance, is widely recognized and publicly approved. It not only provides technical training for Stihl's customers but offers courses in all areas relevant to their customers' businesses. Wella's seminars on the latest trends in hair fashion are popular with hairdressers in many nations. Brita's water filter customers, predominantly retailers, usually open their stores at 9:00 A.M., but between 8:00 and 9:00 A.M. Brita's salespeople train them in selling and handling the filters. Brita wants its retailers to be users of the product as well. "If they are convinced, they will convince their customers," says Heinz Hankammer. Several hidden champions have established separate units to conduct training as a business of their own. Festo Didactic, a unit of Festo, a world leader and the clear number one in Europe in pneumatics for industrial automation, is a particularly successful example. Festo Didactic offers courses to Festo customers and noncustomers on many aspects of industrial automation.

Providing consistent, quick worldwide service is a major challenge for midsize firms. Unlike large companies, they cannot always afford to keep a competent service team in each country. Instead, they have to be fast and extremely flexible. Grohmann Engineering's service slogan is "Reliable and Worldwide"; its service poster displays a high-speed car, a jet plane, and a parachute as symbols that Grohmann's technicians are on their way to customers via the fastest means of transportation. Most hidden champions attempt to achieve twenty-four-hour availability of service technicians and forty-eight-hour availability of spare parts, a big feat for a small company. Hermann Kronseder of Krones, the world leader in bottle labeling machines, describes the problems:

> At all times, we deploy 250 service and installation technicians around the world. Sometimes they cannot come home for weeks and months. Coordinating all of them is an almost unsolvable task for the service department and its manager. But I am proud to say that I am constantly told that our service is the best worldwide. This is the foundation of our success and we owe it all to our service specialists, many of whom have ten or twenty years of service experience.

Kronseder then describes his spare parts delivery system:

> We store the data for each machine, totaling 20,000, in our central computer. These data can be made available at every one of our locations in the world within half a minute. The data are fed directly into the numerically controlled machines, and the spare parts are manufactured immediately, day and night. Parts which are ordered before seven A.M. usually are sent in the afternoon, by truck, to Frankfurt Airport; from there they are airfreighted the same evening to their country of destination. At the same time, our subsidiary receives the flight and freight numbers so that the shipment can be cleared through customs without delay.

It's no wonder that such a company gets top service grades from its customers. A global company should always keep in mind that the customer doesn't care where the company is located. The customers want service wherever they are.

SUMMARY

This chapter has shown that closeness to customers is a pivotal element of the hidden champions' strategy. It's their behavior rather than lip service that contains valuable lessons for every type of company.

- Customer relations are complex and often involve mutual dependence. The unique quality of hidden champions' products makes it difficult for customers to replace them, and their narrow focus induces hidden companies' strong dependence on their customers. Such a situation creates strong commitment on both sides.

- A good customer-supplier relationship is not built on friendship and emotion alone but on sound economic rationale.

- If trust and long-term orientation prevail in a relationship, both sides can substantially reduce their transaction costs.

- While the hidden champions are very close to their customers, they are not marketing professionals. Ideally, a company should be both close to the customer and professional in marketing.

- Closeness to customer comprises performance and interaction; a company should be good in both dimensions.

- Closeness to customer, particularly in interaction, is best achieved through direct distribution, a flat organization vis-à-vis the customer, and much contact of nonsales personnel.

- Customers should and can be extremely valuable sources of information. Gathering market information should include both reliance on surveys and direct personal experience to achieve behavioral impact.

- Direct and regular contacts of top management with customers are extremely important.

- From the success of the hidden champions, it appears advisable to build strategies on superior value and service rather than on price. The firms pay strong attention to customer loyalty and do not exploit their short-term dominant position or their temporary pricing latitude.

- Excellent service is an indispensable aspect of closeness to customer. Especially in an international context, service must be worldwide and fast.

- While the spatial closeness of customers still plays an important role, the hidden champions have begun to transcend this limitation. A global competitor must achieve closeness to its customers regardless of their location.

Again, although these lessons are essentially based on common sense, they are difficult to implement. Customer relations form an essential part of each economic transaction. Mutual dependence and trust develop only when both parties derive their long-term fair share from a business relation. Excellent service requires the closeness to customer of every member of a company, from those in nonsales functions to top management. The hidden champions, having achieved this closeness to an extraordinary degree, are excellent role models.

6

Innovation

The only way to continued success is continuous innovation.

INNOVATION IS CENTRAL to the hidden champions. Almost all of them have achieved world market leadership because at some point they pioneered essential aspects of technology or business practices in their markets. Indeed a number of the markets didn't exist before they were created by their innovators. These companies obviously profit from an environment that is favorable to innovation. Many hidden champions are superperformers in number of patents or in terms of revenue derived from new products.

In their creative endeavors, these firms differ from large companies in not being driven solely by either technology or market. Instead the sample companies prefer to integrate these two driving forces in a well-balanced way. The hidden champions thereby suggest the union of both external and internal elements as a strategic paradigm of innovation.

THE NATURE OF INNOVATION

Like other companies, the hidden champions emphasize the need and the will to invent in their corporate mottos and brochures. But this is true of all kinds of companies throughout the world. Only facts can uncover the difference between lip service and the truth. Therefore I shall concentrate mainly on facts.

Most hidden champions, believing that innovation should not be confined to improving products, invest major efforts in internal and external processes. Underlying this view is a deep and comprehensive understanding of a customer's business and problems. For instance, in 1993, Hoppe AG, European leader in handles for doors and windows, developed a system that radically simplifies the assembly, and has the potential to revolutionize the production, of wooden doors. A trade journal called it "the innovation of the century." When CEO Wolf Hoppe showed me the new product, I said, "It looks so simple; why didn't you arrive at this solution earlier?" Friedrich Hoppe, Wolf's father, replied, "I had the idea thirty years ago, but it takes a very long time and requires very deep knowledge to make such a component as simple as possible. This product is covered by thirty-four patents and patent applications!" It is apparent that Hoppe could develop its improvement only because it studied the role of the lock in door manufacturing more thoroughly than its customers did.

W. L. Gore, Inc., an American hidden champion famous for its semipermeable Gore-Tex fabrics, is another exemplary company. A main source of its success is its exploring the manufacturing and quality assurance processes of its garment and shoe industry customers more intensely than they did. Gore then employed its superior R&D competence to develop problem solutions to aid in the production of its garments and shoes, so that Gore-Tex could live up to its slogan, "guaranteed to keep you dry."

Many hidden champions do not treat innovation as a series of major breakthroughs that occur at long intervals and in discrete steps. Rather, innovation resembles a continuous process of improvement, somewhat similar to the Japanese *kaizen* method (continuing improvement benefiting the customer). At these firms, creative activity is a day to-day process through which each variant of a product is somewhat improved and better than its predecessor. This operating mode is particularly prevalent in the mechanical engineering and systems sectors, where problem solutions rather than tangible goods are the "products." Each new system, because it aims at the needs of a specific customer, is somewhat different and offers the opportunity to innovate.

Wolfram Burger of Böwe Systec, a leader in paper management systems, explains: "Our customers tell us, 'I have this problem; solve it!' Our engineers are most eager to find the best solution, integrating new technology and avoiding past mistakes. In the end, no two systems are identical—each has its own innovative characteristics."

Wolfgang Kufferath of GKD, a world leader in metallic webs, faces a similar situation. "Today our customer is a beer brewer from Dortmund, tomorrow it's a development engineer from Seattle. A typical task for us is the following: we need a metallic web that decomposes the drop of a liquid which hits the web at forty-five degrees. We solve these problems."

Konrad Parloh of Peter Wolters Werkzeugmaschinen GmbH AG, first in the world in ultraprecision machining of parallel and flat surfaces (e.g., Seagate hard disks for disk drives are made on Wolters-machines), faces similar requests from customers: "Our solutions are developed on the basis of customer specifications. Once we have those we design the process and the system. It's a new approach each and every time." There is evidently much more such innovation than one would generally assume.

Gradual improvement is often realized through new applications that require modifications of an existing product. RUD-Kettenfabrik, the world leader in special chains for all types of industrial uses, started in 1875 as a manufacturer of chains for agriculture applications and later became the world leader in snow chains. Today, agriculture accounts for less than 5% of sales, and a myriad of chains for heavy-duty industrial applications like elevators, conveyors, systems for lifting, and tire chains for construction and mining equipment have been added. Biallo (1993, 64) writes: "No other company in the world can compare with RUD's chain professionals." The intense innovativeness of RUD is reflected in its 75% of sales that come from products less than five years old, and there are still innumerable applications for RUD to identify and fine-tune. Automatic parking systems for cars with lifting platforms and high-shelf inventory systems are just two growth areas.

Many innovations are aimed at improving customers' processes to help them save costs, increase speed, and improve quality. Würth, the leader in assembly products, has brought order and systematic inventory handling into hundreds of thousands of auto repair and woodworking shops. Barth, the hops hidden champion (slogan: "Barth facilitates your hopping"), simplified the brewing process by packing hops into pouches— somewhat like large tea bags—according to specified size and taste criteria. Although this may not sound like a radical innovation, it offers big value to the brewer by saving time for weighing and mixing the hops.

Many hidden champions have actually created new markets through their innovations. Did the market for Clean Concept's hygienic toilets exist or did it have to be created? The market for Brita water filters certainly wasn't there before this product appeared. The same is true for the dowels of Fischerwerke, which revolutionized the way things are fastened to walls. Kärcher is trying to create a market for its new window washer, which works on the principle of a water-filled vacuum cleaner for windows.

A strong and lasting need may exist, but customers are often unaware of it or reluctant to change their habits. Livio De Simone, CEO of 3M, the paragon of innovation and an "unhidden" champion in many fields, describes his company's belief: "The most interesting products are the ones that people need but can't articulate that they need" (Loeb 1995, 84). This is exactly the type of commodity on which many a hidden champion's success is built. The introduction of such merchandise requires strong conviction, perseverance, and commitment, if not outright obsession, since a new product runs against customers' entrenched habits. And few things are more difficult and time consuming than changing buyer behavior.

Other hidden champions have redefined the rules of the game in their markets by following McDonald's lead in the fast-food business, namely, by offering a standardized, quality-guaranteed service rather than a local stand's hamburger of uncertain quality. Europe's leading distributor of frozen foods, Bo*frost, a fast-growing hidden champion, falls into this category. Its salespeople deposit frozen food directly into the consumer's deep freezer. This is a convenient and healthy method of delivery, since the food never leaves refrigeration for longer than five minutes. Founded in 1966 the company has grown to more than 4,000 employees and sales of close to $667 million. But Josef Boquoi, Bo*frost's founder, complains that the main problem is still to convince consumers. "Once they are converted, they see the advantage and stick with us," he says.

Similarly, Günter Fielmann has revolutionized the distribution of eyeglasses. Until his appearance, this business was characterized by opticians in lab coats working out of stores with the allure of dentists' waiting rooms, and very high prices. Fielmann turned the endeavor into a combination of aggressive pricing, selling beauty instead of medical devices, and heavy advertising. The firm sells almost one in every three pairs of eyeglasses bought in Germany, is by far the European market leader, ranks number two in the world, and is rapidly approaching $667 million in revenue.

Recycling and the environment have become a highly innovative area. Edelhoff, one of the leaders in the field, is changing garbage collection from a labor-intensive into a capital-intensive business. Its newly developed multiservice transport system (MSTS), a high-technology garbage collection truck operated by one person, performs the same amount of work as a traditional truck with four or five people. In a test in Amsterdam, the MSTS beat all other systems. Waste Management, the largest garbage-handling company in the world, has ordered 200 of them.

Environmental concerns generate a wave of innovation, attracting many hidden champions to this field. Stihl, the chain saw leader, has experienced an explosion of new systems, developing most recently a digital ignition system (sure starting, fuel saving, lower emission); a refill system (no spill, no vapor); a catalytic converter, Ematic (reducing oil consumption by 50%); electric carburetor heating (improved performance in cold temperatures); and Quickstop Super chain brake (increased safety). One may well ask whether the company has outdone itself, to which Stihl commented: "In the last few years we have patented more inventions than any competitor in the world and upheld our claim to technical leadership."

Saving labor costs is a strong driver of innovation. Thus, Putzmeister, the world leader in concrete pumps, has developed a robot for washing airplanes. This high-tech machine, said to be the largest robot in the world, saves the cost of paying a whole cleaning team.

Sometimes hidden champions aim their innovations at rather strange needs of consumers. Junghans's radio-controlled wristwatch is a hugely successful example. Like other watch- and clockmakers, Junghans ran into a crisis in the 1980s because sales of its products fell when cheap electronic watches made in Asia flooded the market. While the Swiss responded to this threat by inventing the Swatch and turning it into a fashion and cult article, Junghans went the high-tech route and developed a watch whose time is controlled by a radio signal emitted by national stations through an antenna contained in the wristband. This watch, with a deviation of one second in a million years, is never wrong. It's unclear why anyone would require and pay an astronomical price for such a watch, but it enjoys an enormous success with techno-freaks.

It has only one competitor in the world, the large Japanese company Citizen (with a 19% world market share of watches), which introduced its product three years after Junghans. Within four years after the introduction, while the rest of the industry was shrinking, Junghans's sales went from less than $133 million to $263 million. The product is also highly successful in Japan—"the mother lode of watches," Junghans CEO Wolfgang Fritz remarked. Interestingly, market researchers advised the company not to introduce the product.

A more recent Junghans innovation with major market potential is a radio-controlled solar wristwatch, which runs without a battery as long as the sun is shining or where there is light. The first model was introduced in 1993. Citizen did not present its first solar-powered watch until May 1995.

These few examples from the hidden champions' arsenal illustrate the extremely wide scope for innovation. The hidden champions take advantage of the most outlandish opportunities to innovate. Their creativity and the variety of their inventions match the variety of the products and services they provide. Rarely taking the beaten path, preferring to follow their own roads, changing or creating their own markets, they are usually far ahead of the pack.

TECHNOLOGY

Technology is the single most important factor behind the competitive advantages and the global market leadership of the hidden champions. Almost three-quarters of the respondents to my questionnaire said that their enviable position is based on technological know-how and innovation. Measuring on a low-technology–high-technology 1- to 7-point scale, 70.6% rated their products as above average, rating these two elements with high scores of 5.9 and 5.6, respectively.

Achieving technological innovation is strongly dependent on an environment conducive to R&D and the implementation of change. The hidden champions' creative activities have to be surveyed against this background. Horst Albach's *Culture and Technical Innovation* (1994) provides a thorough comparison of the conditions for innovation in the United States, Japan, and Germany. The study considers various components of innovation like personality, teamwork, trade unions, companies, users, education, and government and draws conclusions. I do not delve into all these subjects but refer the interested reader to this work.

This chapter sheds light on the conditions for innovativeness of companies in various countries, putting the technological aspects of the sample firms into a country framework to better understand their performance. At the same time, it may correct misconceptions about inventiveness in diverse nations.

The most popular indicators of innovative actions are R&D expenditures and patents. Table 6.1 provides such information for major industrialized countries.

Columns 1 through 3 of the table show R&D expenditures in absolute and per capita figures in European currency units (ECUs) and as a percentage of gross domestic product (GDP). In the last category, Japan, the United States, and the northern European countries are quite similar, but in GDP per capita, absolute expenditures indicate substantial deviation, with Japan clearly in the lead. The table also shows that a large amount of the world total for R&D is concentrated in a few countries.

Columns 4 through 8 show statistics for patents. Column 5 sets forth the number of domestic patent applications, by residents in the home country. One can discern a familiar pattern: in Japan, residents apply for many more domestic patents per capita than those in any other country. In the Western world, Germans lead in domestic patents per capita. In the context of global competition, however, international patents are more relevant than domestic ones. Column 6 contains the number of international patent applications submitted by residents of the various countries. With 295,202, U.S. citizens account for by far the largest number. But on a per capita basis, Germany is well ahead, with 264 foreign applications per 100,000 population, followed by Japan with 162; the United States and France, both with 117, are tied. Column 8 lists the percentages of European Community (Euro 12) patent applications made in the United States according to country of origin. The strong position of Germany is again revealed—with 48.7%, it accounts for almost half the total applications.

Ifo Institute in Munich compiles statistics on international patents for corporations. Figure 6.1 lists the twenty companies with the greatest number of international patents for seven years, 1985 through 1991. This long-term view provides a reliable indicator of the international technological competence of individual companies by neutralizing short-term fluctuations. To a certain degree, it also minimizes the domestic influence in Japan by considering only international patents. Nine of the twenty innovative companies according to this measure are from Japan; Germany is second, with five corporations; and the United States, with four

Table 6.1 **R&D and Patent Applications in Selected Countries**

Country	R&D Expenditures, 1991			Patent Applications, 1990				
	Total (Billion ECU)	Percentage of Gross Domestic Product	Per Capita (ECU)	By Residents in Home Country		By Residents in Foreign Countries (International Patents)		Percentage Share of Euro 12 Patent Applications in the U.S.
				Total Number	Per Capita 100,000 Population	Total Numbers	Per Capita 100,000 Population	
	1	2	3	4	5	6	7	8
Germany	35.5	2.58%	445	30,928[a]	49[a]	161,006[a]	264[a]	48.7%
France	23.5	2.42%	412	12,742	22	66,632	117	17.4%
Italy	12.8	1.38%	224	—	—	29,969	52	6.9%
Japan	77.7	2.86%	627	332,952	270	129,835	162	
United Kingdom	18.4	2.26%	320	19,474	34	80,320	140	17.5%
United States	124.6	2.78%	493	90,643	36	295,202	117	
Other Euro 12 countries (Belgium, Denmark, Greece, Spain, Ireland, Luxembourg, Netherlands, Portugal)	14.0	<1%	150	8,371	9	52,124	56	9.5%

Source: Sam Lloyd, "Western Europe," in *World Science Report* (Paris: UNESCO, 1994).
[a]West Germany only.

Figure 6.1 **Companies with the Largest Number of International Inventions, 1985–1991**
Patents in Two or More Countries

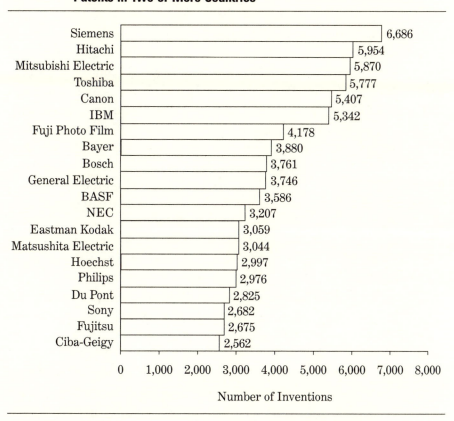

Number of Inventions

Source: Author's calculations based on data obtained from Ifo-Institute, 1986–1994.

entries, is third. The other two countries, Switzerland and the Netherlands, contribute one company each.

Combining these observations with the information about the general international orientation set forth in Chapter 4, one can conclude that the hidden champions work in an economic environment that fosters both technological innovation and globalization. A company's ability to innovate is affected by its local environment, which determines the availability of resources, access to qualified personnel and suppliers, and infrastructure (see Porter 1994). The environment also includes the local competitive forces which play a role for many hidden champions, as discussed in Chapter 8. Thus it seems that the German environment in which the hidden champions operate fosters innovation, particularly with an international scope.

Considering their favorable business climate, it's no surprise that the hidden champions are among the most innovative companies. A glance at the number of patents held by some of these companies reveals their power to effect technological change. Table 6.2 provides the numbers of patents and employees and relates the two. I use the number of patents per hundred employees as an indicator of innovativeness, but should add that some of these figures may not be absolutely accurate. They were taken from company reports and brochures of the companies, which rarely explain exactly how the numbers were developed. The list does not necessarily include the companies with the largest number of patents, because it is difficult to gather complete information on the subject.

To gain proper perspective on the patent performance of the companies listed in the table, one should be aware that Siemens, the most innovative large corporation in the world (see Figure 6.1), has about 40,000 patents and 400,000 employees, so that its number of patents per 100 employees is approximately 10. All the hidden champions represented in Table 6.2 are above this level. Fischerwerke has an incredible 234 patents per 100 employees, and many others are also unusually strong. It is probably not exaggerating to assume that in a global listing of patent productivity per employee, many of the sample firms would be in the top ranks.

Patent statistics provide only a partial picture of the technological prowess of the hidden champions. In addition, patents are not synonymous with market innovations or success. But patent statistics, because they are relatively valid and reliable indicators, have the advantage of allowing one to measure something as complex as technological invention quantitatively. The figures in Table 6.2 substantiate the statement that the surveyed companies operate in and profit from an environment which, in spite of gossip to the contrary, seems to be conducive to internationally oriented technical innovation.

But the creativity of the hidden champions is not totally captured by patent numbers. Many of the companies, particularly smaller ones, are superbly innovative but own few patents or none at all. This is a factor of policy and costs. According to a study commissioned by the European Patent Office, two-thirds of small and midsize companies that are active in R&D don't protect their inventions through patents. The reasons reside in the cost and duration of the patenting process, preference for

Table 6.2 **Patent Position of Selected Hidden Champions**

Company	Main Product	Employees	Number of Patents	Number of Patents per 100 Employees
Fischerwerke	Fastening products, construction sets	2,350	5,500	234
Held	Double-belt presses	90	50	56
Tracto-Technik	Ground rockets	211	100	47
Herion	Pneumatic proportional valves	1,500	600	40
RUD-Kettenfabrik	Tire and snow chains	904	350	35
Sachtler	Camera tripods	130	40	31
Heidenhain	Linear measuring systems for NC machine tools	3,190	800	25
Reflecta	Slide technology	500	100	20
Rittal	Enclosure systems	4,500	949	20
Kiekert	Car locking systems	1,670	300	18
Netzsch	Machines and plants for ceramic industries	2,800	350	12.5
Prominent	Metering pumps	770	90	12
Krones	Labeling machines	7,600	811	11

secrecy, lack of trust in the protective power of patents, and the inability to enforce a patent. Klaus Grohman of Grohmann Engineering, a most innovative company, explains this attitude:

> We don't apply for patents because we don't have the people to do it, and we hate the bureaucracy. Anyway, the speed of innovation in our industry is much too high in relation to the speed of the patenting process. And patents wouldn't help us because we couldn't enforce them. Anyway, in the time it would take to get them, we have usually made enormous progress in development. Patents are like a horse and buggy, and we fly a jet plane.

Quite a few hidden champions share his attitude, but many that are not stars in the patent firmament are highly innovative nevertheless. Of Kärcher's $693 million in sales, 78% come from products less than four years old (with 182 patents and 3,842 employees, Kärcher has 4.7 patents per 100 employees). EOS, a leading, and highly innovative, pioneer in rapid prototyping, operates in a market that literally didn't exist in 1990. The same holds for Fast Electronic, the European market leader in computer compression cards. This is a field in which fast progress is essential, since the computer business as a whole is characterized by short cycles for upgraded products.

In addition, patents are irrelevant in such business sectors as services. Consider Wige-Data Group, which measures time and manages data flows at large sports events worldwide. Wige has a large fund of proprietary knowledge on how to market these events—how best to position cameras and assure data flow to journalists. But none of these capabilities is covered by, or particularly lends itself to, patenting.

Summarizing this section, I conclude that the hidden champions' global success is built largely on superior technological competence and innovativeness and is not a matter of luck or favorable circumstances. The lesson is quite clear. If you want to become a market leader, you'd better do your homework in innovation.

The champions have obviously done just that. This also explains the self-confidence of the CEOs I have encountered time and again in discussing the subject. Many didn't seem to be particularly concerned, which, as someone probably too strongly influenced by the eternal lamenting in the press, astonished me. But the press may simply be unable to look behind the scenes of companies as protective of their privacy as the hidden champions.

THE DRIVING FORCES

After the foregoing techno-talk and the impressive patent statistics, one is bound to conclude that the primary driving force of the hidden champions is technology. A comparison with large corporations reveals that this conclusion is wrong! To the question concerning their driving forces, 50% of the large corporations said they are market driven, 31% named technology as the primary force, and 19% attributed equal weight to both forces. The hidden champions have an entirely different response. A majority of 57% said that market and technology are equally important forces, with 32% naming the market and only 11% citing the technology as the dominant driver. Thus, the percentage of companies that, rather than being one-sided, are integrators of technology and market is three times higher for the hidden champions, as shown in Figure 6.2. This finding almost exactly replicated a result in a 1990 study, which is evidence of the high reliability of this measurement.

In *Polarity Management,* Barry Johnson (1992) suggests that the extremes of any polarity should be avoided and that a middle way is usually superior. Instead of having either a market or technology orientation, it seems better to embrace both aspects. The reason is that each philosophy has advantages *and* disadvantages. At the extremes, however, where disadvantages become dominant, the positive and intended effects of market orientation—listening to the customer, producing exactly what

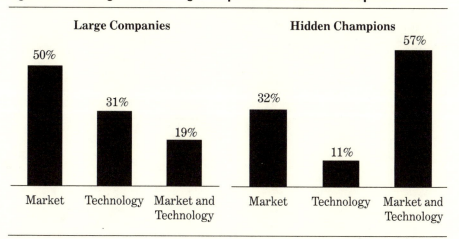

Figure 6.2 **Driving Forces of Large Companies and Hidden Champions**

the customer really wants, being responsive, and so forth (see Chapter 5)—are overwhelmed by disadvantages—lack of focus on technology, loss of technological leadership, low funding of R&D, and so on. Also, technology as a dominant factor intended to stimulate innovation, a strong product line, and high technology can, for example, alienate a company from its customers, drive up costs, and yield overengineered products.

Large corporations encounter problems in managing these polarities. Size, division of labor, functional separation, work "thrown over the wall" to the next department, and compartmentalization are well-known causes of this syndrome. Because the hidden champions are smaller entities, each employee has a more comprehensive understanding of his or her contribution to value creation and can maintain close interaction with customers; these firms are more efficient at balancing the two polarities.

My experience with the sample companies allows me to go a step further. I do not consider technology and market orientation as opposites but as complementary dimensions (see Cooper 1979), as illustrated in Figure 6.3. This represents the view that a company can be both market and technologically oriented, or subscribe to neither orientation. It can have a one-sided orientation, either market or technology prevailing, as in large corporations. The ideal is obviously to be strong in both dimensions. Niels Bohr, the famous Danish physicist, discovered the principle of complementarity, which he expressed in Latin: *Contraria non*

Figure 6.3   Market versus Technological Orientation

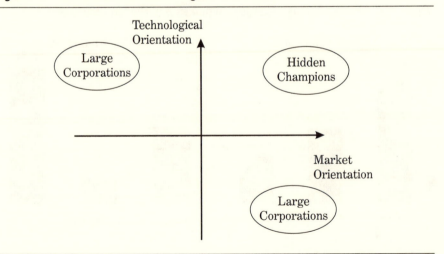

contradictoria sed complementa sunt (Opposites are not contradictory but complementary) (*Scientific American* 1993). The complementarity principle can well be applied to technological versus market orientation, and the hidden champions have found a way to implement it. Norbert Gebhardt of Netzsch, a leader in machines for the ceramics industry and one of the companies listed in Table 6.2, explains his position: "We need both market and technology when dealing with the customer. The salesman is lost when it comes to technical details, and the technician is not well versed in communication. We are aiming for the golden combination."

Deeply ingrained cultural traits underlie the potential conflict between one-sided market or technological orientation. Many Western world firms, particularly large ones, suffer from a cultural schism. In discussing this aspect, it is useful to distinguish between a functional or professional culture and a corporate or customer culture. The former derives its value from the function or profession, for example, an engineer primarily desires to be a good engineer respected by other engineers. The latter, on the other hand, derives its value mainly from the benefit it delivers to its customers. When I asked people the simple question "What are you?" 95% of them answered by stating their profession: "I am an engineer," or a financial expert, a chemist, and so on; they also read professional journals and attend professional conferences. These are all indications that their value system is oriented toward their profession.

I believe that this type of culture is more pronounced in large than in small companies, the reason being simply that people in large companies live mainly within their professional worlds. Those involved in R&D deal for the most part with others involved in R&D. The same is true for production, marketing, finance, and so forth. As a result, these people develop a strong professional/functional orientation. Depending on which side is more powerful, the whole company comes to be one-sidedly driven.

In small companies, however, all personnel continually interact with people in functions and professions other than their own, are closer to the end result of the work, and get more feedback from customers (see Chapter 4). As a consequence, they achieve a better integration of technology and market. One way to bridge the cultural gap is through people. A world leader in several subfields of special chemistry does this systematically by deploying chemical engineers as salespeople. More than 60% of this company's sales force are chemical engineers. Nevertheless, they

carry full responsibility for every aspect of a sale—contract, price negotiation, delivery. In such a system of minimum division of labor, technology and market are reflected in one person. Grohmann Engineering uses
a similar approach. Both companies are most satisfied with the results.

I would like to add that the relative position of market and technology
cannot be defined once and for all—it is a moving target. Sometimes a
customer's voice is irrelevant because the customers don't know or can't
adequately express their true requirements, as noted earlier in this
chapter. Owing to their innovation, hidden champions sometimes have to
teach and convert their customers rather than listen to them.

A manager at Hauni, the tobacco machines hidden champion, recounts:

> For years we were technology driven, not customer driven. Performance
> was the only criterion. We dictated the rules. The customers came to
> Hamburg like pilgrims to order our machines. It was like the old days of
> Hermann Hollerith, who invented a system of recording information on
> punched cards and reading it electrically by tabulating machines. Custom-
> ers had to come to New York and to beg for those machines.

The first U.S. experience of Hermann Kronseder of Krones, world leader
in labeling machines, was also centered around technology: "Though the
price I asked was extremely high, it was not the main problem. The big
barrier was the technology, convincing the customers of the unusually
high performance—they simply didn't believe it was possible." Similarly,
the major problem for Hoppe, inventor of the new door-fitting system
described earlier in the chapter, is to convert door manufacturers to its
revolutionary solution. Wolf Hoppe explains: "Today, as the market
leader, we will probably have the power to do this. If we were a small
guy in this market, we would not succeed in eliminating customer oppo-
sition."

The hidden champions illustrate that one may have to overcome substantial customer resistance against breakthrough innovations. Sometimes customers are conservative or unable to act to their own long-term
advantage. In that event, an innovator should not be customer oriented
for the short term. Of course, this does not preclude the stipulation that
to become a long-term success, a new product must ultimately deliver
superior value.

An opposite problem is that customer inertia may lead to having to cut
back on technology for fear of being considered overinnovative. Robert

Mayr, executive vice president for marketing and sales of Stihl chain saws, reflects on this problem:

> We have so many innovations that I really don't know whether the customers need, want, or accept them. All the ecological novelties are great. But do the customers understand and appreciate the advantage and are they willing to pay for it? My first task is not to push these innovations into the market too fast but to learn what customers are willing to accept and report the information back to our company so as to achieve an appropriate level of innovation. Because we are so inventive, we have to be more customer driven. Attaining that goal is not an easy task.

The dilemma between technology and market suggests a broader strategic issue, that of the two paradigms of corporate strategy. Competitive forces, the primary determinants of profitability principally associated with Michael Porter (1985), stresses the importance of external opportunities. A company must develop the necessary internal capabilities that lead to success by striving to select markets with favorable competitive conditions. Then it must be able to position itself to create and sustain competitive advantage. The paradigm, which suggests an outside-in approach, sometimes translates into the sequence industry structure → conduct → performance.

A more recent alternative paradigm, the so-called resource-based strategy, has received increased attention (Prahalad and Hamel 1990, Peteraf 1993, Hamel and Prahalad 1994). According to this conviction, internal resources and competencies should form the starting point of management strategy, which should be driven primarily by internal rather than external opportunities. This paradigm suggests an inside-out view with the sequence internal resources → conduct → performance. The approach is rooted in the older basic ideas of Selznick (1957), Penrose (1959), and Learned et al. (1965).

My experience with the hidden champions leads me to the belief that one should avoid an either-or view of these paradigms. Internal resources are merely a necessary, but not a sufficient condition for external competitive advantage. A strong internal resource that does not prove its value to a market cannot be turned into an external advantage. If a company can build a car with a maximum speed of 250 kilometers (155 miles) per hour, but there are no buyers for a car that runs faster than 150 kilometers (95 miles) per hour, its technical competence doesn't count.

Figure 6.4   **External Opportunities versus Internal Resources**

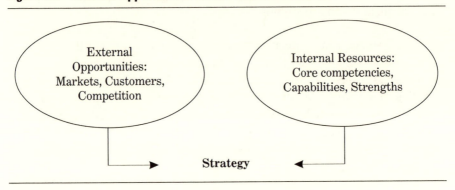

The best steam locomotive manufacturer cannot do any business today. Indeed, some hidden champions went under because their excellent internal competence eventually came to be useless in their markets, as, for example, the company that recorded rolls for mechanical piano players. Ergo, strategy cannot be built on internal resources or competencies alone.

A strategy built solely on external opportunities can be equally deficient. A market may provide a great opportunity, but a company that is unable to develop superior internal competencies is destined to fail. Many diversification projects have fallen into this trap. Large companies tend to deceive themselves into believing that they can develop every competence required in a new venture. Reality proves that this is an illusion.

Only if internal competencies and external opportunities are matched is success likely (see Figure 6.4). The hidden champions achieve this match relatively well, frequently better than large companies, extending the observation that the sample companies are both technologically and market oriented to overall strategy and neither inside-out nor outside-in strategists. The clear focus, the low organizational distance between the carriers of the internal competencies and the customer, and a corporate rather than professional culture are the foundations of an effective integration of internal resources and external opportunities.

THE CUSTOMER AS INNOVATOR

The customer is an extremely valuable source of innovative ideas. Eric von Hippel, who supports this simple message with dozens of examples, sees the innovation process as "distributed across users, manufacturers, suppliers, and others" (Hippel 1988, 3). This is familiar territory that many hidden champions have long taken to heart; some began when dissatisfied customers became their own suppliers.

Bridging the gap between customers and functions that provide new ideas for products is closely related to the general issue of closeness to customer discussed in Chapter 5. It requires either the establishment of direct contact between the two sides, or that functions like sales and service, which involve regular customer contacts, can convey information to technical personnel.

The hidden champions are especially strong in effecting such exchanges. Claas, the leading manufacturer of harvesting combines, ordinarily sells its equipment through distributors that then market it to farmers. But Claas owns at least one retail outlet in each of its major countries, not because it is interested in retailing but as a way of learning farmers' needs on the spot. The company calls these outlets exercise fields, because employees in various internal functions can use them to acquire firsthand experience of farmers' problems and needs.

Interactions between technical experts and customers often happen naturally and spontaneously. Visiting a hidden champion plant, I crossed a factory floor where a group of Volkswagen engineers was working with the company's experts. They were trying to solve Volkswagen's problem with precision grinding an engine part. I was struck by the degree of collaboration between the two groups and the apparent comfort they felt with each other: it was impossible to distinguish which represented Volkswagen and which the hidden champion. Obviously people from the same technical—not organizational!—world had met.

The effects of such close cooperations are interesting. According to a recent study by J. D. Power and Associates, face-to-face contacts between suppliers and customers in the auto industry improve quality and speedy cycle time (see *Harvard Business Review* 1994). Close R&D cooperation is not only advantageous for suppliers in providing input to the innovative process but also helps customers build better quality into their end products and to reduce their own development time: a win-win situation.

The voice of the customer often has to travel a long and hazardous route to arrive at its destination. Hermann Kronseder of Krones personally assures that messages from the field are received by the right people in his company. He explains:

Service technicians' feedback from the field can be quite unpleasant for the design engineers because I am present when the technicians report their findings to them. They clearly state the difficulties they encountered, what has gone wrong, what should be changed and improved. These service people generally have an excellent understanding of such problems. Although they know exactly what went wrong, they cannot translate it into new concepts, or drawings. In most firms, the technicians don't have enough opportunities to bring their complex experience directly to the designers. Sometimes the two groups simply don't come into contact with each other.

The reason I have made it a point to be at these meetings is that if I were not, the technician doesn't stand a chance. Designers, who enjoy a stronger position and are better educated and smarter, push technicians to the wall. The technician usually resigns himself to the inevitable in such a situation, thinking, "Do what you want, it's not my business." Technicians, who are not good at writing and spelling, dislike having to present written reports, which are first read by secretaries who correct the errors like schoolteachers. This is poison for the technicians, who feel humiliated. So they don't have to write reports. Not at Krones AG!

The devil is in the details, and Kronseder's experience proves that communication between the market and the technological people is full of traps. Ultimately Krones's practice may make all the difference between successful and unsuccessful innovations.

Innovative ideas are frequently born when companies observe how their customers work. Reinhold Würth, the guru of assembly products, stumbled on such an idea during a visit to a construction site, where he heard a worker grumbling about how hard it was to read the size numbers of tools and corresponding screws, which, stamped into the metal, were barely legible. Würth subsequently replaced the numbers with colored rings so that workers need only match the colors of screws and tools. This trademark-protected system has become a huge success. Würth also, during such visits, heard workers complaining about soreness in certain muscles and sinews. Nobody had thought about the question of whether standard tools like pliers and screwdrivers were ergonomically optimized. Würth discovered that some tools had not changed their shape for more than a hundred years, so it was highly unlikely that they were at maximum handling efficiency. He initiated a research project with the University of Stuttgart that resulted in a whole set of new tool designs, some of which reduce critical stress by more than 30%.

Codevelopment with customers prevails among hidden champions, often continually and over many years. Schott is the world leader in glass ceramic cooking fields with a product called Ceran, which is $200 to $667 more expensive than traditional cooking plates. But today each household appliance manufacturer in Europe carries the product, and one of two electric ranges sold there has a Ceran cooking field. In the United States, where the product was introduced many years after its debut in Europe, it has a penetration of 15 to 20% and is rising rapidly. There is only one major competitor, the French company Eurokera, whose market share is about 5%. Ceran is available in 2,000 variants, and a team of forty people continually cooperate with manufacturers of appliances, pots, and cleansers, and with designers, to improve the product. Its twenty-year history is one of uninterrupted innovation to which everyone in the value chain has contributed.

Tetra, in the category of hidden champions that originated from customers, was started by Dr. Ulrich Baensch. In the 1950s, as a young scientist, he bred tropical fish for his doctoral research. Finding it difficult to feed his fish because no suitable product was available, he developed his own ready-to-use, fully formulated fish food. Tetra Werke, the company he founded in 1955, is now the leader in the feeding and care of tropical fish with a world market share of more than 50%.

Wendelin Sachtler, a cameraman who experienced all the drawbacks and limitations of existing tripods, founded Sachtler AG on the basis of his ideas about improving them. His company became the world market leader in professional camera tripods in less than twenty years. In the process he drove out a competitor that had a dominant position but became complacent and unreceptive to important technical changes like the transition from film to video.

Carl Spaeter, founder of Stabilus, imported American cars to Germany in the early 1930s. German roads were not built for automobiles; they were so curvy and bumpy that riding in a car was no fun. Spaeter developed an automatically adjusting hydraulic damping system, and soon each luxury car was equipped by its owner with the Stabilus components to make the ride smoother. Today the company is the world leader in gas pressurized springs for vibration damping, which are used in thousands of ways to control vibration—in, among others, washing machines, office chairs, and airplanes.

ORGANIZATIONAL ASPECTS OF INNOVATION

The interdependence of organization and innovation is so complex that it cannot be treated here in depth (see Albach 1994), but I shall touch on some striking aspects of the hidden champions in that respect. Their R&D spending does not appear to be particularly high; they average 6.3% of sales. This picture is corroborated by my subjective perception that amazingly few people work in R&D in most of those firms. My interviews confirmed that R&D and innovation are viewed as a matter of quality rather than quantity. In large firms, I often encounter the attitude that innovation is composed primarily of quantitative input. You throw money and people at a problem, and they will develop a solution, a view the hidden champions do not share because they consider that R&D is primarily a qualitative challenge.

Although most of their R&D teams are surprisingly small, their achievements are impressive. In several firms I found a single, solitary, outstanding figure responsible for R&D, an expert who for years had focused monomaniacally on the problems of the company and produced most of the inventions. While it is hard to generalize from these findings, they suggest that the purely quantitative view of innovation should be suspect. On the other hand, one must be aware that some innovations can be achieved only by large firms with large numbers of people, for example, in software, pharmaceuticals, telecommunications.

I was also surprised to see how several hidden champions mastered technological change. Dr. Werner Pankoke, CEO of Hymmen, market leader in double-belt presses, explains: "We have to go into a great many new technologies to handle wood, plastics, rubber, cork, and composites, all requiring high levels of innovation. But developing the technical competencies and finding the right people has not created a bottleneck so far."

The general flexibility and simplicity of the hidden champions add to their ability to innovate. In many firms, marketing and R&D are under the direction of one leader, who in some cases is the CEO. On occasion marketing reports to R&D, as at Jungheinrich, a leader in materials handling equipment, or R&D reports to marketing, as at Kärcher or Sachtler.

The simplicity of an organization (see Rommel et al. 1995) combined with its entrepreneurial spirit encourages short processing and development times. Innovation in these firms proceeds at a much faster rate than it does in large corporations. Reinhard Wirtgen, founder-CEO of the world leader in street recycling systems, makes this point: "When an urgent problem arose on a Friday, we usually solved it over the weekend. But our competitors needed weeks of discussion to arrive at a decision to do it." Undoubtedly the hidden champions are less averse to risk in their innovative activities than large firms. While the latter test new products for long periods to make sure they really work, the champions introduce them more quickly by adopting a trial-and-error approach to innovation. This, of course, is not without risk, but in a period of increasingly intensive time-based competition, their strategy may be superior. Thus, it doesn't come as a shock that speed and flexibility of innovation are positively and significantly correlated to the overall success of these firms.

Cultural factors play an enormous role in attaining success in creativity. Albach (1994, 17) considers commitment one of the most important determinants of innovative performance. He says:

> Commitment, a personal quality, is a characteristic of firms and a cultural phenomenon. There are individuals who are dedicated to a task, obsessed with solving a problem. The stories and myths about the great inventors of the world are tales of dedication and obsession. Firms that are obsessed with innovation find that commitment is a decisive factor in success. . . . A firm that emphasizes the will to succeed more than developing rules for a research and development project is a more successful innovator in the long run than others. Control of behavior—commitment—is more important than control of results—meeting milestones, staying within budget, writing good intermediate research reports. (Albach 1994, 19)

This statement could have come directly from the innovation laboratory of almost any hidden champion, where commitment is a major determinant of performance and largely a consequence of defined goals and narrow focus (see Chapter 3). Schaudt, a leader in cylindrical and cam contour-grinding machines, says: "Concentration on a single area of specialization has repeatedly enabled us to make headlines with important innovations. We have been setting the pace for eighty-five years."

Once a concept has been developed, it is straightforwardly rendered into a product. Tracto-Technik, maker of ground rockets, expresses this attitude: "Our strength lies in the ability to translate an idea into the simplest possible application suitable for a particular construction site and produce it."

That's what success is all about. It's hard to hold down a person who is committed to innovation in a well-defined market and has the perseverance to pursue a goal.

SUMMARY

Innovation is one of the pillars on which the world market leadership of the hidden champions is built. Many have pioneered a new product or created a market. Some turned their trailblazer status into lasting superiority. Their performance contains a number of important lessons.

- The need to innovate is clearly stated in company guidelines and intensively communicated, and their awareness of it pervades the hidden champions.

- Innovation should not be viewed as narrowly confined to products; rather, each aspect of a business offers opportunities for invention, particularly from customers' requirements.

- Innovation is more than spectacular breakthroughs; the hidden champions innovate continually and gradually. Every business that pursues constant improvement should take advantage of all opportunities.

- Creating a market is one of the most effective routes to innovation; it is, however, demanding and difficult because customers' behavior may have to be changed.

- Technology is the most important ingredient of innovation, and it is helpful to work in a local environment conducive to invention. But companies that do not have such surroundings must not be discouraged even though they may have to undertake particular efforts to compensate for locational disadvantage, for example, in education and cooperation with suppliers and customers. The environment has to be considered a parameter, not a given.

- To realize its full potential, technical innovation should be internationally oriented; the hidden champions are exemplary in this respect.

- The hidden champions are proof that a company should be neither solely technologically driven nor market driven. Technology and market are not opposites but complements to be integrated as equal driving forces.

- In a broader context, a company should reconcile the paradigms of resource-based (inside-out) strategy and competitive forces (outside-in) strategy. Only if internal competencies and external opportunities are matched can a company exploit all its possibilities.

- Customers are a valuable source of innovative ideas; direct contacts of R&D personnel with customers, a systematic bridging of information gaps between functions, and codevelopment are effective ways to activate this fund of knowledge.

- Successful innovation is less a matter of organization or financial resources than of commitment, staff quality, corporate culture, and the will to implement.

The hidden champions prove that small companies can be great innovators. There are no magic formulas for the unknown land of discovery. Innovation is a permanent search, a process of trial and error. The hidden champions' practices can be beneficially adopted by any firm.

7

The Competition

There is so little competition.

THE HIDDEN CHAMPIONS, known as tough competitors, aim their strategy at differentiation rather than cost advantage. However, they do not neglect cost but strive to offer good value at affordable prices. By adjusting their performance to customer requirements, they create competitive advantages in product quality and service.

These are sustainable because they are built on superior internal competencies that are difficult to imitate. When attacked, these firms defend their market positions ferociously, but danger looms for some of them as it is becoming more difficult to separate their niches from volume markets and to evade the increasing cost pressures.

STRUCTURE

There are relatively few competitors in the typical hidden champions' markets. The median number of competitors in world markets is 10, but the much higher arithmetic mean of 55 competitors is misleading because some markets are composed of several hundred competitors. Only about 20% of the sample hidden champions in my research project have more than twenty competitors in their particular world markets. While these numbers may appear small, one should keep in mind that the respective numbers are no greater in many large markets. There are, at most, twenty serious global contenders among the world's automobile manufacturers.

In the framework of Porter's five forces (1985), the competition is principally among existing firms. New competitors are rare (2.7 on a scale of 1 = very rare to 7 = frequent). The probability that the future will see new entries and that those might pose a threat is seen as below average (3.6 and 3.3, respectively, on a 7-point scale). Obviously because the hidden champions' markets are small and their competitive strengths are considered unassailable, these arenas are unattractive to potential contenders. Nevertheless, in some markets mass-produced merchandise is pressing into the hidden champions' niches.

Although a casual observer might expect to find a comfortable competitive life in these markets, this is not the case. Head-on competition is the rule. For the most part, similar competitors appear in every location and at all times (agreement of 5.5 on a 7-point scale) to fight for their share of narrow markets. I was told time and again that the hidden champions take competition seriously. Almost all the interviewees emphasized that their competitors are also strong, so it would be mighty dangerous to consider that their future market leadership had been secured. The highest score for all factors related to competition, 5.8 on the 7-point scale, was awarded to intensity of competition. The hidden champions are constantly aware that market leadership must be earned and defended every day.

Most of these firms do not consider that either substitutes, in Porter's five-forces framework, or suppliers and buyers play a major role as competitive threats. Hidden champions tend to maximize their share in the value chain, avoiding outsourcing whenever possible. This makes them less dependent on suppliers but may have a negative effect on their cost competitiveness. Cost as a weak point is discussed below.

The regional structure of competition is interesting. For answers to the question Which country is your most important competitor's home? see Figure 7.1. Although I requested a single reply, many respondents gave multiple answers, so the percentages total more than 100%.

Competition is really global—72.6% hold that one or more of their most important competitors is from a foreign country; nevertheless, more than half the respondents (55.4%) say that one or more is in Germany. This percentage confirms almost exactly a result in a 1988 study in which mechanical engineering companies were asked a similar question—52.8%

Figure 7.1 **Home Country of Most Important Competitors**

Percentage of Hidden Champions

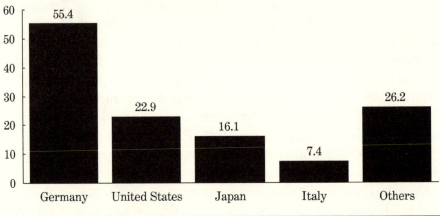

answered that their main competition is in Germany (Informationsdienst des Instituts der Deutschen Wirtschaft 1988). Domestic rivalry is an important element in Porter's "diamond" of international competitive advantage. Porter (1990a, 117) states: "Among the strongest empirical findings from our research is the association between vigorous domestic rivalry and the creation and persistence of competitive advantage in an industry. Nations with leading world positions often have a number of strong local rivals."

These conclusions are corroborated by my observations. Tough domestic competition is an essential element in making the hidden champions fit for world markets. It is not the only determinant but one of several national traits like international orientation, demanding customers, and innovativeness, which interact to work in the same direction. I see domestic rivalry as a factor for global fitness. The effect is not related to collusion but a kind of permanent top challenger for a championship like in a sports contest. They are seldom friends, but by competing against each other, the rivals drive themselves to higher levels of performance. That phenomenon exists for some hidden champions such as when the two leading companies in the world are in the same small town or village. Chapter 8 considers specific relations of sample firms with various partners.

The competitive perspective is not confined to region; 39% of the hidden champions believe that one or more of their most important competitors are in the United States or Japan. Italy, specifically in the north, comes next as a location for strong competitors, the Italians having done well in international business over the past two decades. Other companies cited include Switzerland, the United Kingdom, Sweden, and the Netherlands. Southeast Asian countries were rarely mentioned, as companies from this region are active in mass markets. Also Central and East European countries are not yet playing in this league, but I expect to find Czech Republic on the list in ten years. The hidden champions, with customers and competitors around the world, chart their course on a truly global mental map.

In sum, these companies compete in markets with relatively few competitors worldwide. Their typical markets are oligopolistic. Competitive intensity is high, as each company has to fight for its share in narrowly defined markets. Consistent with the theory that intense domestic rivalry prepares companies for world markets, most hidden champions have strong competitors in their home country, but they do not confine their activities to specific regions. Aiming for world markets, they are confronted by strong companies throughout the world as competitors. The lesson is plain: any company that wants to play a leading role in the global market must actively seek competition with the world's best, wherever they are. World class is attained only by confronting the best, not by competing in the minor leagues.

PRINCIPLES OF COMPETITIVE ADVANTAGE

To lay the groundwork for this subject, I suggest a look at the strategic triangle in Figure 7.2. The three C's at the angles—for customer, company, and competitor—denote the players whose interaction results in success or failure. Marketing has traditionally focused on the customer-company relation. The company trying to meet the customer's needs offers a certain value, for which the customer pays a price. An analogous relationship exists between customer and competitor.

In modern markets—including the hidden champions' markets—several competitors almost always deliver high value at competitive prices. Therefore the third relationship in the triangle, company-competitor, highlights the crucial importance of competitive advantage. It is no

Figure 7.2 **The Strategic Triangle**

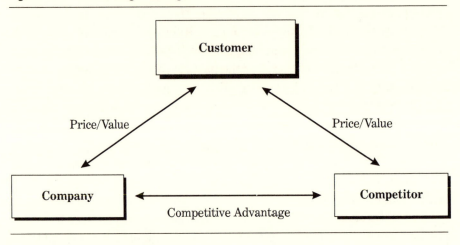

longer sufficient for a company to offer a customer good value at a good price. The company must be better than the competition in at least one component of value or price, that is, to have a competitive advantage. In addition to the question How well do we serve our customer? a firm must ask itself, What is our competitive advantage? It's amazing how many companies, but not the vast majority of the hidden champions, have difficulty answering this simple question.

A competitive advantage can be defined as a superior performance relative to competition that meets the following three criteria:

1. It must be important to the customer.

2. It must be perceived by the customer.

3. It must be sustainable.

If, for instance, a product's packaging is irrelevant to a customer, it is unlikely to create a competitive advantage. If the durability of a product is superior to that of similar merchandise, but a customer doesn't know about or perceive this advantage, it doesn't count. If a company cuts its price without effecting a cost advantage, the competition can follow suit and the advantage is therefore not sustainable. Fulfilling the three criteria simultaneously presents a major challenge. In an earlier study, only 60.4% of a cross section of German industrial companies said they have a competitive advantage that meets the three requirements (Simon 1988).

In managing competitive advantages, a company must observe and adhere to a number of simple principles of which the hidden champions are well aware.

Survival Principle

To survive, a company needs at least one competitive advantage. Why should a customer buy a product from or be loyal to a company if it does not offer at least one feature superior to the competition's goods? A principle of evolutionary theory, Gause's law of mutual exclusion, offers an analogy: "A species will survive only if it masters at least one activity better than its enemies do." It must be able to run faster, dig deeper, climb higher (see Henderson 1983). The same applies to competition; like evolution, it is a perpetual battle for survival. The hidden champions are well acquainted with this principle. The average claimed by the companies is 1.2 competitive advantages that meet the three demanding criteria. Compare this to the 0.6 advantages found in Simon (1988).

Know Your Competitor Principle

To create and defend competitive advantages, one must be well acquainted with one's competitors. The Figure 7.2 triangle suggests that all three players and the relations between them be equally well known. Only if a company knows the strengths and weaknesses of its competitors can it adjust its own strategy to its advantage. Competitive intelligence has to comprise both the external market advantages and the internal competencies about which information is not readily available. Though the situation has improved over the past decade, owing to increased awareness and better methods, in the context of the strategic triangle, competitive intelligence, particularly on internal competencies, is still hard to come by.

This is not fundamentally different for the hidden champions. Chapter 5 showed that they acquire valuable knowledge of their customers by maintaining close contact and on-site experience with them rather than relying on formal market research. The same holds for competitive intelligence. Few hidden champions have instituted formal competitive intelligence systems, but by being close to their competitors, they usually understand them well. They almost always have personal contacts with the important people in the competing companies, which is probably the most important aspect of competitive intelligence. They meet the same

Figure 7.3   **Opportunities for Competitive Advantage**

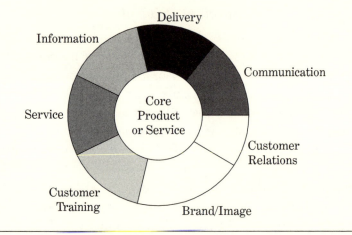

Advantages of Product versus Software

representatives at almost every turn so they acquire knowledge of the competitors' behavior quasi-automatically and unavoidably.

While close relations with customers produce useful feedback on competitive behavior, some company behaviors impede the collection of competitive information. Prominent among those is secrecy; many hidden champions allow access to only a minimum amount of written and publicly accessible information. Some interviewees stated that they refrain from collecting competitive information because they don't care to compare themselves with competitors. One said, "We don't compare ourselves with the competition. They look at us." Another agreed: "The competition is not our standard. We set our own standards." Such companies aren't interested in others' benchmarks because they set their own, an attitude that should be taken seriously.

Leadership cannot be attained by mimicking competitors. Hans-Jürgen Warnecke, president of the Fraunhofer Society, an industry-oriented research institute, warns: "Once you get into the vicious circle of looking for problem solutions from your competitors, rather than from within your own company, you focus on imitating existing solutions and you will stay second forever" (Warnecke 1992, 8). A person who steps into someone else's footprints is unlikely to overtake him. I might add that competitive intelligence and imitation are not the same, though the line of separation may be blurry. For the hidden champions, competitive intelligence is useful mainly to check on whether they are still ahead, not as a primary source for innovation ideas and problem solutions.

Opportunity Principle

Each competitive parameter offers an opportunity to create a competitive advantage. There is a long list of potential candidates. A superior performance can be attained not only in core product and service parameters such as quality, technology, durability, and price, but in numerous "software" parameters like service, delivery, sales/distribution, information, advertising, customer relations, and customer training. Figure 7.3 illustrates the software circle.

A glance at Figure 7.4, the hidden companies' competitive advantages tabulated from their responses, shows that both the core product and the software circle are well represented. One notes, however, a focus on core product, particularly quality and technology. Product quality, at 38%, was

***Figure 7.4* Frequency of Hidden Champions' Competitive Advantages**

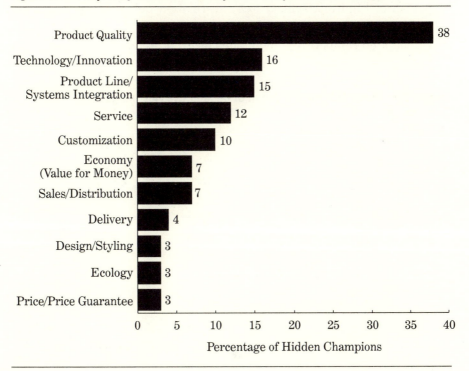

by far the most frequently mentioned advantage. Technology/innovation, in second place, confirms the Chapter 6 finding that this factor is a foundation of the companies' superiority. Product line and systems integration are also important areas (see Chapter 4). Separately, software parameters like service, customization, sales/distribution, and delivery were less frequently cited, but taken as a whole they have a major impact. Price plays a role in competitive advantage for only a tiny minority of the firms.

One can learn from these exemplary competitors that, in spite of talk to the contrary, superior performance results from the creation of competitive advantages primarily in core product and service, which largely determine customer value. The best advantage is product quality because, as the hidden champions prove, most products are not equal.

I am not denigrating competitive advantages in the software circle, but the priorities set forth in Figure 7.4 are right. In many markets it is becoming more and more difficult to sustain superiority in core product, particularly where competitors can quickly imitate one's advantages. One must recognize that sustainability of software advantages is gaining in importance. Figure 7.5 illustrates the relation between the origin and sustainability of competitive advantages.

Unpatented competitive advantages incorporated in a product are usu-

Figure 7.5 Sustainability and Origin of Competitive Advantages

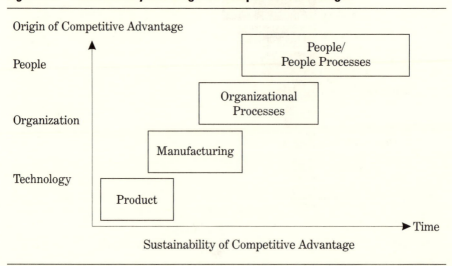

ally easiest to copy—in many modern markets a competitor needs only a few weeks or months to reproduce a new product by buying and reverse-engineering it. It's considerably more difficult to replicate manufacturing and other organizational processes so that these areas are more sustainable. For instance, a competitor like Komatsu would require much more time and money to replicate Caterpillar's global spare parts delivery systems than to rebuild Caterpillar's most recent grader.

The most difficult to duplicate, therefore the most sustainable, advantages are those that rest in people and their processes. Customer relations, superior service based on highly qualified technicians, responsiveness, and friendliness shown by willingness to serve belong to this category. But time is an essential input toward building trust and confidence between a supplier and a customer, because that requires repeated opportunities to cement such relationships. The same is true for education, which, like these competencies, is not for sale in a market. Therefore, consumed time automatically creates sustainability. Of course, the distinction between external advantage and internal competence in these areas becomes blurred. However, with sustainability based on factors cultivated in employees and corporate culture, it is mighty difficult and time consuming for a less efficient competitor to catch up.

Though such competitive advantages in this highest category were rarely mentioned by those whose responses are illustrated in Figure 7.4, they played a prominent role in unstructured interviews. Superior customer relations was a recurring theme. "Our competitive advantage clearly lies in our customer contacts" was a typical comment. Time was also emphasized: "We have been in this business for more than a hundred years, and our customers know and trust us, so the competition has a hard time coping with us." I see these advantages as add-ons to a core product position that has to be at least equivalent to that of the competition. Software advantages cannot compensate for inferior core product or service. Which brings me to the next precept.

Consistency Principle

The performance of a competitive parameter should be consistent with the importance customers attribute to it. Excellent performance counts for a great deal in parameters important to customers, yet low performance is acceptable if a parameter is unimportant to them. Their closeness to customers enables the hidden champions to adjust their performance

Table 7.1 **Principles of Competitive Advantages and Hidden Champions' Position**

Principle	Statement	Hidden Champions' Position
Survival	Survival only with competitive advantage	Well aware of this principle; have one or two competitive advantages
Know Your Competitor	Competitive intelligence as important as customer research	Good knowledge of, through closeness to, competitors; little formal competitive intelligence; do not fall into imitation trap
Opportunity	Each competitive parameter offers opportunity for competitive advantage	Main focus on advantages in core product or service; software advantages under aspect of sustainability
Consistency	Performance should be consistent with importance	Well adjusted; some exceptions in technology-driven firms
Perception	Only perceived advantages count	Generally good, but problems with new, complex products; communication skills sometimes weak

to customer requirements. This aspect is more fully discussed below in the analysis of competitive advantage.

Perception Principle

Only those competitive advantages that customers perceive count—having an objective advantage is not enough unless it is conveyed to the customer. While most hidden champions think they master this communication challenge well, some expressed concern as to whether they get their message across. This is particularly true for complex and new products and systems, like Clean Concept's hygienic toilet, or when a large number of customers precludes intensive one-on-one conversations. Because mass communication in markets with many customers is not a hidden champion strength, some may not translate their full potential into perceived advantages. This is a problem when growing companies have to switch from a personal direct style of communication to an indirect one.

The foregoing information is summarized in Table 7.1.

Again the hidden champions have no magic formulas of competition but use a great deal of common sense. Adhering to the principles outlined above, all have at least one competitive advantage. They know their competitors without relying on formal competitive intelligence; they do not fall into the imitation trap. They exploit opportunities to create competitive advantages but focus on core product and service. They attempt to employ software parameters, particularly in customer relations, to build sustainable advantages, and in observing the consistency principle adjust performance to customer requirements better than their competitors do. Some find it difficult to communicate their complex advantages to customers.

ANALYSIS OF COMPETITIVE ADVANTAGES

To present the hidden champions' competitive advantages more formally and quantitatively, I employ the COMSTRAT system (for *COM*petitive *STRAT*egy), which has proved useful in many consulting projects for my company, Simon, Kucher & Partner, Strategy and Marketing Consultants. COMSTRAT contains several modules, including one that concerns external competitive advantages, and one that analyzes internal competitive competencies. Both are illustrated in Figure 7.6.

Both modules have the same structure: first, the relevant parameters are determined; next, the importance of their weight is estimated; and finally, performance is evaluated. The importance weights and the performance evaluations can be calibrated on various scales, usually a scale of 1 to 5, sometimes by rank. Sophisticated methods like conjoint measurement and analytical hierarchy process can be used for this calibration.

Since performance and competencies are evaluated for all competitors, the system contains a large amount of data (e.g., for 10 competitors and 15 attributes, we get 300 data points), the volume of which impairs interpretation. Therefore the data are condensed into two matrices: the matrix of competitive advantages and the matrix of competitive competencies, again with the same structure. The vertical axis shows the im-

Figure 7.6 **Competitive Advantages and Competencies in the COMSTRAT System**

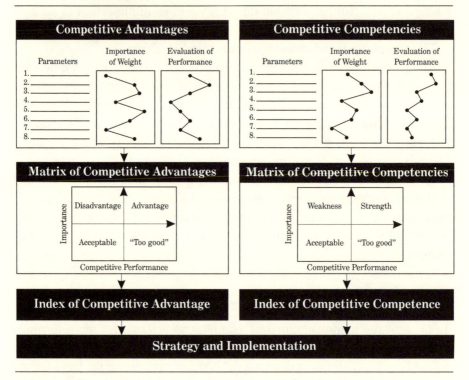

Source: Simon, Kucher & Partner, "Strategic Analysis and Action" (Bonn: Simon, Kucher & Partner, 1995), brochure.

portance weights, while competitive performance and competence are displayed on the horizontal axis.

The competitive performance is either measured in ranks or relative to the strongest competitor with regard to the parameter under consideration. The idea is to compare your company against your strongest, not the average, competitor. (This is comparable to the portfolio of The Boston Consulting Group, in which relative market share is calibrated against the strongest competitor's share.) If the evaluation of your product quality is 4.8 on a 5-point scale and the strongest competitor's is 4.0, your competitive performance is 4.8/4.0 × 100 = 120. Your product is 20% better than that of the strongest competitor. If your quality evaluation is only 3.2 and the strongest competitor's is 4.0, your competitive performance is obtained as 3.2/4.0 × 100 = 80; yours is 20% below the strongest competitor's. The competitive competence score is calculated the same way.

These aspects can be further condensed into an index of competitive advantage and an index of competitive competence. Totaling the products of importance weights and competitive performance across all parameters results in a number that measures overall competitive position. An index of competitive advantage of 95 means that on the weighted average you are 5 points below the strongest competitor for each attribute.

The matrix of competitive advantages in Figure 7.6 helps explain the consistency principle of the preceding section. Only parameters in the upper right-hand box of the matrix (labeled advantage) form competitive advantages because their importance is above average and their performance is better than the strongest competitor's. Accordingly, parameters in the upper left-hand box are competitive disadvantages—high importance, inferior competitive performance. Positions of parameters in the lower right-hand corner of the matrix of competitive advantages are too good—below average importance, superior competitive performance. This combination does not create a relevant competitive advantage. It would be better to shift resources from these parameters to those with above-average importance to improve performance there. Similarly, positions in the lower left-hand quadrant are acceptable. The analogous interpretation can be applied to the matrix of competitive competencies. The consistency principle says that a profile along the diagonal from the upper right to the lower left corner is optimal because it conforms to consistency between importance and performance.

Figure 7.7 displays the matrix of competitive advantages for the sample hidden champions. Importance and competitive performance are measured by rank scale. Remember that the figures are averages across all the sample companies. The shaded diagonal illustrates the consistency principle, with which the hidden champions are in excellent accord. Compared to the hundreds of such matrices I have seen, the consistency between importance and performance here is superb. Product quality, the most important parameter, shows the best competitive performance. This unparalleled consistency enforces the earlier finding on the competitive role of product quality. Closeness to customers (see Figure 5.1), which includes openness, receptiveness, and contacts, the third most important parameter, is also perfectly positioned as are some of the less important ones in the lower left quadrant.

Figure 7.7 **Matrix of Hidden Champions' Competitive Advantages**

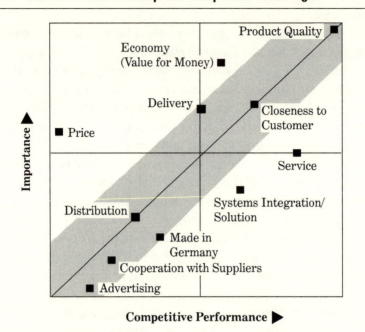

Economy (value for money), the second most important parameter, which could stand improvement in performance, partially reflects the only major violation of the consistency principle, namely, price. Service, second in performance, is of average importance. In the future, the fine service performance may be desirable, since the importance of service is likely to increase. Of course, in specific industries, for example, machinery and mechanical engineering, service is more important, frequently ranking second after quality. In these cases the hidden champions tend to deliver outstanding service. Wolfgang Wilmsen, CEO of Weinig, the world leader in automatic molders, displays great self-confidence: "In our industry, we are by far the best company in the world in service." He emphasizes that the superior service relaxes the price pressure of recent currency fluctuations, which have favored competitors in other countries, principally Italy. Hermann Kronseder of Krones and Berthold Leibinger of Trumpf see similar competitive advantages for their companies on the service side.

Price is the only competitive parameter of above-average importance with a disadvantageous position, but it is acceptable just as long as other important parameters are superior. Nevertheless, most hidden champions have become aware of increased price sensitivity and pay more attention to price, some employing it as a competitive tool. Fielmann, the European leader and number two in the world in eyeglasses, offers a money-back guarantee. The consumer who finds the same product at a lower price gets a refund. Paul Binhold, world leader in anatomical teaching aids, applies the same principle worldwide. In addition to fending off aggressive price cutters, Binhold considers the action a worthwhile way to gather information on competitors' pricing practices from around the globe.

From this, one can conclude that the hidden champions' competitive performance is in synchronization with the importance of the parameters. The firms have competitive advantages in product quality, closeness to customer, and service, a hard-to-beat triad. While the overall matrix provides information on the average competitive position of the hidden champions, it is interesting to consider a specific case in depth because it sheds light on problems some of the companies face in competitive dynamics. This case concerns Procon, a pseudonym for a hidden champion that makes propulsion drives. The data were collected through customer interviews in all relevant regions of the world—North America, Europe, Asia, and Australia. Procon is a world leader in a submarket, a "special" market. In addition, Procon has a much smaller share in a larger "volume" market. Customer requirements in the two markets are markedly different.

In its special market, elasticity of the drives, which includes power and acceleration, is the most important parameter; in the volume market, price is of paramount importance. It is therefore necessary to analyze the two markets and the company's respective competitive positions separately. Figure 7.8 shows the matrix of competitive advantages for both. Procon's competitive position is fundamentally different in the two markets. In the special market it has three competitive advantages: elasticity, product quality, and closeness to customer. In the volume market it has no advantage.

The price disadvantage in the special market is feasible because it is offset by the superior performance in several other parameters, but it is totally unacceptable in the volume market. The overall index of competitive advantage in the special market is 118, indicating that on the weighted average Procon's performance exceeds the best competitor's

Figure 7.8 **Matrices of Procon's Competitive Advantages in Special and Volume Markets**

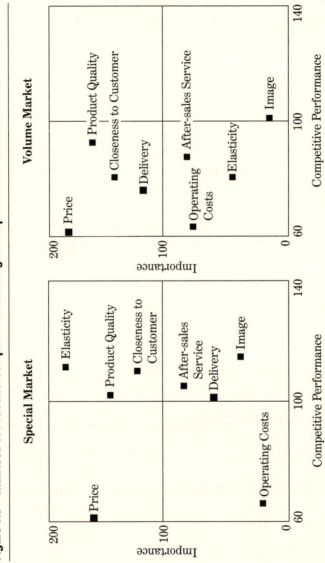

performance by 18%. In the volume market, the company's index of competitive advantage is 89, indicating that relative to the strongest competitor here, Procon underperforms by 11% on average. So it is no wonder that Procon is the world leader in the special market but merely an also-ran in the volume market.

The strength associated with the company's focus in the special market turns into weakness in the volume market. When Procon's management was seeking opportunities for expansion, the volume market appeared to be a natural target. Its size and growth pattern attracted attention while the specialty market was stagnating. As the undisputed technological leader, Procon felt confident of success in the volume market.

My analysis of competitive advantages confirmed the strong specialty market position but revealed that Procon is in a disadvantageous situation in the volume market, in which its current competitive position violates practically every principle of competitive advantage. Consequently, Procon questioned whether it had the internal competencies to improve that competitive position. Companies must realize that internal competencies are prerequisites for external competitive advantages in relation to a specific market.

Following the COMSTRAT system pattern shown in Figure 7.6, I developed the matrices of Procon's competitive competencies in the special market and the volume market reproduced in Figure 7.9. In its special market, Procon has five competencies with great importance and superior performance: R&D, sales, manufacturing flexibility, marketing, and implementation. It is evident why these parameters count in the special market, and its historic experience accounts for Procon's superiority there. It is exactly these parameters that propelled the company to world leadership. In the volume market, however, the picture of competitive competencies is disastrous, with the consistency principle almost reversed: Procon shows inferior competencies in all the parameters that are significant in the volume market. Even the relatively good parameters are not worth much in this market. Procon has three strategic options.

1. Continue the hidden champion strategy of staying in the special market, defending and strengthening its position there. The risk here is that cost disadvantages become too large and customers start to buy the standard products originally conceived for the volume market.

Figure 7.9 Matrices of Procon's Competitive Competencies in Special and Volume Markets

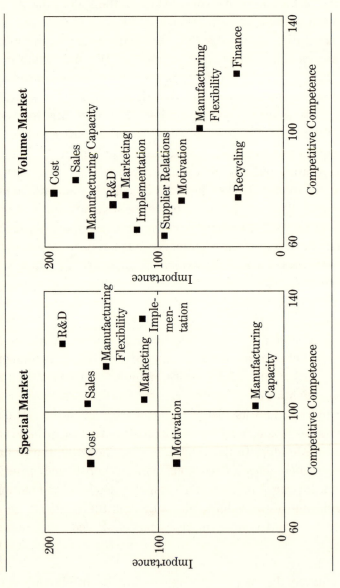

2. Develop the competitive competencies required to succeed in the volume market and turn them into competitive advantages. It would take years to implement this time-consuming option successfully.

3. Find a partner strong in the volume but weak in the special market. The company adopted this option. Forming a strategic alliance with a Japanese partner, it began to operate on a worldwide scale in early 1995.

This case also serves to illustrate competitive risks hidden champions commonly face, which are discussed in the following section. Dynamic shifts between volume and special (niche) markets carry both risks and opportunities for these companies.

My analysis has determined that the hidden champions generally maintain a consistent competitive position. Their competitive advantages lie in product quality, closeness to customer, and service. The Procon story revealed that both competitive advantages and internal competitive competencies in a narrow market can easily become disadvantages in a broad market. These observations shed light on potential competitive risks of narrowly focused hidden champions.

COMPETITIVE RISKS

Chapter 3 surveyed market risk, particularly in the hidden champions' narrow market focus, which implies that these companies put all their eggs in one basket. A market decline or disappearance can lead to disastrous consequences. If people smoke fewer cigarettes the demand for Hauni's cigarette machines will be directly and negatively affected, but that risk is somewhat moderated by geographical spread, since business cycles vary across regions. Relative to market risk, however, the more prevalent and threatening competitive risks can assume many forms.

Probably the most threatening risk concerns the niche positions of the hidden champions and results from a complex combination of performance, cost, and price dynamics. As noted, the competitive position of the hidden champion is almost always one of, in Porter's (1985) terminology, "focused differentiation," that is, a combination of narrow target market and superior performance in one or several parameters. This position can be endangered in various ways. One scenario is of improving mass product performance that gradually neutralizes the traditional differentiation advantages of the hidden champions. This occurred in numerous markets, like cameras, motorcycles, cars, pharmaceuticals after patent expiration, machine tools, and hi-fi equipment, when standard products achieved a quality or performance level formerly available only from premium niche products.

Erosion of a premium product's advantage frequently results from increased versatility of a standard product. Standard electronic machines are more and more capable of handling what were once specific and individualized problems. With a desktop personal computer everyone can create publications that once were the province of specialists in printing, graphics, and layout. Computer-controlled standard machines perform jobs that formerly could be accomplished only by dedicated machinery.

The upgrading of standard products is almost always supported by major cost and price advantages stemming from economies of scale and experience curve effects associated with much larger volumes of output. The Japanese makers of plastic injection molding machines produce about ten times the volume of the German companies, and the same relation holds for the largest company in each of the two countries. Relative size is bound to lead to major cost and price differences for which superior performance often cannot compensate. One respondent, a leading manufacturer of machining centers, reported a Dutch customer's comment: "Your price is $1.60 million, and an Italian firm's price is $990,000. I acknowledge that your product is better, but it's not 60 percent better." The Dutch customer bought the Italian product.

This has become a familiar situation, and it is not confined to the hidden champions. Every company that operates in a premium market has to face this risk. Essentially the same happened to Mercedes-Benz and BMW in the early 1990s, when they were attacked by cheaper Japanese luxury cars like Lexus and Infinity. But the consequences of the risk are particularly menacing to the sample companies because, unlike Mercedes-Benz, these firms have no broad base to carry them through such a crisis.

How can one respond to this threat? No company can take for granted that it has secured its current competitive advantage for the future. Advantage must be defended and fought for continually, in one of essentially only two ways. First, a company has to learn faster than its competitors—in innovating, cost cutting, and improving quality faster. If it succeeds in doing that, it can retain its lead. Of course, one must realize that most parameters have a saturation level and that costs increase exponentially as this level is approached.

The alternative is to change the parameter of the competitive advantage by creating a new advantage. If further product quality improvements are no longer possible or economical, a company may have to switch to a software parameter or build a strong brand name that may be important to consumers to accomplish this end.

Hidden champions pursue all these routes. Tetra Pak and Kärcher are on the way to building brand names. Many firms put extra efforts into services. Even small changes can add up to a service-based competitive advantage. Smithers Oasis, the German subsidiary of U.S.-based Solaris, the world market leader in floral foam, introduced a toll-free fax line, regularly organizes seminars for florists, and publishes books of advice for its customers. When the company receives a complaint, an employee responds to resolve it within thirty minutes. That doesn't sound extraordinary because many companies aspire to process complaints rapidly. But to avoid the impression of giving lip service to such goals, one must work conscientiously every single day to implement them. There are myriad ways to add services to a product, but the greater their potential as a competitive advantage, the greater the difficulty implementing them.

Improving or shifting a differentiation strategy must not be a deterrent to cutting costs massively if that is required. Many companies that have pursued this tactic were misguided in overemphasizing differentiation-based competitive advantage and neglecting cost considerations. As was true of Procon, when hidden champions are not well enough equipped to compete in a mass market, they must nevertheless pay maximum attention to cost. Even if the primary foundation of a competitive strategy is superior performance, costs are of utmost importance. In the long term, no company can afford to neglect being cost-effective. The self-deception that customers pay any price for a superior product so that costs can be treated lightly is probably the most serious error of companies that deal in premium products. The golden rule of competition is that performance *and* costs are the two almost equally important parameters, allowing only for slight variation by more or less emphasis on one or the other.

Most hidden champions had to learn these painful lessons in the early nineties. While some didn't survive as independent companies, for example, machine tool manufacturers Maho and Deckel, most did what was considered impossible by redesigning products and slashing costs. In my study, the majority of the companies reported that they coped with the recession better than their competitors did. Such are the fruits of major efforts in product and process redesign (see Chapter 1). Most hidden champions introduced target pricing and target costing into their development plans. Instead of generating a "perfect" product and then determining its cost, they increasingly project definite price and cost targets before starting a project. The resulting products frequently are simpler than first visualized. Trumpf, world leader in sheet metal cutting devices, one of the first to institute target costing, has reported cost reductions of 30% for products with superior performance.

Of course, all the familiar techniques, like simultaneous engineering, reengineering, and lean management, are employed to reduce development and manufacturing time. However, while the hidden champions were already very lean compared with larger companies, many told me that they derived little profit from such buzzwords because they had implemented many of them long before those principles appeared in the literature. This is largely consistent with what I experienced on my tour through their places of business, where I saw some of the most efficient operations in the world. For instance, five of the plants have areas which are off limits to Japanese visitors. Perhaps the biggest difference between the hidden champions and large companies is that the former require much less time for implementation—my guess is a half to two-thirds less.

In development aimed at improving their competitive position, many companies have learned that they must not yield volume markets to mass producers. If experience curve effects and economies of scale are important and standard products come close to performing as premium products, the companies must defend or attack the turf of their mass markets. Nicholas Hayek, the man who created the Swatch, was one of the first to point out this lesson by recommending that companies which want to defend their niche markets refuse to cede them to mass marketers. Junghans, the maker of radio-controlled and solar wristwatches, has adopted this philosophy by introducing less expensive models. The company now enjoys market leadership in Germany through this aggressive strategy. Junghans overtook Citizen in 1991 and in 1993 had a relative market share in value of about one and a half times that of its rival.

Hidden champions often defend their markets ferociously when attacked. An aggressive Italian company was the prime competitor of one hidden champion. When in 1992–1993 the Italian lira experienced more than a 20% devaluation, the Italian company took the opportunity to attack through very hostile pricing, increasing its world share by 7 percentage points during 1993. The hidden champion commissioned a detailed competitive intelligence study focusing on cost. Discovering that its competitor had an overall cost advantage of 27%, it set a cost reduction target of 30%. The project included redesigning its product, creating a new low-price "attack" product, and relocating parts manufacturing to low-wage Central European countries. The company achieved the cost reduction within a short time. From the moment the hidden champion recognized that reduction was a realistic goal and before it actually lowered costs, prices were slashed. Since then, the company has regained its lost market share points and is in the best shape ever.

The spread of international locations provides the hidden champions with a degree of flexibility and a buffer against currency and cost fluctuations. One firm reduced its workforce in Germany by 300 and increased it by the same number in the United States. Since U.S. hourly gross wages are about one third lower than those in Germany (Institut der deutschen Wirtschaft 1994, 6), this relocation results in substantial cost reduction. At the same time, the company shifted additional work to its newly founded subsidiary in Poland, where the cost of wages is about one-sixth that in Germany. But be aware that the flexibility gained through such relocations is limited. The high qualifications of some hidden champion employees can be only partially replicated in other locations.

In assessing threats, it is absolutely crucial to understand the factors critical to success. While I emphasize the relevance of cost, that is not always the decisive factor. In many markets experience curve effects and economies of scale don't play a role. One of the bigger errors of the 1970s and 1980s competitive strategy was to posit a universal validity of that curve, which simply doesn't exist. Also, such more recent trends in competitive strategy as time-based competition, total quality management, and reengineering claim undeserved universality whose danger lies in one-sided emphasis on one factor (see Porter 1994). One must carefully scrutinize the competitive parameters to determine which are decisive on a case-by case basis. Frequently the key parameter may not be cost or time or any other single factor. Generally, the art of competitive strategy lies in doing several things somewhat better, not doing one thing much better.

The Japanese market still poses a major competitive challenge to the hidden champions. A few years ago I conducted a study of the competitive position of German products in Japan, for which I interviewed sixty-six managers in Japan (33 expatriates, 33 Japanese). While this study was not confined to hidden champions, it sheds light on the challenges facing companies in Japan. Figure 7.10, which shows the matrix of competitive advantages, has the same structure as Figure 7.7. Both the importance on the vertical axis and the competitive performance on the horizontal axis are rank ordered.

The Japanese ranking of importances is quite different from that shown in Figure 7.7, which relates to the average "global" customer. Again product quality is the most important parameter with service and delivery second and third. Although price plays the lowest role in the Japanese market, that seems to be changing in the second half of the nineties. Consistent with Figure 7.7, German products have a strong

Figure 7.10 **Matrix of Competitive Advantages, German Products in Japan**

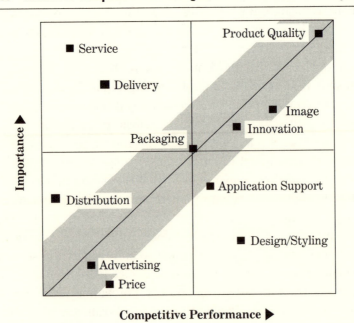

competitive advantage in product quality, with image and innovation following. But the competitive position in service and delivery of German products in Japan is totally unacceptable. The long distance between Germany and Japan, which is responsible for this weakness, is irrelevant to Japanese customers, who require fast and competent service as well as punctual and flexible delivery. A company that wants to succeed in Japan had better take care to avoid such competitive disadvantages from the very beginning. A large number of hidden champions that are successful in Japan, for example, Binhold, Weinig, Heidelberg, Karl Mayer, Trumpf, and Wella, are not burdened by the drawbacks that plague the average German company. They have gone the extra mile in the Japanese market to match the competitive performance of the local competitors. The motto of Paul Binhold, "to checkmate the Japanese in Japan," and its effective implementation prove that foreign firms can build superior competitive positions in Japan, which should encourage other companies.

SUMMARY

The hidden champions are not immune to competition; they are exposed to the same pressures as other companies. They operate mostly in intensely competitive oligopolistic markets. Generally tough competitors, they consciously pursue a focused competitive strategy, basing their advantages on differentiation rather than cost. Their performance suggests a number of lessons on competitive strategy.

- A company must strive decisively for at least one competitive advantage that is important to its customers, perceived by the customers, and sustainable.

- The foundation for competitive advantage lies in superior knowledge of customer requirements.

- Knowledge of competitors is as important as knowledge of customers, and competitive knowledge comes from closeness to competitors and formal competitive intelligence.

- Competitive advantages should be created in the core product; the software circle should not be neglected, for software parameters frequently allow for better sustainability.

- Competitive performance requires excellence in important parameters, but lower performance in less important parameters is acceptable. The hidden champions are exemplary in creating competitive advantages in product quality, closeness to customer, and service.

- Competitive advantages and competencies should be quantitatively analyzed in the framework of a formal system, a merely qualitative view being insufficient.

- To attain or retain world-class status, a company should actively seek out rather than avoid competition with the best in the world.

- Even if competitive advantage is built on differentiation, cost must not be neglected, being given only a slightly lower priority.

- Companies must be aware that a competitive advantage or superior internal competence in one market can become a weakness in another market.

- A niche or premium competitor should be alert to threats from a volume market. Standard products can attack premium products by either increasing their performance or realizing major price advantages.

- When a competitive position is attacked, it is preferable for a company to defend it immediately and ferociously rather than adopting a wait-and-see-attitude.

- As the successes of some hidden champions in Japan prove, companies can prevail in a difficult environment by implementing a decisive competitive strategy. Avoiding competitive disadvantages is critical in such a situation.

Competition involves a permanent battle for survival. The hidden champions have no wonder weapons in their arsenal but in a fight employ the arms that are available to all others. Their most effective weapon is adhering more closely than competitors to commonsense rules. They offer customers superior quality, which they support with close personal contact and excellent service. If customers discern that they are receiving superior value, they are willing to pay a fair price premium. Competitive advantage is built through doing many things a little better, not one thing much better. In implementing their competitive strategies, the hidden champions act speedily and decisively. A company that observes these simple principles encounters little real competition.

8
The Partners

The strong one is most powerful alone.
—Friedrich von Schiller

IN ADDITION TO CUSTOMERS AND COMPETITORS, other categories of potential partners have relevance for the hidden champions' excellence. Suppliers are just as critical as strategic alliances and other types of cooperation. I first look at outsourcing, which like strategic alliances, has become a cure-all for many problems. Neither of these holds much attraction for the hidden champions. They prefer to maintain depth in manufacturing and conduct their own R&D. They tend to go it alone even in foreign markets, relying on their own strengths rather than the illusion that an outside force will solve their problems.

But they are not solitary; they are surrounded by suppliers, customers, locational conditions, and companies outside their particular industry, all of which form the contingent that drives them to their unusual achievements. While difficult to explain and impossible to measure, this environment may play a much larger, almost invisible role than external observers realize. Why else would one find several hidden champions in one small town? Occasionally a newcomer adopts one of these firms as a role model and becomes one of the elite group itself. Every company must be aware of the relevance of such forces and try to take advantage of them or create propitious conditions for itself.

SELF-RELIANCE

The hidden champions strive to retain work within their companies. On average, value-added accounts for 50% of revenue, which is amazingly high for modern industrial companies. (Value-added is defined by what a company adds to the value of purchased materials and services, namely, the sum of wages, taxes, interest, and profit.) The sample companies' annual value-added per employee is $88,435, which is high by any standard. A study of the German machine tool industry (Rommel et al. 1995) found an average annual value-added per employee of only $68,667.

Self-reliance is particularly pronounced in manufacturing and R&D. The mean depth of manufacturing (the percentage of total manufacturing done in house) is 57%. A quarter of the hidden champions even have a manufacturing depth of more than 70%. Only a quarter have less than 40%, which appears to be an upper limit for lean production companies. And 69.2% of the sample firms say that a high depth of manufacturing is important or very important for them. The statement "Our depth of manufacturing is lower than that of competitors" earned the lowest rate of agreement among twelve items on corporate issues, and "We try to outsource as much as possible" received the third lowest agreement. The fierce self-reliance in manufacturing reflects the belief in specialization and concentration. The critical relevance of product quality as the outstanding competitive advantage (see Chapter 7) does not, in the eyes of the hidden champions, allow for outsourcing the production of key components. To protect both competitive advantages and core competencies, they prefer to keep such activities in-house in spite of potential cost disadvantages. In the choice between make or buy, the decision is usually to make.

Heidelberger Druckmaschinen, world leader in offset-printing presses, is typical. It still runs its own foundry because management is convinced that the ultra-high quality and precision required of its products cannot be met without the closest control of the manufacturing process. The company probably sacrifices some economies of scale it could effect through outsourcing but believes that quality is more important than cost. The same sort of thinking can be found at Miele. This leading manufacturer of premium washing machines and dishwashers reflects the same values. "Miele manufactures as many components as possible, preferably within a small region with firmly rooted workers. This is not going to change soon," reports *Frankfurter Allgemeine* (1995). In a private conversation, Dr. Peter Zinkann, Miele's CEO, commented that this attitude refers to core competencies, not noncore activities. And of Braun, the Gillette subsidiary which is the world market leader in four of its six businesses, it is said: "Braun manufactures almost everything it needs, even the special machines for its production and the small screws for its razors. The company holds that its quality requirements are extremely high, and this quality cannot be procured at reasonable prices on the market" ("Ein echter Braun wird mit Nüssen und Kirschkernen beschossen" 1995).

Mercedes-Benz has a similar attitude concerning critical components. Its truck division, world leader in heavy trucks, is the only German automobile manufacturer that operates its own foundry for axles, cylinder heads, and crankcases. Another proponent of full production control is Helmut Aurenz, founder of ASB Grünland, world leader in potting soil. Because he wasn't satisfied with the quality of the packaging soils he could buy on the market, he started to produce and print his own. Aurenz's motto is: "You can fully trust only what you make in your own shop." Other hidden champions echo this value system. A manager of a construction equipment manufacturer recounts:

> Whenever possible, we keep work in the company. I find out how much a certain component costs in the market, then challenge my people to produce it at the same cost or less. They usually succeed, and I can then be certain of its quality. We really dislike letting work out to others.

Hidden champions that have increasingly outsourced in recent years are reconsidering their position. The managing director of one such company, which makes special engines, describes his thinking of late 1995:

> In the late 1980s we had a CEO who tried to outsource almost everything. I think this was a big mistake. I am now trying to get as much work back as possible, because the outsourcing has made our processes very complex, particularly in R&D. We have also experienced serious quality problems, but our developing self-confidence leads us to a counteroutsourcing view. What are we good for if we can't make the better quality pistons and crankshafts at the same costs as others in the market?

A largely neglected problem with outsourcing originates with customers. A hidden champion executive in the electrical sector explains:

Our customers realize that all competitors use the same components from the same suppliers. So they question having to pay a premium price for our product if it's so similar to the others. In the end, only the assembly and the external appearance are different. No, we absolutely need proprietary core components that are available in our, and nobody else's, products.

Outsourcing complete subsystems is a modern trend. Instead of buying single components and assembling them as a system or subsystem, the supplier is asked to deliver the whole subsystem. This approach reduces the number of suppliers and parts, relays overall responsibility to that supplier, and is usually cost efficient. Particularly popular in the automobile industry, it has also attracted increasing attention by manufacturers of industrial equipment. But that approach can lead to new problems as some of the sample firms have learned. A leading maker of equipment for the food industry gave suppliers the essential know-how and asked them to produce various subsystems. For a while this venture went very well, achieving substantial savings in cost. But in the process several suppliers, with the knowledge they had acquired, started to sell their subsystems directly to food industry customers. Thus, the hidden champion educated its own competitors, which caused it serious difficulties. It discontinued outsourcing these subsystems and is striving to win back its sales volume for the complete system.

The attitude against outsourcing is not confined to product components but includes an earlier stage of value creation. Many hidden champions prefer to make the machines necessary to manufacturing their products, which, again, can hardly be justified on the basis of cost. Only partially motivated by keeping value-added in house, it is rather viewed as an effective way to protect the companies' production expertise. Friedrich Hoppe, chairman of Hoppe, the European market leader in door and window fittings, says, "About ten percent of our workforce is in our machinery shop, which is a closely guarded operation. We develop and make our own machines and don't sell them to anyone. They contain our matchless skills."

When Heinz Hankammer, the founder-CEO of Brita water filters, led me through his factory, he included the machine shop in the tour. He said, "Why should anybody be better at making these machines? Brita is world market leader because it has a unique product made on unique machines." Haribo, world leader in Gummi bears, which develops and builds its own machines, prefers to keep them hidden from visitors. The same is true for the Schlatterer woven belts used in cigarette machines. Schlatterer, whose overall world market share is 70 to 75%, produces everything it needs in-house. Because nobody else produces the weaving equipment the company needs, Schlatterer does that for itself, replacing the machines with advanced models every three years.

I presume that the in-house development and production of machinery has the further purpose of keeping and motivating highly qualified engineers and technicians. I had the impression that the firms' most able employees generally worked in these departments rather than in the routine jobs involving production of the end product. The hidden champions' competitive advantage is not solely attributable to a better product fashioned from third-party manufactured machines any company can buy. The sample firms' advantage is rooted in their ability to develop and manufacture equipment unique to a company's requirements and unavailable to competitors.

Jürgen Nussbaum, executive vice president of Sachtler, world leader in professional camera tripods, emphasizes this point: "In some countries, competitors try to imitate our products. But they fail because they don't have the same tools. We make our own tools, which can't be bought on the market. This is our best protection against pirates." Seen in this light, the issue of manufacturing depth assumes a totally different meaning as an essential cornerstone of a competitive strategy aiming at differentiation. The core of the advantage resides in the capacity to supply in-house a piece of equipment that cannot be reproduced so that the value creation process starts at an earlier, unique stage and is not confined to the production of the end product.

This insight can be directly transferred to R&D, where the hidden champions' self-reliance is even more pronounced than in manufacturing. Eighty-two percent of the respondents said that they strive for great depth in R&D for two reasons. First, their specialization requires that they conduct their own research. Others are simply not specialized enough to contribute anything of value. Second, these firms are extremely sensitive to protecting their idiosyncratic knowledge. The CEO of a leading supplier to the furniture industry describes his experience: "We once entered into an R&D cooperative arrangement with another company. We learned very little from this cooperation, but they gained a great deal of information from us. Since then, our independent R&D has become a top-secret activity. It's the only way to protect our superior know-how." I heard dozens of similar comments from the hidden champions.

Of course, there are also serious risks associated with an anti-outsourcing attitude. If cost and price become more important competitive parameters, and economies of scale can be realized through outsourcing, the prevailing attitude has to be reconsidered. Many sample firms have increased the share of their outsourced value-added. Outsourcing, and R&D, like any other issue, must not receive a one-sided or ideological assessment. Overreliance on one's own strength may turn into a weakness if competencies required for new technologies cannot be developed internally or quickly enough. On the other hand, if R&D—a core competence in most businesses—is bought on the open market, it is unlikely to create a competitive advantage since it is accessible to everyone. The literature on outsourcing has been focusing too narrowly on costs, neglecting the effects on competitive differentiation. The hidden champions teach us that this is an incomplete interpretation and that a more holistic consideration of outsourcing is necessary.

While the negative attitudes toward outsourcing apply to core activities like manufacturing and R&D, they almost reverse to positive for noncore elements, in which the hidden champions do a great deal of outsourcing. While large companies often strive for autarky in noncore fields such as law, tax accounting, and other services, the vast majority of the hidden champions employ external suppliers for these activities. Their usual argument is that they can't afford such departments and the fixed costs associated with them. But I think there is more to it than that and again suspect a trade-off between cost and quality. When I discuss this issue with representatives of large corporations, they can generally prove that it is cheaper for them to have their own tax people, lawyers, and internal consultants, even taking into account the trade-off between variable and fixed costs. But they rarely discuss quality, which may be understandable because quality differences between internal and external suppliers of sophisticated services are difficult to measure. The hidden champions have a different view of these issues.

A CEO of a trading company explains his fairly common position:

> We outsource all noncore functions like tax, law, public relations. We want to keep our company very lean in these activities, and we hate fixed costs. In addition, I am convinced that we get a much better quality of service than we could generate internally. Why should an excellent lawyer, tax adviser, or any such expert work for us as an employee? If he is really excellent, he can earn much more money as a freelancer or a partner in a specialized firm. I think that large companies deceive themselves enor-

mously when they think they can hire top staff in these fields. Outsourcing is the only way to buy the best expertise in noncore activities. Once a company finds an excellent external consultant, it must build a permanent relationship with him. The consultant gradually acquires the knowledge of an internal expert but is nevertheless obligated to prove constantly that he is still top because he is not a permanent employee.

From my experience with both large corporations and hidden champions, I agree with this statement. The sample firms' suppliers of sophisticated services often outperform the internal staff of large corporations. It is probably true that large companies need certain internal noncore services, but the hidden champions' experiences suggest that the decision on outsourcing in these fields should not be confined to aspects of cost but include those of quality as well.

SYSTEMS INTEGRATORS

At first glance, some hidden champions appear to be heavy outsourcers and in this way contradict my foregoing contentions. The value-added in these companies may account for only 15 or 20% of sales revenue. Dürr and Brückner belong to this category. Both build large plants, the former for the automobile industry and the latter for the chemical industry. Their outsourcing percentages do not contradict my statements because these companies are essentially systems integrators rather than manufacturers. Their core competencies are in the integration of highly complex systems, in project management, and in engineering.

Brückner, the world-leading manufacturer of biaxial film-stretching systems, exemplifies this type of company. Only 260 employees are responsible for sales revenues of $120 million, and its $461,538 of sales per employee are extremely high for an industrial firm. The reason? Brückner doesn't manufacture but confines itself to designing and completing the plants.

Dr. Wolfgang Pinegger, president of Brückner, describes its role:

Our core competencies are in designing these complex machines, finding the suppliers of the hardware, then putting everything together. It's an extremely complex job. We are not really outsourcing because we do not manufacture. But in systems integration, our core activity, we don't outsource anything. We protect our know-how very carefully. We hold the essential patents and have strengthened our position during the recent crisis years.

This company is another example of a hidden champion guarding its core competencies. Outsourcing has a different meaning for systems integrators than for manufacturers.

STRATEGIC ALLIANCES

The hidden champions' negative attitude toward outsourcing core activities extends to strategic alliances. Most of the firms would subscribe to what Michael Porter (1990b, 93) said: "Alliances as a broad-based strategy will only ensure a company's mediocrity, not its international leadership." Deciding whether to form a strategic alliance or go it alone in entering a foreign market is particularly difficult. Peter Drucker (1989) suggests that "for small and medium-sized businesses [strategic alliances] are increasingly becoming the way to go international." But this does not apply to the hidden champions; a majority of 56.5% said that their policy is to do it themselves. The questionnaire statement "We cooperate in foreign markets" received the second lowest number of agreements among twelve items. These companies don't want middlemen between themselves and their customers. Only 23% said that they generally enter foreign markets with a partner.

The Japanese market represents an exception. Alliances are much more common in Japan than in other countries owing to the difficulty of cracking this market. Many cooperative arrangements started in the 1960s and have proved to be quite successful. Lenze, a world leader in small gears, has a long-standing relationship with Miki Pulley, a similar-size Japanese company that dates back to the early 1960s. The relationship has helped Lenze to sell its products in Japan; in return, Lenze markets Miki's products in Germany. Over the years the owners' families have developed close personal ties, for instance, attending one another's wedding and birthday celebrations.

Trumpf, world leader in sheet-metal cutting machines, entered the Japanese market in the early 1960s through a Japanese distributor, with whom it cooperated closely for more than a decade. Kreul, a world leading manufacturer of top-of-the-line oboes, did not enter the Japanese market until the 1980s, cooperating from the very start with a Japanese importer.

Hans-Joachim Kreul, the owner-CEO, emphasizes the importance of a long-term relationship and patience. He and his Japanese partner cooperate successfully and visit each other several times a year to cultivate their relationship.

But even if they enter foreign markets with a partner, most hidden champions prefer to gain full control of their operations in the long run, as Trumpf did by establishing its own subsidiary in the mid-1970s. BMW is particularly enlightening: its successful expansion in Japan started only when it took over its Japanese distributor in the early 1980s. One hidden champion, a supplier to the auto industry, has entered many foreign markets through partnerships with local firms. But over the years this company consistently pursued a strategy of gaining full control and now totally owns sixteen of its nineteen foreign subsidiaries. This is a standard pattern for many sample companies.

While the hidden champions are demanding but fair partners in transactions along the normal supplier-customer chain, they are difficult to deal with in less well-defined strategic alliances. Their idiosyncratic corporate culture and management style (see Chapters 9 and 10) can make cooperation with outsiders troublesome. Zealously guarding their cherished independence, these companies are very demanding vis-à-vis their partners, from which they expect the same standards of performance and the same values as their own. Their goals (see Chapter 2) may be incompatible with those of a less-ambitious partner.

I distinguish between "barricade of wagons" companies and "amoeba companies." While amoeba companies maximize their contacts with outside partners, the barricade of wagons type are withdrawn from and reserved with outsiders that are neither customers nor suppliers. Most hidden champions belong to the barricades category and can be characterized by a description of Mars, the candy bar giant: "Mars has its go-it-alone strategy and is not an outfit into idea sharing and strategic alliances" (Saporito 1994). Note, however, that neither the barricade nor the amoeba culture is generally superior. The preeminence of one or the other depends on specific conditions. The observation that the hidden champions lean toward the barricade-type culture should be not be construed as a recommendation. That culture can be dangerous because it fails to perceive or understand environmental changes. An amoeba culture, on the other hand, involves the risk of too much expertise being released and shared with outsiders.

Table 8.1 **Hidden Champions' Attitudes toward Outsourcing and Strategic Alliances**

Outside Activity	Hidden Champions' Attitude
Outsourcing in Manufacturing	Generally negative; quality more important than costs, particularly for core components and sometimes machinery
Outsourcing R&D	Negative, with in-house R&D seen as critical for protection of core competencies
Outsourcing Noncore Activities	Positive, owing to variability of cost and quality; continuing relationships with suppliers
Strategic Alliances/ Cooperation	Generally negative; preference for full control; barricades of wagons mentality prevalent, particularly in foreign markets, except for Japan

The hidden champions teach one to be wary of the illusion that strategic alliances can solve problems a company cannot unravel by itself. First and foremost, every company should rely on its own strengths and assume the responsibility of building the critical competencies necessary to compete and thrive in a market. According to these firms, strategic alliances should be a last resort, not a first choice.

The hidden champions' opinions about outsourcing and strategic alliances are summarized in Table 8.1.

These attitudes deviate strongly from prevailing opinions in the literature. Lean management and similar concepts suggest extensive use of outsourcing and alliances, but many such recommendations result from overemphasis on costs. The effects on quality, on commitment to a market, on employee motivation, on protecting know-how, and on differentiation are rarely considered in depth. I am far from suggesting that the skepticism of the hidden champions is always right, for it certainly can lead to the danger of missing economies of scale or technological developments or wasting too much time in entering a foreign market. What the hidden champions can teach us is the benefit of suspicion toward searching for problem solutions in other companies instead of one's own house.

PARTNERS

While the foregoing analysis may suggest the loneliness of a hidden champion (which is largely true), many formal and informal connections and networks contribute to the unusual performance of these companies. Some fall into strategic groups or families or industry clusters, but others are simply formed on the basis of some other sort of regulation.

In a discussion of these aspects, it is useful to draw on Porter's framework of competitive forces and environmental conditions (1985, 1990a). Figure 8.1 provides a simple example of such a structure. I have already touched on several environmental conditions that affect the hidden champions. Chapter 4 showed that they operate in an environment with a strong international orientation, thus favoring their own globalization. Chapter 6 indicated that they profit from an environment conducive to technological innovation.

Chapter 7 treated competitive strategies, focusing on competitive advantage; from this perspective, competitors are adversaries. But in the context of Figure 8.1, and as Porter (1990) has correctly pointed out, competitors are also "training partners for fitness." This does not imply

Figure 8.1 **Outside Forces Affecting the Hidden Champions**

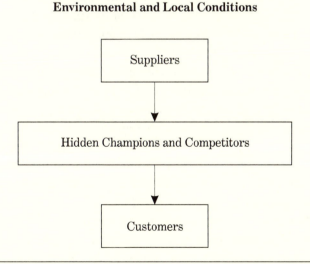

that they must be on friendly terms; the opposite is usually true. But companies that compete against each other cannot afford to neglect to continuously improve relations if they want to survive. Their relationship is comparable to that of two top athletes competing against each other. Even if they don't exercise together, they drive themselves to new heights of performance as long as they remain ambitious.

Close competitive relationships are fairly common among the hidden champions. Table 8.2 lists companies whose closest—and usually toughest—competitor is nearby. Sometimes the first and second in the world are located in the same small town, such as Würth and Berner, for assembly products, in Künzelsau, and Zahoransky and Ebser in Todtnau. The latter two lead in the world market for brush-making machines. Two leading firms in ceramic ware, Hutschenreuther and Rosenthal, are in Selb, close to the border with the Czech Republic.

Faber-Castell, the world's number one in pencils, and its closest competitor, Staedtler-Mars, are both in the Nuremberg area. One of their many battles, over which is the oldest pencil maker, took place in 1994. Faber-Castell was founded in 1761, Staedtler-Mars in 1835. In 1994 Staedtler launched a lottery to celebrate the 333rd anniversary of the production of the first pencil by Friedrich Staedtler, the first member of the founding family to ply the trade. Faber-Castell fought back ferociously to defend its position as the older company. The fact that in 1978 Staedtler acquired Eberhard Faber, the U.S. company founded by a black sheep of the Faber-Castell clan in 1904, adds spice to the feud. Another competitor, Lyra Bleistift-Fabrik in Nuremberg, founded in 1806, also claims to be older than Staedtler.

My interviews with the hidden champions always addressed the issue of the strongest competitors, but quite a few respondents didn't care for this subject. My impression is that as competitors they are not on friendly but on very competitive, perhaps hostile, terms. In any case, I have no doubt that they are driving each other toward competitive fitness. Albert Berner, a former Würth employee, is the world number two in assembly products with sales of more than $533 million. Berner has publicly declared that it intends to penetrate the $667 million (DM 1 billion) barrier in 1997. Of course, the race between Berner and Würth, which has four times more sales, spurs both of them to faster growth. The same is true for most of the other listed pairs. Sometimes the fight ends in defeat or takeover, as in the case of RUD. The war between RUD and Erlau, the

Table 8.2 **Pairs of Hidden Champion Competitors**

Market/Product	Competing Hidden Champions	Competitive Position and Conduct
Assembly Products	Würth	Würth uncontested number one; relative market share ca. 5;
	Berner	Berner, the offspring, fierce attacker
Offset-printing Presses	Heidelberg Roland	Intense competition for more than 100 years
Bottling Systems	KHS Krones	KHS is number one in complete systems, Krones in labeling machines; fierce competitors
Gas-pressurized Springs, Vibration Control	Stabilus Suspa	Each number one in certain submarkets
Industrial Chains	RUD Erlau	Intense competitors for 100 years; in 1988 RUD took over Erlau
Double-belt Presses for Continuous Heating and Pressing	Hymmen Held	Each number one in certain submarkets; extremely intense, unfriendly competition
Brush-making Machines	Zahoransky Ebser	Zahoransky distant leader; fierce competition in submarkets
Pencils	Faber-Castell Staedtler-Mars	Faber-Castell founded in 1761, Staedtler-Mars in 1835; intensive battle over which has longer tradition and better reputation

top producers of chains and both in the town of Aalen, had been waged for almost a hundred years. Although RUD acquired Erlau in 1988, it has retained the latter's brand name.

One can find similar competitive patterns in other countries. The world's two largest producers of sparkling wine, Freixenet and Codorniu, are in the same village in Spain. Jointly these two companies dominate a large chunk of both the U.S. and the European sparkling wine markets. Freixenet alone sells more bottles in the United States than all French champagne producers combined. Their success, according to the *Wall Street Journal Europe*, "owes a lot to the heated rivalry of Freixenet and Codorniu" (1994). Pairs and groups of competitors are also a phenomenon in the Italian shoe industry, the Dutch cut-flower industry, the American software industry, and wherever one finds world leaders (see also Porter 1990a).

As noted in preceding chapters, the hidden champions don't see competition as being limited by a regional scope. Nevertheless, it seems that proximity of a strong competitor has an enormous impact on competitive fitness. This leads to a seemingly perverse implication. It might be better for a company to have strong than weak competitors nearby. As in sports, the lonely athlete is less likely to gain the gold medal than the one who trains close to other top contenders. The top athletes in a discipline frequently congregate in one place. The same is true for companies. One should, however, view both sides of the medal. In head-on competition, a company either atttains world class or goes under. If unwisely waged (e.g., through aggressive pricing), this kind of competition can be disastrous for both parties. The smart approach to close and tough competition seems to hold promise of world market leadership.

Another important force for the development of the hidden champions is vertical relations. The customers of several of the companies are world leaders in their own markets. Together they form vertical pairs of hidden champions. The leading maker of gelatin, DGF Stoess, belongs to this category. Haribo, with Gummi bears, the largest gelatin user in the world, is DGF Stoess's largest customer. Another customer, partially owned by DGF Stoess, is R. P. Scherer, the world's largest manufacturer of soft gelatin capsules for the pharmaceutical industry. DFG Stoess and R. P. Scherer are both residents of Eberbach. Schlatterer, a producer of special woven belts for the manufacture of cigarettes, used to have a 100% world market share for original equipment and between 90 and 95% for replacement. Schlatterer has become large through Hauni, the cigarette machine leader. Thomas Beckh of Schlatterer comments, "We didn't need to sell or do any marketing; we just distributed our products. And because we lacked enough capacity, our delivery times were much too long." Today, Schlatterer is fully engaged in marketing its products and has a world market share between 70 and 75%. Its relation with Hauni is still fruitful for both sides. The same is true for ebm Electrobau Mulfingen, a world leader in specialized electric motors.

Koenig & Bauer with about 90% of the world market for money-printing presses and Giesecke & Devrient, number two in money-printing services following De La Rue, form another vertical pair of hidden champions. Wirtgen and SAT combine expertise in on-site recycling machines and services. Such pairs are difficult to beat, as they share expertise, cooperate in R&D, and can create additional barriers to entry. These vertical pairs flourish only if both partners attain the utmost level of performance. None is forgiving in that respect, for they create a market relationship, not a strategic alliance. The fact that both partners have similar corporate cultures fosters the cooperation.

Demanding and strong local customers as an essential ingredient to becoming a world-class organization is not a new idea (see Porter 1990a). Indeed, dozens of hidden champions are suppliers to industries in which Germany has a strong international position.

Table 8.3 lists some of them in five industries selected because they are in various stages of their international life cycle (Wells 1972). The German auto industry was and still is strong and, although it has lost market share in places like the United States, Germany seems to be in no danger of losing its competitiveness in car manufacturing. Conditions are different for the chemical industry, in which environmental restrictions have caused large German corporations to increase investment abroad rather than in their domestic market. The United States has already become the largest market for Bayer AG, and the supply markets are gradually shifting from Germany to other countries. This movement, proceeding apace in the furniture industry, is furthest along in the textile industry, many of whose companies have already relocated to lower-wage regions.

Nevertheless, despite the current locational structure of all these industries, a number of strong hidden champions maintain their base in Germany, which points out two important lessons. First, they can retain customers even though those move; second, if customers internationalize, a supplier, to remain at the front of the pack, has to follow its customers wherever they go. Close location may be critical to attaining a leading position in the first place, but once a company gets there, it should be flexible enough to serve customers in the entire world.

The hidden champions in the furniture and textile industry seem to

Table 8.3 **Hidden Champion in Industries at Various Stages of the International Life Cycle**

Customer Industry	Hidden Champion Supplier	Major Product
Auto	Weingarten, Schuler	Heavy presses
	Gehring	Honing machines
	Kiekert	Door locks
	Webasto	Sunroofs, auxiliary heaters
	Dürr	Paint shops
	Glyco	Gliding rings
	Hella	Lighting equipment
Chemical	Uhde, Lurgi	Chemical engineering
	Barmag	Fiber machines
	Brückner	Machines for biaxial film stretching
	Göttfert	Rheological test equipment
	Automatik-Apparate	Underwater pelletizers
Furniture	Weinig	Automatic molders
	Hymmen, Held	Double-belt presses
	Homag	Machines for the furniture industry
	Glunz, Hornitex, Pfleiderer	Wooden materials like pressboard, fiberboard
	Hoppe	Door and window handles
	Siempelkamp	Hydraulic presses for chipboards
Textile	Erhardt & Leimer	Web-handling technology
	Karl Mayer	Rashel machines
	Grosse	Jacquard machines
	Helsa	Shoulder pads
	Union Knopf	Buttons
	Groz-Beckert	Needles
Electronics	Aixtron	Thin film equipment
	Convac	CD-coating equipment
	Grohmann	Electronics assembly systems
	Leybold	Vacuum technology
	Wacker	Silicon
	Meissner & Wurst	Cleanroom technology

have mastered this challenge well, but so have others in industries like paper, food processing, medicine, optics, and even electronics. At least to date, they have been able to defend their leading position as suppliers despite their customer industries having left the domestic market. Other industries have fared less well. With the decline of the shoe industry in Germany, the shoe machinery manufacturers largely collapsed, and Italy has taken over the lead. In the long-run, however, staying in touch with customers that have moved may require relocation of a supplier's main activities. Since many industries are wandering from country to country following changes in comparative costs, exchange rates, technologies, and demand, a supplier to those industries must ultimately become a true global competitor with the ability to deliver and operate anywhere. Many hidden champions have achieved this level of globalization.

The vertical view of the sample firms suggests that a good way to international leadership is to team with demanding world-class customers. Only a company willing to meet the requirements of such customers can become and remain a global leader. It may be possible to attain this goal from an original location, but if physical closeness is important, as in many instances it seems to be, relocation of core activities is necessary. Some hidden champions, for example, Karl Mayer and Dürr, are far advanced in this regard.

Beyond direct horizontal competition and the vertical supplier-customer relationship, further environmental factors affect the hidden champions. Many of them operate in an environment that fosters their development of an industry-specific mind-set. Though it is somewhat similar, it goes beyond Porter's (1990) idea of industrial clusters. Several industries include numerous hidden champions that neither compete directly against nor act as suppliers to one another. Nevertheless, they seem to profit from the existence of others that comprise the wider industry, as shown in Table 8.4.

The hidden champions in these groups seem to profit from the overall position of the industries. Sports equipment, for one, lends itself to a discussion of possible explanations and implications. First, there are resource-based causes. Top athletes can create strong demand for these products—Germina, an East German producer of high-performance cross-country skis, was once supplier to the East German team. If a sport originated in an area, it is no surprise that the suppliers are also located there. Nor is it astonishing that Fischer, world leader in skis, is from

Table 8.4   **Industries with Numerous Hidden Champions**

Industry or Market	Hidden Champion	Major Product
High-Performance Sports Equipment	Spieth	Gymnastic apparatus
	Sport-Berg	Discuses, hammers, shots
	Uhlmann	Fencing equipment
	Germina	Cross-country skis
	Carl Walther	Sports guns
	Anschütz	Sports guns
	BSW	Sports floors
	Wige Data	Timing devices for major sports events
Scales	Bizerba	Retail scales
	Söhnle	Household and personal scales
	Sartorius	Laboratory, scientific scales
	Seca	Medical scales
	Mettler-Toledo	Industrial scales
Pumps	KSB	Industrial, centrifugal pumps
	Prominent	Metering pumps
	ABS	Submersible pumps
	Putzmeister	Concrete pumps
	Schwing	Concrete pumps
Laser Technology	Rofin Sinar	Industrial lasers
	Trumpf	Sheet metal punching machines
	EOS	Rapid prototyping
Photo/Film	Cullmann	Camera tripods
	Sennheiser	Earphones
	Neumann	High-performance microphones, camera chairs
	Arnold & Richter	35-mm film cameras
	Sachtler	Professional camera tripods
Welding	Cloos	Welding technology
	LSG	Ion sources for welding and soldering
	Linde	Welding gases

Table 8.4   *continued*

Industry or Market	Hidden Champion	Major Product
Plants/Nurseries	Bruns	Nursery
	von Ehren	Large, living trees
	Dümmen	Poinsettia plants
Assembly	EJOT	Direct screw joints
Products	Würth	Assembly products
	Berner	Assembly products
	Böllhoff	Screws and nuts
	Fischerwerke	Dowels
Books	Kolbus	Bookbinding machines
	Bamberger Kaliko	Bookbinding textiles
	Heidelberger	Printing presses
	Roland	Printing presses

Austria or that Gallagher, the world's number one supplier of electric fences for cattle and sheep, comes from New Zealand. But resource base offers only a limited explanation, because other conditions seem to be equally important. An international customer that wants to buy sports equipment may find it more convenient to purchase it in one particular place rather than in many different ones.

Frequently complex infrastructures develop around such an industry. A customer interested in participating in a fair knows that the largest sports goods fair is ISPO, held in Germany. Or the organizer of Olympic Games, requiring, in addition to sports equipment, huge tent and catering facilities, would find the world leader just around the corner from Frankfurt where he probably intends to shop anyway. Röder Zeltsysteme, located in this area, is the major tent leaser in the world and regularly supplies large events like the Olympics. In addition to ISPO, many other internationally important fairs are held in Germany. Hannover Messe is the largest industrial goods fair in the world, CeBIT the largest fair featuring information technologies and all their accouterments. Both are held in Hanover, home of the largest fairground in Germany. Other German cities regularly hold internationally significant world fairs. Cologne itself is the site of twenty-five fairs that are the biggest of their kind in the world. Having these fairs in Germany provides local firms with the valuable asset of easy access to important players in their respective markets. On the other hand, strong local firms are to a considerable extent responsible for the existence and importance of such fairs.

Resource and demand relations differ from case to case. Sometimes accidents of history offer explanations, as, for instance, in Basel, Switzerland. The city is a fortress of the chemical industry because, centuries ago, it welcomed alchemists who were expelled from other regions. Whatever the specific resource or demand conditions are for the emergence of leadership in an industry, this kind of environment seems to assist in gaining dominant world positions. Silicon Valley and the biotech centers in the United States are recent examples. Every company should be aware of these phenomena when it decides on location.

Further effects of location, unrelated to industry proximity, can have an impact on hidden championship in totally separate industries. I remember, from my youth, a tiny village with seven farms. Almost every boy of my generation who grew up there established his own business in one of a variety of industries. These guys motivated one another to become entrepreneurs. So it is not particularly amazing to find local clusters of hidden champions, as can be seen from Table 8.5. Is it an accident that just across the highway from Wirtgen, world leader in recycling machines, one finds JK Ergoline, number one in professional sunbeds? Or is it chance that not only Würth, the largest assembly products company, and its largest competitor, but also Sigloch, one of the largest European bookbinding companies, originated in Künzelsau? Or that Stihl and Kärcher, two of the toughest hidden champions, are situated in the neighboring towns of Waiblingen and Winnenden, near Stuttgart, where they eye each other closely?

A huge proportion of the world's surgical instrument industry is concentrated in the region of Tuttlingen, southern Germany, where one finds about 600 firms that produce these tools. They partially compete against but also complement one another, since the market is highly fragmented. While Aesculap is the overall world market leader, Karl Storz is clearly the leader in endoscopic instruments.

Few of the hidden champions would admit that these relations and comparisons have affected their own behavior. But there are effects! If a person has the right motivational setting, a company that has made it in

Table 8.5 **Local Clusters of Hidden Champions**

Region/Town	Companies in Local Clusters	Major Products
Windhagen, Horhausen, Bad Honnef/Rhenania	Wirtgen	Street-recycling machines
	JK Ergoline	Professional sunbeds
	Birkenstock	"Birkenstocks," natural sandals
Palatinate	SAT	Street-recycling services
Künzelsau/ Baden-Württemberg	Würth, Berner	Assembly products
	Sigloch	Bookbinding and printing services
Solingen/North Rhine-Westphalia	Henckels Zwillingswerk	High-quality cutlery
	Pfeilring	Manicure sets
	Boeker	Ceramic knives
Waiblingen, Winnenden/Baden-Württemberg	Stihl	Chain saws
	Kärcher	High-pressure cleaners
Neutraubling/Bavaria	Krones	Bottling systems
	Zippel	Minibreweries
Holzminden/North Rhine-Westphalia	Dragoco	Fragrances
	Haarmann & Reimer	Fragrances
Nuremberg/Bavaria	Faber-Castell	Pencils
	Staedtler-Mars	Pencils/writing instruments
	Lyra Bleistift-Fabrik	Pencils/writing instruments
	Schwan Stabilo	Pencils/writing instruments
Tuttlingen/Baden-Württemberg	Aesculap	Surgical instruments
	Gebr. Martin Medizintechnik	Surgical instruments
	Medicon	Surgical instruments
	Karl Storz	Endoscopic instruments

the individual's neighborhood becomes a strong challenge and role model. Georg Schmitt of SAT, the street-recycling company, touches on this mental bridge when he says,

> The success of my friend Reinhard Wirtgen offered a real challenge to me. Relative to Reinhard, I made a mistake. While he started his own business after his apprenticeship at the age of eighteen, I first studied, then worked in a large company. I didn't start my own business until I was forty-five. Now, after thirteen years, both Reinhard and I are world market leaders, but his turnover is four times greater than mine.

Hidden champions are created and driven by entrepreneurs, and motivation is one of the essential ingredients of entrepreneurship. There can be no doubt that business environment has a strong impact—and that hidden champions breed other hidden champions.

HIDDEN CHAMPION TEAMS

Carrying the findings on the advantages of market leadership one step further, a few companies have begun to build their corporate portfolio around the idea of hidden championship. Large companies like General Electric, Siemens, or Hoechst, which have declared that they strive for number one or number two positions in the world market may be considered forerunners of this trend. Gillette and particularly its subsidiary Braun are far advanced in this strategy. Braun is the world leader in four of its six businesses. Heraeus, a maker of specialties in chemistry and metallurgy, holds many world leader positions. Its Electronite subsidiary, which makes sensors for the steel industry, is the market leader in each and every of the more than fifty countries it does business in.

Some companies in my sample are in double hidden champion positions: Webasto is world market leader both in sunroofs and in auxiliary heating systems; Steinbeis Holding has two units that hold world leader positions, Peter Temming in linters, a special kind of cotton fiber, and Zweckform Etikettiertechnik in battery labels. Hauni/Körber seems to be proceeding systematically in building an empire of hidden champions. Besides its unique position in the cigarette machine market, it owns E. C. H. Will, world leader in cut-size sheeters for paper products, and the U.S. company Wrapmatic, which is a world leader in special packaging machines. Hauni's portfolio contains other very strong companies: all the thermal paper for telefaxes in Germany is produced on Pagendarm machines, and many of the world's passports are manufactured on machines of Kugler Automation, and both are Hauni subsidiaries.

Firms in other countries also appear to be building organizations around the hidden champion concept. Hallmark is world number one in greeting cards, and its subsidiary Revell-Monogram is world leader in plastic model kits, mainly through its German subsidiary, Revell AG. The English company De La Rue is the world leader in bank-note printing with a 57% share of the market accessible to outside contractors. It is also the parent company of Garny, the world market leader for safes and bank fittings. In late 1994, De la Rue acquired Portals, which has about 50% of the world market for security paper. This trio of hidden champions seems quite powerful, since there are substantial synergies in their three businesses. In 1995, Lonrho, an English company, and Gencor, a South African firm, merged to attain world market leadership in platinum.

It is hard to conceive of smarter strategies than those built around combined hidden champions' positions. These companies' major challenge is to retain the original focus and strengths that brought them into world leadership in the first place. Teams of hidden champions that work together without losing the focus on their core businesses look like very strong constellations—and are highly interesting targets for investors.

SUMMARY

Leaders are lonesome, and this is not different for the hidden champions. Leadership requires that a company cannot delegate the core activities on which its dominant role is built. At the same time, every company works in a wider environment from which it can profit. The attitudes and experiences of the hidden champions contain many important lessons:

- High depth in manufacturing of core components often seems superior to outsourcing whenever possible.

- The outsourcing decision should depend not only on cost considerations but take into account the effects on quality, know-how, and core competencies.

- It may be advantageous to integrate vertically, for example, to build one's own machines, because things that cannot be bought in a market are highly effective in creating competitive advantage.

- Outsourcing whole subsystems can be dangerous, because it enables suppliers to sell directly to end customers. This does not apply to systems integrators, whose core competence is integrating such systems.

- High R&D depth appears to be an effective way of protecting core expertise.

- The hidden champions outsource a great many noncore activities, not only because they want to keep costs variable, but also because it leads to better quality.

- Hidden champions have a negative attitude toward strategic alliances, even in entering foreign markets. They teach one to beware of the illusion that strategic alliances are the solution to the problems a company cannot solve for itself. Japan is an exception.

- Competitors should be seen not only as adversaries but also as training partners for fitness, for in the long term a company may benefit from having strong competitors. This suggests that a company should actively search confrontation with the strongest competitors in the world, as it is the only way to world market leadership. This competition should be performance-oriented rather than price-aggressive.

- A company should also seek the most demanding customers, and, to retain leadership, follow them to wherever in the world they go.

- The overall environment and industry mind-set are important prerequisites for world class. A company should not take them as givens, but should actively seek and create—or if that's impossible, relocate to—that type of productive environment.

The hidden champions adhere to the motto of William Tell, the Swiss national hero in Friedrich von Schiller's drama: "The strong person is most powerful alone." They mistrust modern concepts that advise looking to others to solve problems that should not be delegated. Nevertheless, these firms are parts of networks and systems which drive them to ever better performance. They are alone, yet not alone at one and the same time. I think that this is good advice for any company. In some areas, presumably core activities, one should stand alone, but in noncore activities and in motivation from customers, competitors, and the environment in general, one should welcome cooperation.

9
The Team

Always more work than heads!

THE HIDDEN CHAMPIONS are partial to a strong, idiosyncratic corporate culture. Their employees identify with the companies' goals and values more intensely than employees in average firms do. Such high motivation is reflected by markedly lower rates of worker sick days and job turnover. Acting as a team, the employees pull in the same direction, wasting minimal energy on internal friction. The hidden champions in my research project are tough employers; demanding in their standards, they don't tolerate underperformers and weed out people who are not in sync with their practices. Regarding it as part of their selection process, the employers are quick to terminate new hires who do not accept their modus operandi.

The rural location of most of these companies creates mutual dependence between employer and employees. This tends to foster employees' lifelong commitment to the organization and employers' flexibility in offering continuing education opportunities and multifunctional deployment to workers. Employee creativity is an important source of ongoing improvement, and the hidden champions seem to be able to attract and retain well-qualified staff.

CORPORATE CULTURE

I hold that one gets a feeling about the corporate culture of a company ten minutes into a first visit to its site. Its appearance, the behavior of

the receptionist, the decor, symbolize its spirit. My first impressions of
the hidden champions were usually admiring, lasting, and sometimes,
following an interview, even awe. But I could rarely single out a particularly striking element, except for a sense, akin to gestalt, of energy and
efficiency.

I define corporate culture as a company's set of goals and values to
which, ideally, all employees are committed. These, not the surface characteristics of buildings, rituals, and furnishings, are the substance of the
culture. It need not be formally set down as written principles or guidelines but must be anchored in the heads (cognitively) and the hearts
(emotionally) of all employees and respected by leaders and followers
alike.

Some hidden champions do have written guidelines or creeds, a few of
which are a bit bolder and more marked than those of large corporations,
but they do not differ fundamentally. Because I don't attach much importance to such statements, I refrain from citing any here. The hidden
champions usually do not cast their corporate principles in stone, their
most distinct characteristic being that the values are accepted. As its size
increases, it probably becomes necessary for a company to publish guidelines, but those cannot replace personal communication. Annett Kurz,
manager of Clean Concept, expresses a typical attitude: "You can write
it, even write it well, but ultimately you have to communicate it personally
to motivate your people." The difference between strong and weak corporate cultures lies not in the formulation but in the degree of enthusiasm
with which all employees accept the values. In this, the hidden champions
provide noteworthy models.

My survey addressed various aspects of corporate culture and employee commitment. Figure 9.1 provides the hidden champions' evaluation of selected traits related to employees and corporate culture. The
complete list contained many additional traits, but for comparative purposes I chose to show long-term customer relations, which was selected
as a strength by the largest number of companies, and production costs,
selected by the fewest. The figure illustrates that all traits from company
loyalty to working climate received scores of about 75% or more, so that
a majority of the respondents believe that their companies are strong in
these traits. Such positive identification is the foundation for the superior
competitive competencies outlined in Chapter 7.

Corporate culture is not an end in itself but a means to increasing

Figure 9.1 **Evaluation of Traits Related to Employees and Corporate Culture**

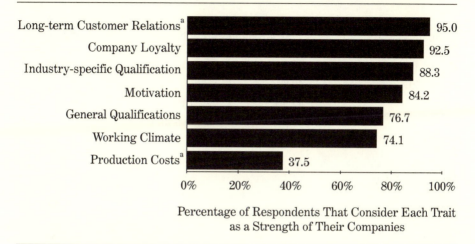

Long-term Customer Relations[a]	95.0
Company Loyalty	92.5
Industry-specific Qualification	88.3
Motivation	84.2
General Qualifications	76.7
Working Climate	74.1
Production Costs[a]	37.5

0%   20%   40%   60%   80%   100%

Percentage of Respondents That Consider Each Trait
as a Strength of Their Companies

[a]Long-term customer relations, with the maximum score, and production costs, with the minimum score, are included as a basis for comparison.

productivity. A strong culture is an effective deterrent to internal frictions. I frequently ask managers what percentage of their energy they waste fighting internal resistance. In large corporations, the answer usually lies between 50 and 80%, small to midsize firms usually cite a range of 20 to 30%, and the hidden champion companies tend to assign 10 to 20%. Interestingly, managers of large Japanese corporations provide similarly low estimates. While not exact measurements, these figures indicate that the substantial differences from firm to firm can translate directly into productivity, speed, and competitiveness.

I refer here to concrete and measurable economic effects such as the rate of absenteeism on account of sickness; high motivation can lower such rates. The sample hidden champions have a mean sick rate of 4.9%, 40.8% of them reporting a figure of less than 4% and only 16.3% more than 6%. These figures and those for large automobile companies in Germany for 1992 are given in Table 9.1. Since sick rates vary across industries, comparisons should be made cautiously. Among the large industrial sectors, the auto industry provides a good comparison to the hidden champions since many of them operate in the mechanical engineering sector.

The differences between the two categories of firms are striking. The

Table 9.1   **Hidden Champion and Auto Company Sick Rates**

Company	Sick Rate in Percentage		Employees (in thousands)
Hidden Champions	Mean	4.9	239
(n = 122)	40.8%	under 4	
	42.9%	4 to 6	
	16.3%	more than 6	
Audi		8.2	38
Mercedes-Benz		8.6	222
Ford		8.6	48
Opel		9.8	53
Volkswagen		8.2	123
BMW		6.3	60
Auto Industry	Mean (weighted)	8.3	544

8.3% average sick rate in the large auto companies is almost twice that of the hidden champions. If the auto companies with an accumulated workforce of 544,000 could attain the same rate as the sample companies, they could reduce their workforce by 18,946 employees. At gross total cost for each additional worker of $100,000, the high sick rate costs the auto companies $1.9 billion, a figure close to their joint profit of $2.07 billion in 1992, a year of record sales. Compared with the auto companies, the survey sample companies save $813 million through lower absenteeism owing to illness. Extending this calculation to all 500 hidden champions, the savings would amount to $3.3 billion. Such comparisons prove that a single factor like reduced sick days can have a tremendous economic effect.

A factor that can have a negative economic effect on corporate culture is employee turnover. The high rating for company loyalty shown in Figure 9.1 is confirmed by the rating of employee turnover. While the mean rate is 5.3%, owing to a few outliers, the median is a considerably lower 3%. Many managers emphasized the virtual absence of frequent employee movement from company to company. For example, Heinz Hankammer of Brita water filters says, "We have virtually no turnover," and is echoed by Hermann Kronseder of Krones, who declares, "We hardly know what turnover is."

There is, however, one important exception. Many new employees leave, or are terminated by, a hidden champion shortly after joining its work force, both sides having learned quickly that a worker does not fit into the firm's culture and cannot stand its pace. Later I discuss recruitment and reconsider this important trait, so it's not exactly right to say that the sample companies experience practically no turnover, but it is true that once employees have "bought into" the corporate culture, then turnover is very low.

Average company loyalty usually means that employees remain with the companies for twenty to thirty years, but loyalty itself is not a goal. What counts is that by selecting and retaining, often for a lifetime, highly qualified and experienced people, the hidden champions are rewarded with that invaluable asset. This is in sharp contrast to my experience in the United States. During my years there I found that in many U.S. companies, the constant rotation of people in jobs and frequent employee turnover are a highly disturbing, efficiency lowering factor. Customer relations suffer every time a contact person is replaced. Valuable expertise and competencies are lost when qualified employees leave. The hidden champions take these insights to heart and cherish the devotion of their able coworkers.

PERFORMANCE

The hidden champions' corporate cultures are oriented toward performance. In my survey, about two-thirds of the respondents attributed their success to the entire team and its coherence, with only one-third believing it came through individual achievement, findings that suggest the prevalence of a team culture. In *Built to Last*, Collins and Porras (1994) similarly hold that the key factor to sustained success of their visionary companies is a cultlike corporate culture. However, leading hidden champions seem to consider the leader a more important factor than the large corporations investigated by Collins and Porras do.

The hidden champions liken business to a team sport, such as soccer or football, in which weak players affect performance adversely and are therefore unacceptable. This attitude is not imposed by a top-down hierarchy but is part of the team's value system. Group or social control of performance works under such circumstances and is much more effective than formal control. Large corporations have complex prescribed systems, for example, time measurement and incentives, but beating them is considered a socially acceptable sport. As a result, many large companies suffer from overacceptance of underperformers. Philips Electronics stumbled into a serious crisis in the early 1990s. According to Jan Timmer, who then took over as CEO and rescued the huge company, Philips got into trouble because there was simply too much tolerance of weak performance. The sample companies' team culture is not likely to tolerate such a situation. Those who shirk their duties are booted out.

Of course, smaller companies have a structural advantage in that poor performance can quickly be detected. Annett Kurz of Clean Concept comments: "In our company of eighty people, we can't afford to have even two idle employees. Because we have no excess capacity, everybody has to roll up his or her sleeves. Slackers may escape detection in a large company, but in a small one like ours—never." During my visits with the hidden champions, I could observe the fast pace of the work. In such companies the employees apply themselves to their tasks during working hours because they feel an obligation to their jobs.

This aspect is extremely important. One CEO hit the nail on the head:

> We have always had more work than heads to do it, and that's how it should be. This is not only good for productivity but it actually keeps people happier. If people are not challenged to work hard, they resort to unproductive activities like writing memos, holding meetings, occupying themselves. Most of the intrigue and bureaucratic hassle that plagues large companies is avoidable when there's an abundant amount of work.

Of course, the relation between workload and capacity is a delicate matter and must not be carried to an extreme, but a certain surplus of work is an excellent means of keeping internal friction and the associated waste of energy to a minimum. Parkinson's Law applies only when a company has more people than work. When employees have to invent work to appear to be occupied, they produce little value-added.

In this context it is critical that people know what they are working for and can recognize their contribution to the end result. Only then are they willing to invest time and effort. With less division of labor, this prerequisite for motivation is more easily achieved in small companies than in large ones. In a growth situation, a surplus of work develops almost automatically, because the demand is always greater than the internal resources. That's why some hidden champions give their full attention to continual growth. One CEO said, "We must grow to stay productive; growth keeps us busy and alert. A company is like a tree; the day it stops growing, it begins to die. Growth is part of our culture."

But growth ultimately leads to large size, which presents a danger. Many hidden champions are confronted with the challenge of retaining their small-company culture because they are becoming too large. This is one aspect of what Clifford (1973) called "growth pains of the threshold company." Putzmeister, world market leader for concrete pumps, is a case in point. Karl Schlecht, the owner-CEO, fears that as size increases, a corporate bureaucracy emerges, more people attend meetings, and making decisions takes more time. As of 1995, he started to separate various units—concrete pumps, aircraft washers, industrial pumps—into companies that operate as independent hidden champions. Hauni-Körber, the cigarette machine world leader, did the same as of 1995, splitting into three independent operating companies: Hauni, the cigarette machine specialist; PapTis, holder of several world leader positions in paper- and tissue-processing equipment; and Schleifring, machine tool manufacturer.

The challenge of retaining its performance-oriented culture in a growing company is a difficult one. Few of today's large companies that were once the size of smaller typical hidden champions have managed to conserve the strengths of their corporate youth, and many have succumbed to the large-company syndrome. There is evidence that Putzmeister's route may be effective. Hewlett-Packard has had success in applying a similar system: units of usually fewer than a thousand people manage for the most part to operate like small companies. W. L. Gore, Inc., maker of Gore-Tex, a semipermeable material used in such applications as outdoor wear, medicine, and insulation, is another company that pursues this approach. Gore's units are made up of no more than 150 employees so that within a unit everybody knows everybody else, individual performance is obvious to all, and direct personal communication is effective.

It is fascinating to think about breaking up large corporations into small hidden champion-type units. I am referring not merely to divisions that are still handcuffed by corporate bureaucracies but to truly independent companies. One of the few that has taken this path is the British chemical corporation ICI, which in 1993 split into Zeneca, which comprises the life sciences business, and ICI, the industrial businesses. It seems to be as successful as the U.S. "baby Bells," which were born courtesy of the 1984 divestiture of AT&T. In 1995 AT&T announced a further breakup into three independent companies. More large companies should consider this alternative, even though it runs counter to the usual imperial concept of sheer size as a goal and an indicator of one's place in the economic pecking order.

A further aspect of the performance culture is the availability and flexibility of employees with regard to working time. While large companies are relatively inflexible, the hidden champions display pronounced strength in this respect. Almost all interviewees said that they can mobilize their forces to work longer hours, even on short notice. Dr. Wolfgang Pinegger, president of Brückner, the world leading manufacturer of biaxial film-stretching systems, explains the situation at his company:

> Our people can't expect to have regular eight-hour workdays. We have to be more flexible and faster. For instance, we often have to travel over the weekend, and people who stay with us aren't rigid about Monday through Friday as the workweek. We are very demanding, but we also offer more than just monetary compensation.

Though Brückner has fewer than 300 employees, it operates its own kindergarten and has vacation houses for its employees in the Caribbean, among other benefits. Reinhard Wirtgen concurs: "We have beaten our competitors over weekends." A CEO who spends about half the year in incessant worldwide travel said about his company, "We fly by night and work by day." The hidden champions' toughness extends to availability of personnel and flexibility of working hours, so such requirements are a major consideration in the selection and tenure of employees.

Flexibility is also necessary in the organizational and functional deployment of employees. In 1992, Reinhold Würth realized that he had to increase his sales force dramatically, but because of the recession he couldn't expand his total workforce. The only alternative was a major reshuffling of personnel from internal services to the sales department. Figure 9.2 illustrates what Würth achieved in one year. The total workforce increased only slightly, from 12,730 to 12,860 (+1%), but the sales force was expanded by 509 people (+8%) and internal service personnel were reduced by almost 400 (−6%). The change was achieved largely

Figure 9.2 Evidence of Hidden Champion Flexibility, Würth, 1992–1993

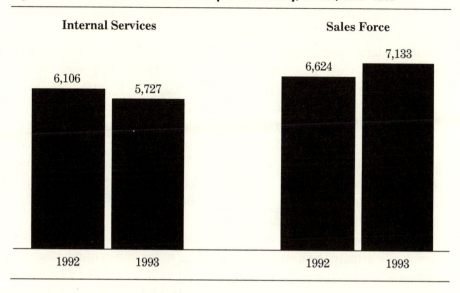

through reshuffling. Anyone who knows how difficult it is to effect such a shift in the German environment, where employee councils are strong, can appreciate the extraordinary flexibility of this organization. Most similarly sized companies would have needed a much longer time to effect such a major reallocation.

To recapitulate, hidden champions are partial to demanding and performance-oriented corporate cultures. While they may be instituted from the top down, they are accepted and practiced by virtual teams of employees that exert social control more effectively than any rigid rules could do. The firms usually have more work than personnel to complete it. Although the situation causes the firms to put a demand on employees' time and flexibility, it minimizes internal friction and conflict. While the hidden champions are not easy to work for, the commitment of their workers makes them strong.

RURAL LOCATION

What are the roots of hidden champion employees' solid commitment? Besides obvious factors like clear focus, closeness to end results, and team mentality, location plays an important role. Few hidden champions are headquartered in large cities like Berlin, Frankfurt, Munich, and Düsseldorf. Only Hamburg is home to a sizable number of these firms: Jungheinrich, logistics equipment; Fielmann, eyeglasses; Rothfos-Neumann, green coffee; Eppendorf-Netheler-Hinz, medical products; von Ehren, large living trees; Paul Binhold, anatomical teaching aids; and others. The vast majority of the companies are located in small towns and villages with names like Harsewinkel (Claas), Aichtal (Putzmeister), Kandel (David + Baader, a world leader in sterilization for baby bottles and the like), Holzminden (Dragoco, Haarmann & Reimer, two leaders in fragrances), Mulfingen (ebm, world leader in fans for domestic appliances), Plettenberg (Plettac, world leader in scaffolds), and so on. There are not many people who have ever heard of these places. Interestingly, Japanese companies also prefer such locations over large cities when they establish manufacturing plants.

Rural location has several important effects. First, because the hidden champion is usually the only major employer in town, its employees have no alternative. On the other hand, the town provides a limited reservoir of qualified workers, so the company must depend on the goodwill of its employees. For better or worse, these conditions create a mutual dependence: the employer needs the employees, and the workers need the company jobs.

The fact that often the owner-manager of a company was born and raised in the same small town as his employees leads to intimate relationships that cannot be duplicated in large city corporations. In many of these small towns, several generations of a family work or have worked for the company. Managers help foster such closeness. When walking through factories with CEOs, I have been astonished to find that they know most of their employees by name, sometimes addressing them by their first names and in the second person, which is rather unusual in Germany. It is also customary for the company owners to sponsor local sports clubs, particularly for soccer, which adds to the company's popularity in the town. A world-class company is frequently the pride of a little town. All these factors contribute to unusually strong employee commitment.

Another effect of rural location is the absence of distraction. Klaus Grohmann, who focuses on the thirty top electronics firms in the world as his target customers, explains that advantage:

I am from Düsseldorf, a big city, and my first company was there. At the time we had a successful worldwide engineering business with customers in the steel industry. But what we are doing for the electronics industry today couldn't be done in Düsseldorf because there would be too many distractions for our superior performers. We require deep concentration that can be evoked only in quiet surroundings. I decided to go to the little town of Prüm in the Eifel, close to the Belgian border because I wanted to create a permanent bond between employees and company, and it worked. Our job turnover rate is less than one percent, our employees' average age is thirty, and we don't waste time in traffic jams. We live close to the fields and the forest, and when we go home we can relax. Our employees can afford their own homes, for land is cheap. We have some trouble attracting people from large cities, but it's not too serious a problem.

Again, this is the typical attitude of many, if not most, of the hidden champions. It echoes Livio De Simone, CEO of the 3M company in Minneapolis-St. Paul, who said, "We're sitting back here in the Midwest— you know, farmer types" (Loeb 1995, 83). Hidden champions around the world subscribe to this belief. Melroe, maker of the world-renowned Bobcat skid-steer loader, is in Gwinner, North Dakota, of all places. Gambro, the Swedish world market leader in renal care products, with revenues close to $500 million has its headquarters in the small Swedish city of Lund. Beneteau, one of the oldest builders of fishing vessels in France, is now the leading yacht builder in the world. The company employs some 1,100 people far from large cities in six production sites in the region around Saint-Hilaire-de-Riez, France. Freixenet and Co-dorniu, the world's two largest producers of sparkling wine, operate out of the Spanish village Sant Sadurni d'Anoìa. Two Swiss world market leaders, both of which capture about 60% of their respective markets, are located near each other: Flytec, world market leader in hang glider flight instruments, and Uwatec, world market leader in scuba diving instruments, are sited in the midst of mountain peaks and lakes close to the village of Hallwil, Switzerland.

One had better take those farmer types seriously. While smart urban employees may fall for the enticements of the big city, the hidden champion guys are probably dreaming up nasty competitive tricks in their backwoods locations—even on weekends.

QUALIFICATION AND LEARNING

The key factors in international competition vary across markets. In mass markets, where low costs are decisive, ability to manufacture at the

lowest possible cost, with access to cheap labor, becomes a core competence. In the hidden champions' markets, quality and service are the most
important competitive parameters, so the workforce's expertise and ability to learn are core competencies. In sophisticated markets, education
is increasingly becoming a determinant of international competitive advantage. For a country to achieve and maintain competitive, superior
education, opportunities must be directed not only to the elite but also
to the masses of workers.

Figure 9.1 illustrates that the hidden champions rate their workers'
industry-specific qualifications highly. On average, 8.5% of their employees have a university degree. In many companies the percentage of
employees with higher education is much greater. Of the 250-member
workforce of Aqua Signal, world leader in ship-lighting systems, 50 are
engineers. At Hauni/Körber, the more than 1,500 engineers on its payroll
represent almost one in four employees. Twenty-two percent of Trumpf's
employees have an academic degree.

In an international comparison, however, the education of the workers
is an even more outstanding factor. Practically the entire nonacademic
workforce of the sample companies have completed vocational training
programs. That system is one of the pillars of Germany's international
competitiveness. The programs consist of three and a half years of combined practical work and theoretical education. The entire practice experience, during which the apprentice receives a modest salary, is provided
by the employer. The theoretical portion is provided by state schools.
Both facets of learning are coordinated by special councils, forming a
private-public partnership that is unique in the world. At the conclusion
of the programs, the Chambers of Industry and Commerce administer
an examination. Dr. Gerhard Neumann, head of General Electric's Aircraft Engine Group (world leader in jet engines) for seventeen years,
holds that his apprenticeship years in Germany were the most important
formative period of his professional life, even more important than his
academic engineering studies. Those who attain the best scores go on to
the next educational phase, which leads to the title *Meister* (master, not
to be confused with the academic master's degree), requiring additional
practical work and theoretical schooling.

Apprentices in vocational training programs make up 4.5% of the
hidden champions' workforce. Relating this percentage to their median
735 employees, a typical hidden champion has about 33 apprentices.

Added to the aforementioned low incidence of turnover, this figure assures a permanent source of talented personnel.

In the late 1980s the vocational training system was justifiably criticized for being too inflexible, unable to cope with rapid technological change. As a consequence, the programs underwent reform in the early nineties and have attained state-of-the-art standards. The 1980s training centers differed hardly at all from those of the 1960s, but the ones I've seen lately resemble electronics laboratories. The state schools encounter problems, largely financial, keeping abreast of new equipment, but even that situation has improved. The hidden champions' apprentices have generally acquired a good fundamental education by the time they enter the program. At Hymmen, world leader in double-belt presses, virtually every apprentice has completed the required thirteen years of primary and secondary education leading to a high school diploma. The same is true for numerous other sample companies.

Many hidden champions, as well as large corporations like Siemens, have "exported" elements of the vocational training systems to their foreign subsidiaries. Stihl, the chain saw world leader, uses the German concepts for training purposes in the United States and in Brazil. Others institute extensive exchange programs with their subsidiaries to guarantee that their young employees all over the world are exposed to the same fund of knowledge. While it may be difficult to emulate this training system countrywide, every company can learn from the Germans that educating its skilled workers is a rewarding investment. However, unless the company imbues its workers with sincere loyalty to their employers, the investment does not pay off.

The hidden champions are also active in sponsorship of continuing education. The study of Rommel et al. (1995) has shown that successful companies spend almost four times as much on education per employee— $551 versus $150—as their less successful mechanical engineering competitors. But these numbers reveal only part of the small-company picture because on-the-job training plays a greater role than formal programs. High rates of innovation induce a quasi-automatic continual learning process; unlike large organizations, the smaller companies rarely budget for education systematically, making it difficult to make intercompany comparisons.

An important ingredient of the learning process, which escapes translation into a statistic, is interfunctional exchange. As noted in Chapters

5 and 6, the flexibility to deploy staff across jobs is prevalent among the hidden champions. Winterhalter Gastronom requires that every employee learn to handle at least one other job, preferably two. Production personnel customarily jump into a service department job and vice versa. Rommel et al. (1995) report that such transfers occur about four to five times more frequently in successful than in less successful companies.

My interviews addressed the issue of organizational learning. The respondents almost never complained that their teams were unwilling or slow to learn, in contrast to large companies that often refer to such attitudes. It may well be that the hidden champions' employees feel less secure and perceive a stronger need to learn than their colleagues in other companies. They understand that the law of survival through learning requires them to adapt speedily to change in their work environment and act accordingly.

My respondents consider an educated workforce as still another foundation of their competitive superiority. A combination of many such factors is indispensable for success in international competition.

WORKER CREATIVITY

Every company should constantly be on the lookout for new ideas on increasing productivity, cutting costs, improving products, and reducing process time. Everyone professes allegiance to these ideas, but few companies make full use of the most obvious and closest source of betterment, the creativity of their workers. The Japanese, through *kaizen*, their system of continuing improvement, are much better than Western companies at exploiting this source.

Table 9.2 presents dramatic evidence of the differences between Germany and the United States on one hand and Japan on the other. These calculations are based on statistics collected by the German Business Institute (Deutsches Institut für Betriebswirtschaft). The numbers are probably not fully comparable across countries, but the differences are so staggering that slight errors in measurement seem to be irrelevant.

The German companies with 16 suggestions and U.S. companies with 21 suggestions per 100 employees are similar, but Japanese companies achieve a whopping 2,500, surpassing Germany by a factor of 156 and the United States by 119. In Germany and the United States, only 39% and 35%, respectively, of the suggestions are implemented, whereas in Japan the implementation rate is 86%. What ultimately counts are the net

Table 9.2 **Employee Suggestions in Germany, 1993, and in Japan and the United States, 1992**

	Germany	Japan	United States
Suggestions per 100 Employees	16	2,500	21
Average Bonus per Suggestion in U.S. $	621	4.1	461
Implementation Quota	39%	86%	35%
Implemented Suggestions per 100 Employees	6.2	2,150	7.4
Net Savings per Implemented Suggestion in U.S. $	2,609	139	
Net Savings per Employee in U.S. $	161	3,921	

Sources: Deutsches Institut für Betriebswirtschaft, various dates; Informationsdienst des Instituts der Deutschen Wirtschaft, various dates; Simon, Kucher & Partners, Strategy & Marketing Consultants, 1995.

savings per employee. U.S. figures for that category are unavailable, but they are probably similar to those for Germany. The Germans achieve net savings of $161 per employee and the Japanese $3,921, the factor of the difference being an unbelievable 24!

The German data are from a survey of 245 companies in various industries, 17 of which are hidden champions. The latter fare substantially better than the average German company. They achieve 47 versus the average 16 suggestions per 100 employees and savings of $229 per employee versus $161 for all German companies. Thus, the hidden champions, although considerably better than the average German company, are still way behind the Japanese. But the hidden champions, at least those in the institute's sample, are definitely not good enough at mobilizing their workers' creativity. Two companies in Germany have proved that enormous increases are possible: in 1993 the General Motors unit in East Germany, Opel Eisenach GmbH, had 924 suggestions per 100 employees and savings of $1,000 per employee; in 1994, Porsche AG, the sports car maker, achieved 600 suggestions per 100 employees and realized savings of $1.53 million. For 1995 it is reporting an increase to 1,500 proposals per 100 employees and savings of $5.2 million.

I believe that the hidden champions in general would reveal better statistics than those of the 17 companies in the study. Most hidden champions, particularly the smaller ones, do not have a formal suggestion system—in one of my earlier surveys only 12.8% of the respondents had such a procedure. Hidden champions shun the bureaucracy inherent in such systems. Rather, like the Japanese *kaizen*, they demand and expect that all employees actively engage in seeking possible improvements, which, I am convinced is superior to a formal process. Trumpf, world leader in sheet metal punching machines, asks that "each employee feels the need and has the ability to influence processes in the company and to act creatively." My company, Simon, Kucher & Partner, has three principles: correct, quick, and creative. "Creative" means that everyone is supposed always to think of ways in which we can improve our services.

A second reason for the hidden champions' not faring particularly well in suggestion numbers is that they are already marvelously efficient and productive. A young executive who is now with an auto company shared the following observation: "In my current company, workers make lots of suggestions, and there is really much to improve. Before I came here I worked with a hidden champion, where many fewer suggestions could be implemented, simply because the company was so damn good that there was much less room for improvement than here." The same may be true for improvements in productivity. The hidden champions' numbers on suggestions for the most part may not be very impressive because they have already achieved a high degree of productivity. One should not be deceived by change alone; ask at what point the change started. I have often found that reports on impressive productivity gains (such as those in the reengineering literature) related mostly to processes that had formerly been extremely inefficient.

Concerning the creative thinking of workers, I take the liberty of quoting a statement made by Konosuke Matsushita, the founder of Matsushita Electric Industrial Corporation, which Professor Philip Kotler included in a personal communication.

> We are going to win and the industrial West is going to lose out; there's not much you can do about it because the reasons for your failure are within yourselves. Your firms are built on the Taylor model, and even worse, so are your heads. With your bosses doing the thinking while the workers wield screwdrivers, you're convinced deep down that this is the right way to run a business. For you the essence of management is getting the ideas out of the bosses and into the hands of labor.

We have gone beyond the Taylor model. We realize that business has become so complex, the survival of firms so precarious, and our environment increasingly unpredictable, competitive, and dangerous that firms' continued existence depends on their day-to-day mobilization of every ounce of intelligence.

I don't know whom Mr. Matsushita had in mind, but his statement certainly does not apply to the hidden champions, except for the last sentence. There they would fully agree with him. They may not be tops in formal procedures, and probably could improve in that direction, but as far as I can tell from my experience, they are really good at tapping workers' creativity in many areas, large and small.

Once again, I emphasize that each and every company must strive to tap the full mental potential of its workers. Most companies have huge repositories of undiscovered gold mines of ideas. While no one has unearthed the magic password to these mines, the hidden champions reveal that worker commitment to and integration of group thinking into the job itself may be preferable to suggestion systems.

ATTRACTING AND KEEPING THE BEST

If employee quality is a keystone of superior competencies, attracting and keeping the best talent available is, obviously, vitally important. Since the early 1980s, my company has regularly made empirical studies on the attractiveness of companies to graduates of university and vocational training programs. From these studies we know that midsize companies are increasingly becoming more appealing to young graduates than large corporations.

Figure 9.3, employing the competitive advantages matrix of Chapter 7, presents the findings from a study of mechanical engineering graduates. The rank order of importance of items is depicted on the vertical axis and the performance of a medium-size company relative to a large corporation is shown on the horizontal axis. Volkswagen, a typical large organization, is used for comparison. On the right-hand side, the medium-size company is more attractive, and on the left, Volkswagen scores better. A superior relative performance related to an item of higher importance is more valuable.

The medium-size company has advantages in the two most important items, working climate and realization of one's ideas, and is regarded as

Figure 9.3 **Attraction of Medium-size Company and Volkswagen for Mechanical Engineering Graduates**

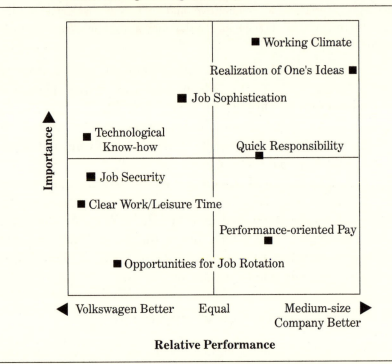

Source: Hermann Simon, Kai Wiltinger, Karl-Heinz Sebastian, and Georg Tacke, *Effektives Personalmarketing* (Effective personnel marketing) (Wiesbaden: Gabler, 1995).

superior in quickly offering responsibility. Volkswagen, representing a typical large corporation, has advantages in job sophistication and technological know-how. The items with below-average importance are less crucial to the graduates' decisions.

Overall, the medium-size firm is a more desirable employer than the large firm. Medium-size firms probably attract the more entrepreneurial types who appreciate the opportunity to have their ideas put into practice and to assume responsibility quickly. While large firms are preferred by some technical freaks, the smaller companies lure doers who fit into their corporate culture.

These findings are consistent with my observations of individual hidden champions, which generally have no serious difficulties in hiring excellent people. In their regions they are usually considered to be desirable employers. The management of Würth, for instance, reports that with five times more highly qualified applicants than the company can hire, it can be really selective. Heidenhain, world market leader in measuring lengths and angles, has 3,000 employees. The company once advertised two jobs for graduate physicists, for which it received more than 1,000 applications. Manfred Bobeck of Winterhalter Gastronom said in late 1994: "Today it is easy for us to attract good people. The reputation and the attraction of Winterhalter have improved so much that academic graduates line up for jobs. These young people know that they receive excellent training, can assume responsibility very quickly, and have a future rich in opportunities." Some hidden champions experience problems in hiring top-level graduates from faraway universities. Their rural location and the fact that they are not well known outside their region can be a liability because such candidates may be reluctant to relocate to a small town. But once these people succumb to the environment and feel at home, they are likely to stay with the company a long time.

Attracting the right people is only the first step; retaining the right ones and terminating those who don't fit into the company culture are equally important aspects of building an excellent workforce. While, as previously mentioned, the hidden champions' employee turnover rate is very low, it can be fairly high in the early stages of an employee's joining a company. The strength of the commitment and the corporate culture militate against new employees who don't buy into it. Heinz Hankammer of Brita water filters describes the situation in his company: "New employees who don't fit into our culture disqualify themselves. I don't have to tell anyone, 'You don't fit into this company.' It just develops without my intervention."

There are alternative means of building an outstanding workforce. One is to test candidates very carefully before they are hired. The Japanese companies seem to pursue this route when hiring people to work in foreign countries. The hidden champions seldom employ this method, for they would rather hire promising people and test them on the job. Those who don't perform satisfactorily are separated in a short time. In Germany a labor contract usually specifies a six-month trial period, but large companies, in contrast to the hidden champions, rarely dismiss a new employee during that time. More complex jobs may require a longer test period. One CEO told me that the real quality of a new employee can be judged only after a year or two. "Even after two years," he said, "we are very rigorous in terminating an employee if we recognize that he or she doesn't meet our expectations. One has to be patient and give them time, but ruthless if they don't fit." The advantage of this method compared with extensive pretesting lies in its greater validity because the only way to measure a person's true performance is on the job. It's more intuitive and less scientific than testing, but overall it may be more effective.

The hidden champions are quite successful in attracting and retaining excellent employees. They are appreciated as entrepreneurial employers that provide leeway for responsibility and the quick realization of new ideas. These traits make them attractive to go-getters who tend to fit into their corporate culture. Those who don't are quickly let go. This "unconscious" selection process is most effective.

MITTELSTAND

Underlying the cultural traits of the hidden champions described in this chapter is the broader philosophy of the *Mittelstand*, the middle class. Mittelstand, which encompasses all small and medium-size companies, describes a complex network of distinct values shared by thousands of German firms. At its core are values like desire for independence, fascination with quality, and good labor relations. Thus, strikes are almost nonexistent in the sample companies. RUD, the world leader in industrial chains, calls its plant an island of peace. There has never been a strike in its 120-year history. In 1910, the company voluntarily established a form of workers council. In general, Germany is always at the low end of strike statistics, and the hidden champions are among the lowest in this respect. About 50% of them offer profit-sharing programs and many provide clubs and organize activities for employees and their families. But I don't consider these traits unique because many other companies, small and large, offer similar amenities.

All in all the Mittelstand philosophy is traditional and conservative at its core. It believes in giving value and quality to customers and in demanding fair prices. "Keep it simple" is a recurring theme. Mittelstand thinking is sober and not prone to new buzzwords. The subtitle of Tom Peters's *The Tom Peters Seminar* (1994), *Crazy Times Call for Crazy Organizations*, provokes only a sneer from hidden champion CEOs. There is nothing spectacular about their organizations and cultures. With no single key factor to success, they just do a thousand little things a little better than their competitors.

Mittelstand values are not unique to Germany. I found the same attitudes in first-class companies throughout the world. Obviously, there are principles and values on conducting business that exceed space and time, and every company would be well advised to heed them.

SUMMARY

The role of the corporate culture in the long-term success of firms has generally been underestimated. Strong corporate cultures are an important characteristic of the hidden champions' identity. Their team-type cultures contribute strongly to the continued competitiveness of these firms. The main lessons one can take from them are:

- A corporate culture as a set of accepted values and goals is a means to efficiency in aligning resources and minimizing internal friction.
- A shared culture is the foundation for employee identification and motivation.
- Motivation in turn yields hard economic advantages by reducing sickness and job turnover rates.
- A corporate culture should be oriented toward performance and intolerant of underperformers; social control is much more effective than formal control.
- It seems advisable to have more work than heads to do it; this imbalance also prevents internal friction.
- A company or its units should remain small enough to make performance transparent; once a company grows too large, it might consider splitting up into smaller units (if possible).
- A location that offers little distraction may contribute to improving performance.
- To succeed in dynamic markets, companies should strive for flexibility of the workforce regarding work hours and deployment of personnel.
- A company should pay close attention to employee qualification

not only at the professional, but also at the worker level. Vocational training programs are recommended.

- Worker creativity is an untapped source of productivity whose full potential can better be realized through motivation of the entire workforce than through formal suggestion systems.

- A superior workforce is created only by attracting, selecting, and retaining top-quality people. The hidden champions suggest that hiring people, testing them on the job, and rigorously weeding out those who don't fit is an effective means to that end.

Its corporate culture is the soul of a company, and the hidden champions have a strong soul. Their values are built on simple principles strictly implemented throughout the company and accepted by all employees. A value-sharing workforce forms a team that's hard to beat.

10

The Leaders

In you must burn what you want to ignite in others.
—*St. Augustine of Hippo*

IF I HAD TO CHOOSE ONE common, outstanding characteristic strength of the hidden champions, it would be the leaders, or more specifically, the incessant drive and energy of those leaders. They are as different as people in general, but all are imbued with the power and enthusiasm that move their companies forward. Most are highly focused on their business. Continuity of leadership is another outstanding trait. The average hidden champion leader remains at the helm for more than twenty years. Leadership styles are authoritarian where the fundamental goals and core values are concerned and participative and empowerment oriented where the process and details of implementation are concerned. Leadership is a prime ingredient whether a company is owned by a family or by a substantial concern. Large organizations that acquire a hidden champion are wise to let it continue on its proven path if they want to keep it successful.

STRUCTURES AND IMPACT

In small and medium-size companies, ownership and management structures are closely associated. Of the hidden champions, 76.5% are owned by families or a few individuals, and only 2.4% are widely held public

Figure 10.1 **Hidden Champions' Ownership and Management Structures**

Other Companies/ Concerns	Public Ownership/ Many Owners	Family Ownership/ Few Owners
21.1%	2.4%	76.5%

Foreign Parent	German Parent		Owners in Management	No Owners in Management
12.5%	8.7%	2.4%	62.3%	14.1%

corporations. The remaining 21.1% are owned by concerns. Figure 10.1 summarizes the ownership structure and management composition of the family-owned companies. In the others, the managers are, by definition, hired hands.

In four out of five family-owned or closely held companies, at least one owner is in management. Altogether, owner-managers are active in almost two-thirds of the hidden champions, 62.3% to be exact. Combining ownership and management functions naturally places such leaders in a strong position. In almost one-fifth of the companies, 17.6%, this position is further enhanced by there being a single person at the highest level of management.

The educational background of the leaders is divided almost equally, with 49.1% having received a business education, 38.6% a technical or science education, and 5.3% having formally studied in both fields. However, many of the managers are well versed in both disciplines because they have constantly been confronted with problems in all functions and regimens. There is much less division of management tasks in small than in large companies.

It is interesting to note that many hidden champion founders have not had academic training. Hermann Kronseder (Krones, producer of labeling machines), Heinz Hankammer (Brita water filters), Reinhard Wirtgen (street recycling machines), and Reinhold Würth (assembly products), like dozens of others, belong to this category. They have usually gone through an apprenticeship program, during which, with their natural talent, they acquired sufficient and usually excellent technical knowledge. Hermann Kronseder, a *Meister,* holds 151 patents.

Whether they received a formal education is closely related to the age of the company founders. Most who started a new organization or drove an existing small company to world market leadership began at an early age. Würth was nineteen when his father died suddenly, Wirtgen started at eighteen, as did Lothar Bopp of LoBo Electronik, a leader in laser shows. Those who didn't found their own business until they were older consider it a mistake. Thus, Georg Schmitt of SAT, world leader in on-site recycling of road surfaces, said, "It was wrong of me not to start my own business until I was forty-five. SAT could have been much larger today if I had begun earlier, as my friend Reinhard Wirtgen did."

The founder's age is a recurring theme in the investigation of the origin of companies. Landrum (1993), who studies the leaders of innovative companies like Microsoft, Apple, and Federal Express, finds that most started when they were very young, and quite a few, like Steve Jobs of Apple and Bill Gates of Microsoft, dropped out of a college or university. The same is true for the founders of the "visionary companies" studied by Collins and Porras (1994). For instance, William Hewlett and David Packard were both twenty-six when they founded Hewlett-Packard; J. Willard and Allie Marriott were twenty-six and twenty-two, respectively, and Howard Johnson was twenty-seven when they started their companies. Though there are exceptions, entrepreneurial energy seems to be strongest in people between the ages of twenty and thirty. This suggests an interesting analogy to the discoveries of young scientists in their twenties, Einstein for one.

These age and behavior patterns point to a potentially serious conflict between the increasingly long educational process and ambitious entrepreneurial dynamism. In Germany, students rarely complete their academic studies before reaching their late twenties. Students who engage in doctoral research, which is quite common in certain fields, are unlikely to leave their university until they are in their early thirties. By then their entrepreneurial energy may well have burned out. Their optimistic "can-doism" has vanished. Those who wish to pursue the entrepreneurial route should seriously consider shortening their academic career or abandoning it altogether. Entrepreneurs are the fuel that drives

economic growth, and at the moment I am aware of a dearth of entrepreneurs with hidden champion potential rather than a scarcity of well-
educated academicians.

The hidden champions prefer to promote their leaders from within, a
statement with which 64.2% of the respondents in my survey agreed or
strongly agreed. Accordingly, the in-house sourcing attitude observed in
the core activities extends to management promotion and development.
On the other hand, only a minority believed that the integration of outside
managers is problematic, with which I tend to disagree. My observations
confirm that the idiosyncratic corporate cultures make entry into a typical hidden champion difficult for an outsider, unless the person comes
from a company with a similar culture. The stronger a corporate culture,
the more difficult it becomes for someone well advanced in a career to
adjust to a new one. Many of my interviewees confirmed that the best
future leaders grow up in their own company culture.

The personality of the leader at the helm of a company was seen as a
strength by 73.9% of the respondents, and continuity in leadership received an even higher approval rate, 79.8%. These direct assessments are
confirmed by a multiple regression analysis, in which we tried to explain
the overall success of the companies, as defined in Chapter 1, by independent variables related to internal resources. (Although external variables
were also included, they are of no interest here.) Figure 10.2 shows the
impact of the four internal variables that turned out to have a significant
influence on success. Leadership has the strongest impact, but professionalism of management is almost as important. These remarkable findings are fully consistent with my subjective observations: the leaders of
the most successful hidden champions are both strong in leadership and
in professionalism. Leadership and management professionalism must
not be either-or but both-and constructs. These unusual people combine energetic, motivational, visionary traits and technical, methodical,
instrumental capabilities. Reinhold Würth distinguishes these two aspects when he speaks of "leadership culture" and "leadership technique."
A good leader has to master both. According to Würth, the culture trait
is rarer than the technique trait and the combination of both is very rare.

LEADERSHIP TEAMS

In most companies with one leader, the founder holds this position. In
the second generation, hidden champions are typically led by teams.

Figure 10.2 **Internal Variables with Significant Impact on Overall Success**

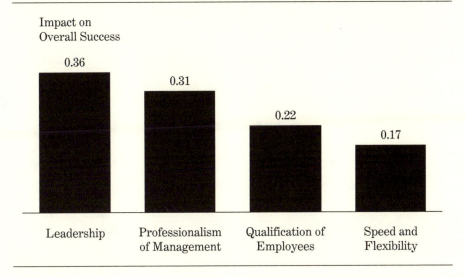

Overall, a vast majority of the sample companies, 82.4%, are led by a team of up to five members. It is interesting to look at the structures of these teams, which include all variants of family and nonfamily combinations. Table 10.1 lists several patterns.

In the first generation, we found, in addition to a single founder-leader, cofounder-leaders. In some companies they are siblings, like Rainer and Jürgen Wieshoff who began Interface, a leading company in locks for computer disk drives. In others they are unrelated, as in SAP, the world leader in standard business software, which was founded by Dietmar Hopp, Hasso Plattner, Hans-Werner Hector, and Klaus Tschira, all former colleagues at IBM. Fast Electronic, one of the world's leading companies in computer compression cards, was founded by Matthias Zahn, who started the company with university friends and roommates, all of whom still have top positions in the firm.

Founder-leader pairs or teams comprise an interesting phenomenon whose potential is not well researched and understood. They combine to supply technical and business expertise, which are seldom found in the same degree in any one person. Many large companies owe their origin and growth to such teams. They include, besides William Hewlett and David Packard, Paul Dubrule and Gerard Pelisson, who created the French company Accor, now the largest hotel chain in the world; Masaru Ibuka and Akio Morita, who built Sony; and Carl Zeiss and Ernst Abbé,

Table 10.1 **Leadership Structure of Selected Hidden Champions**

Leadership Structure	Examples			
	Company	Founded	Primary Product	Leaders
One Founder-Leader	Brita	1966	Water filters	Heinz Hankammer
	SAT	1982	Road recycling services	Georg Schmidt
	Grohmann Engineering	1982	Electronic assembly systems	Klaus Grohmann
Several Founder-Leaders	Interface	1983	Floppy disk locks	Rainer and Jürgen Wieshoff
	SAP	1972	Client/server applications	Dietmar Hopp, Hasso Plattner, Hans-Werner Hector, and Klaus Tschira
Intergenerational Family	Hoppe	1952	Door and window hardware	Friedrich Hoppe (founder), Wolf and Christoph Hoppe
	Reflecta	1967	Slide projectors	G. Junge and wife, and daughter and her husband
	Sandler	1879	Nonwovens	Christian Heinrich Sandler, Dr. Christian Heinrich Sandler

who founded Schott and Zeiss, two German sister companies in optics and glass, bringing with them a model combination of technical and business expertise.

The most critical problem the hidden champions face is that of succession, which is discussed in depth below. Ideally, founders want to pass the baton to the next generation of the family, and there are indeed numerous instances of second- and even later-generation members of a family on a

Table 10.1   *continued*

Leadership Structure	Examples			
	Company	Founded	Primary Product	Leaders
Second-Generation Family	Stihl	1896	Gasoline chain saws	Hans-Peter Stihl, Eva-Mayr-Stihl, Robert Mayr
	Haribo	1920	Gummi bears	Dr. Hans and Paul Riegel
	AL-KO	1931	Caravan chassis	Herbert, Kurt, and Willy Kober
Mixed Family–Nonfamily	Binhold	1948	Anatomical teaching aids	Paul Binhold and daughter and her husband, Otto H. Gies
	Krones	1951	Bottling systems	Hermann and Volker Kronseder, Paul Hinterwimmer
Nonfamily	Dürr	1895	Auto painting systems	Hans-Dieter Pötsch, Rolf Haueise, Walter Schall, Bernward Hiller
	Sachtler	1967	Camera tripods	Joachim Gehrt, Jürgen Nussbaum
	Heidenhain	1889	Measuring instruments for lengths and angles	Rainer Burkhard, Dr. Walter Miller

management team. Frequently two, sometimes three siblings step into the shoes of the founder-leader. An almost perfect case is Haribo, where Dr. Hans and Paul Riegel took over after the death of their father in 1945. Hans is in charge of external relations and marketing, while Paul runs the internal operations. Sometimes brothers- and sisters-in-law join a leading team, as at Stihl, Binhold, and Reflecta (see Table 10.1).

In sibling management teams, one—usually the first-born—almost always plays a dominant role. This is not surprising because their child-hood relationship is simply continued at the company. But even the hidden champions are not immune from the behavior displayed in such TV series as *Dallas* and *Dynasty,* so there are cases in which siblings don't get along and split up.

In the initial phase of companies, the founders' spouses provide an important supportive function. They are also capable of taking over after the sudden death of a leader. When founder Alfred Kärcher died in 1974, his widow, Irene Kärcher, replaced him as CEO of Kärcher and with the manager Roland Kamm, who is not a family member, led the company to its current world leader position in high-pressure cleaners. And Elisa-beth Belling, founder Hans Lenze's daughter, took over at Lenze when her husband died in 1981.

Mixed teams of family and nonfamily members can work very well. While the family supplies technical talent, the outsiders often introduce professional management techniques like controlling systems and mar-keting. In the course of the transition from a single founder-leader to a team of specialized members, a company may gain a new impetus toward growth—or it may face a crisis. On the other hand, a power discrepancy between family and nonfamily team members may continue. Ownership plus a management contract carry heavier weight than a management contract alone. An important internal aspect of this power structure relates to employees. Those who grew up and worked under the foun-der-leader may accept an heir as their new leader but find it difficult to extend their loyalty to a new, hired boss.

In 18.5% of family-owned hidden champions, no family members par-ticipate in top management. Among them are many companies that are quite well managed and have successfully negotiated the hazardous tran-sition from a family-oriented to a merit-based selection of leaders. For them, as for the hidden champions owned by concerns, the succession problem is much less serious than for the family-owned companies. On the other hand, manager-led firms lack some of the attractive charac-teristics of family firms. Ultimately every company may be forced to make such a transition since there is no guarantee that a person with sufficient management potential can be found in the following generation.

The real message of Table 10.1 is not that the origin of the managers or leaders ultimately counts. Whether or not they are family members is irrelevant compared to how well they cooperate as a team. I have come across intergenerational and sibling family teams that display a great deal of tension and dysfunctional behavior and mixed teams that cooperate very smoothly.

Communication and information are the most obvious areas from which to draw illustrations of cooperation. In one very competitive company the three leaders share one large office. Going through the mail together every morning, each of them is fully and equally informed at all times. In another company, all the members of the management team who are on site lunch together every day and discuss current issues. Dr. Wolfgang Pinegger, president of Brückner, the world leading manufacturer of biaxial film-stretching systems, describes his company's communication style:

> We never know where anybody is, because all of us are always traveling. But we are all reachable. We have built a global communication structure which allows us to contact each member of our team any time any place. And three or four times per year we all come together for several days to discuss everything in depth. There we gather the body of knowledge from which all of us can live for the following months. Such a system works only if the team is small enough and the members are perfectly attuned to one another.

Comparing the typical large company with the hidden champions, I see a huge difference in the interpersonal relations of the management team members. In large firms they are often formal, governed by spheres of responsibility and territory with accompanying power fights. Of course, the hidden champions are not free from quarrels and internal friction, but such problems are much less prevalent and the resulting loss of energy and time is not nearly as great as in large organizations.

A more subtle difference between management teams in large and small companies is that the leadership role of the number one person within a team is more pronounced in the smaller companies. In large German companies, the power within a management team is rather equally distributed, sometimes the chairman or the speaker of the team being a primus inter pares rather than a boss. This is more true for German than for American large companies. In this sense, the sample companies' power structure is relatively more similar to that of American than of German corporations. The leader's strong role does not necessarily conflict with the good team spirit described above. If the other team members recognize the leader's role, strong leadership and team spirit can coexist nicely. One explanation for the difference between large and small companies is that the founder's strong leadership is passed on to succeeding leaders. The solid continuity of leadership, which I address in the following section, contributes to the transcendence of the founder's legacy. Unfortunately, the larger a company, the more quickly this effect dissipates.

CONTINUITY

Continuity of leadership as such is neither good nor bad. A long tenure of a bad leader is obviously disadvantageous. A good leader who continues for a long time can be a great advantage. Collins and Porras (1994) compare the average tenure of the CEOs in their "visionary" companies with those of a matched sample of less successful "comparison" companies. In the visionary group, which the authors call the "best of the best," the CEOs have an average tenure of 17.4 years while the mean figure for the comparison companies is only 11.7 years. All the companies in their study are at least fifty years old, all having been founded before 1946.

However, the length of CEO tenure in the best of the best companies pales against those of the hidden champions. Across all hidden champions their leaders' average tenure is 20.6 years. This comparison with the best of the best is even biased because the majority of the hidden champion sample firms have been in existence less than the visionary companies' minimum of fifty years. If one considers only the companies in my sample that were founded before 1946, their average CEO tenure is 24.5 years.

Many hidden champions have been led by the same CEO for an unusually long time. Table 10.2 lists a number of older companies whose CEOs have completed terms of thirty years or longer, and a large proportion of these firms have had only three or four leaders in their more than hundred-year existence.

One should be overly cautious in interpreting long CEO tenure as a factor of the hidden champions' success. Is a company successful because the CEO has a long-term vision and stays to carry it out, or is the CEO allowed or invited to stay on because the company has been successful in the first place? Both reasons are plausible although the first is the more likely, but the other may also be true.

Table 10.2 **Average Tenure of CEOs in Selected Hidden Champions**

Company	Founded	Primary Service/ Product	Age of Company	Number of CEOs	Average Tenure per CEO
Netzsch	1873	Machines and plants for ceramics industries	121	3	40.3
Glasbau Hahn	1836	Glass showcases for museums and exhibitions	158	4	39.5
Böllhoff	1877	Screws and nuts	117	3	39
seca	1840	Medical scales	154	4	38.5
Haribo	1920	Gummi bears	75	2	37.5
EJOT	1922	Direct screw joints for plastic material	72	2	36
Stihl	1926	Gasoline chain saws	68	2	34
von Ehren	1865	Large living trees	130	4	33.3
Carl Jäger	1897	Incense cones, incense sticks	97	3	32.3
Loos	1865	Industrial steam and hot water boilers	129	4	32.2
Bizerba	1866	Electronic system retail scales	128	4	32
Merkel	1899	Industrial seals	95	3	31.6
Probat Werke	1868	Industrial coffee-roasting technology	126	4	31.5
Bruns	1875	Nursery	120	4	30

The critical relevance of continuity has to be seen in connection with the audacious goals discussed in Chapter 1. If the founder of a small company sets a goal of becoming a world market leader, he does better to think in terms of a generation. Some spectacular modern markets, for example, telecommunications and computers, which have been global since their very inception, may deceive one as to the length of time required to penetrate markets in many different countries. It usually takes decades to build trust and distribution and service networks, to learn how to succeed in faraway markets, and to develop management teams and human resources. Continuity is an essential prerequisite to success under these conditions. Accompanied by perseverance, it may eventually result in world market leadership. Discontinuity, on the other hand, has to be seen as one of the most disastrous factors of both small and large companies. How can a long-term plan be successfully implemented if the person in charge changes every few years? This is a serious problem with business units in large corporations, which in the course of rapid job rotation frequently experience quick turnover of their managers.

PERSONALITIES

Who are these leaders? What types of personalities do they have? What makes them outstanding? Meeting them on the street one wouldn't recognize them. Externally and in most of their characteristics they are ordinary people like you and me. There is no way to describe them in simple uniform terms, for they are as varied as humankind in general. Among them I have found ebullient extroverts and withdrawn introverts. Some are great communicators who enjoy speaking while other are men of few words. Extracting comments from the latter was like pulling teeth. When I visited, some were always surrounded by their people while others hid in the privacy of their offices.

But in spite of all these variations, these leaders have a number of traits in common. From my observations, I have distilled five traits that, to a greater or lesser degree, are common to the leaders of the hidden champions.

Unity of Person and Purpose

It is said of Dr. Hans Riegel of Haribo, a representative hidden champion leader, "His person and his company have always been a unit." This reminded me of a finding on artists and scientists. In their collection of twelve case studies of famous creative people, Wallace and Gruber conclude: "For many creative people the life is the work. Some creative people integrate rather than separate their personal life and their work" (1989, 35). The same could be said for most of the hidden champion leaders I met. They are genuine people who identify totally with their companies. Unlike many managers in large corporations, they live what they are and what they want to be. Helmut Brähler of Brähler International Congress Service contends that his company is his hobby and recommends that everybody try to make his hobby his profession, as he himself has done. "Try to do what you like and plan for a few years ahead," he advises.

This attitude toward work implies that money isn't the primary driving force. While some of the leaders admit that this is easy to say when one has enough money, I believe that this attitude is essentially true. Their motivation is the result, first, of these leaders' identification and satisfaction with their work and only then of economic success. My conclusion is corroborated by the fact that many of the leaders, despite their wealth, continue to lead relatively modest lives. Hermann Kronseder exemplifies this style: "My family and I have never lived extravagantly. I don't like to spend money for unnecessary luxuries. I don't have a yacht, and I don't wear expensive designer suits or an expensive watch. I have a pilot's license but don't own a plane."

Some have extravagant hobbies, but there I got the impression that they are somehow connected with the business. Reinhold Würth, who has an all-weather jet pilot license, at age sixty may well be the oldest possessor in Germany of such a permit. I've never been able to determine whether that's really his hobby or a means to arriving at his many destinations in the shortest possible time. Although it is uncommon in Germany, quite a few of these men have pilot's licenses. I think of their activities as aids to efficiency rather than as true hobbies. Theo Schroeder says that flying fire balloons is his hobby, but he happens to be among the largest manufacturers of fire balloons in the world. All this amounts to integration rather than a separation of work and private life.

Their full devotion to and identification with their work give these leaders enormous credibility with employees and customers. They impose no limits on what they do and assume full responsibility for their companies. Some historically acclaimed industrialists expressed much the same attitude. Robert Bosch, the founder of Bosch, once said, "I

would rather lose money than trust. It has always been unbearable for
me to think that someone could say on examining my products that I
produce something of inferior quality." Henry Ford concurred. "When
one of my cars breaks down, I know I am to blame" (Ford 1922, 67). Such
a sincere stance is transferred to employees and contributes to their
motivation and identification. True leadership can never be play-acted; it
must reside in the leader's genuine core of beliefs and values.

One rarely discerns such attitudes in modern large corporations. I
have met many of their managers who feel relatively alienated from their
work, which may explain the sometimes astonishing ease with which they
switch from company to company.

Single-mindedness

In his biographical *Adventures of a Bystander,* Peter Drucker recounts
meetings with two famous professors in their fields, Buckminster Fuller
in physics and Marshall McLuhan in communication sciences. Drucker
(1978, 255) says:

> They exemplify to me the importance of being single-minded. The single-
> minded ones, the monomaniacs, are the only true achievers. The rest, the
> ones like me, may have more fun, but they fritter themselves away. The
> Fullers and the McLuhans carry out a "mission"; the rest of us have
> interests. Whenever anything is being accomplished, it is being done by a
> monomaniac with a mission.

Applied to hidden champion heads, this description may be a bit of an
exaggeration, but it is pretty close to reality. Their focus and concentration are founded largely on single-mindedness. A person may not want
to become a monomaniac, but must be aware that one is likely to be a
loser in competition against such a fellow. Reconsider Drucker's last
sentence regarding accomplishment, and recall Klaus Grohmann's words
cited in Chapter 9: "We require deep concentration that can be evoked
only in quiet surroundings."

Beneath such focus and concentration sometimes lies an amazing con-
scious strategy called EKS. It stands for *Engpass-konzentrierte
strategie,* which means "bottleneck-concentrated strategy." EKS was invented in the sixties by consultant Wolfgang Mewes and marketed as a
distance learning product. It has been particularly popular with medium-
size companies. Several years ago, Mewes sold his educational product
to *Frankfurter Allgemeine Zeitung,* the leading German national news-

paper whose information service arm continues to market it. The simple idea behind EKS is that every development is limited by one bottleneck factor that tends to limit growth. EKS suggests that one first has to identify the bottleneck factor, then concentrate fully on removing it. After that factor has been excised, it is, by definition, replaced by another limiting factor that must be identified and attacked.

EKS provides details and methods for employing this essentially simple and correct concept, recommending strong concentration on one factor at a time, but also dynamic adjustment of concentration. I have frequently encountered this philosophy in my interviews. Some hidden champion CEOs have become such convinced adepts of this method that they teach it to their own customers. Manfred Bobeck of Winterhalter Gastronom, world leader in commercial dishwashers for hotels and restaurants, tries to convince his distributors of the value of this highly focused approach to strategy. He is fully convinced that this method will make them, and indirectly him, more successful. The surprisingly frequent adoption of EKS may be one of the few "secrets" culled from the hidden champions.

Fearlessness

A third common characteristic of hidden champion leaders is fearlessness. I prefer this word over courage because it seems to me to convey absence of fear rather than presence of courage. One may also perceive from it the absence of inhibition. In my experience, the Chinese proverb "Ignorance of your freedom is your captivity" applies to most people, myself included. Most of us could achieve greater heights if we were really aware of our freedom and our opportunities, for many of the limits we perceive are within ourselves.

But the proverb does not apply to many of the hidden champion leaders, who don't have the same inhibitions and fears as normal people and accordingly are better at exploiting their potential.

They just proceed to any country, any market, any customer, and start doing business. They are essentially uninhibited by risk, limited knowledge of foreign languages, and other mental barriers. Heinz Hankammer simply started selling his filters in a Salt Lake City drugstore; Reinhard Wirtgen unhesitatingly traveled all over the world to deploy his machines. A company with only 110 employees, which prefers anonymity, began producing household products in Russia and China in 1995. Many mistakes are probably made in the course of such actions, because many involve great risk. But the hidden champion leaders are not gamblers willing to bet all their assets on risky ventures. Rather, they consider them the only quick way to elicit reliable, valuable information about new markets.

Stamina and Perseverance

As noted in the introduction to this chapter, the hidden champion leaders appear to possess inexhaustible energy, stamina, and perseverance. Helmut Aurenz of ASB Grünland, world leader in potting soil, considers perseverance the most decisive factor of all. The fire continues to burn in them, even beyond retirement age. Some never retire, which may be a problem in itself. Thus, Paul Binhold, at eighty-two, and Prof. Friedrich Förster, at eighty-six, are still active presences in their companies.

In addition to their intrinsic drive, I believe that interaction with their clear goals and their single-mindedness is an essential factor for their stamina. Success and the achievement of goals inject new energy into these leaders. Tony O'Reilly, CEO of H. J. Heinz, expresses this nicely: "Nothing energizes an individual or a company more than clear goals and a grand purpose" (Smith 1994, 71).

It is also amazing to see how experiences that might discourage others have the reverse effect on hidden champion leaders, for instance, Günther Fielmann, European leader and the world's number two firm in eyeglass retailing. On his entry into city after city, he fought against entrenched competitors, engaging in numerous legal battles, being attacked on many fronts, and surviving other nerve-racking incidents. A popular joke about Fielmann goes, There are two things opticians don't like: people with perfect vision and Fielmann. His blunt reply: "It would be much worse if my competitors ignored me." Richard Branson of the U.K. Virgin Atlantic Group, another of the same ilk, attacks wherever he can—most recently Coke, with a look-alike product—rejoicing increasingly the tougher the counterattacks become.

As I entered the office of many a hidden champion leader, I had an almost physical sense of the energy that emanated from the person, a kind of unknown force that certain people possess. I have no explanation for this phenomenon.

Inspiring to Others

Artists may create their own world fame, but in an economic enterprise nobody can single-handedly create a world market leader. He or she always needs others' work and support. Therefore, the fire that burns in a leader alone is insufficient; he must ignite it in others, usually in many others. According to Warren Bennis (1989), we still don't know why people follow certain leaders and don't follow others. I can only say that the hidden champion CEOs are mighty effective in building a following. It cannot be attributed to their style of communication because many of them are not great communicators in the usual sense. I think that the first trait, the identity of person and purpose, plays a crucial role in the ability to light the fire in others.

The five personality traits are certainly not a definitive description because the relative importance of these traits varies from individual to individual, but they serve adequately to characterize leaders I have met. The five traits are summarized in Figure 10.3. Of course, these are not static characteristics. The demands on these leaders change over time and the leaders must change with the demands. Many of them had to make enormous transitions in this respect. Günther Fielmann's experience is somewhat illuminating:

Figure 10.3   Personality Traits of Hidden Champion Leaders

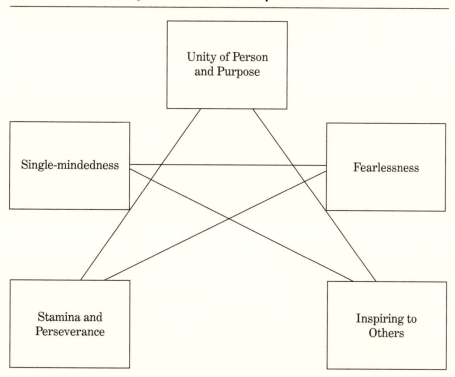

I started out as an optician, an expert on eyeglasses. Later on I had to become a cheerleader, a missionary, someone who could attract exceptional people and instill spirit in them. Then I had to learn how to deal with the media. Now I have to supervise a large organization and devote my time to things like finance for which I may not have sufficient talent.

The demands on the adaptive abilities of the hidden champion leaders are enormous. While large organizations have become more dynamic of late, the changes their leaders experience are hardly as radical as those that occur in the course of developing a hidden champion.

LEADERSHIP STYLES

The leadership styles of the hidden champion executives are not easy to describe, for they are ambivalent and sometimes contradictory. As I have pointed out repeatedly, the hidden champions are tough, demanding employers and it is not to everyone's liking to work for them.

Berthold Leibinger of Trumpf, world leader in machines for punching and nibbling sheet metal, calls the prevailing leadership style enlightened patriarchy. Alfred K. Klein of Stabilus, number one in gas-pressurized springs, described his company style paradoxically as both group oriented and authoritarian. How can these apparent contradictions be reconciled?

The uncomplicated answer is quite apparent. The leadership styles are authoritarian, centralized, and dictatorial where the principles and fundamental values of a company are concerned. There is no discussion about such core aspects as mission, strategic goals, market focus, quality, and service. These core values are decided and dictated from the top down. There is, however, a great deal of leeway in the participation of individuals and group in deciding how these principles are to be executed. Hidden champions' employees are usually faced with far fewer rules and regulation in carrying out details than their colleagues in larger, more bureaucratic organizations.

This tight-loose leadership style is illustrated in Figure 10.4. Typical hidden champions, whose leadership style is rigorous in principles and flexible in details, are shown at the lower left. Some large firms, which are participative or lax in principles but authoritarian and highly regulated in details, are placed in the upper-right box. Other firms are par-

Figure 10.4 **Prevailing Leadership Style of the Hidden Champions**

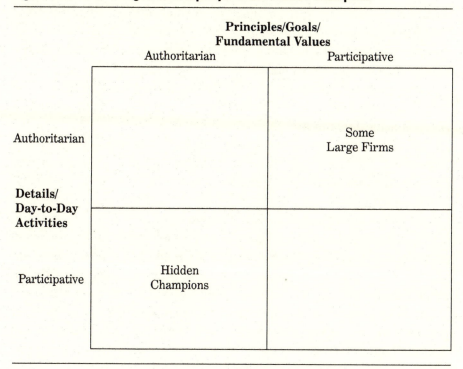

ticipative in both dimensions, which may present a problem when various players in the company pursue different goals.

These differences result in concrete consequences. While large organizations tend to operate under the assumption that trust is good but control is better, the reverse is true for many hidden champions. One company has a simple rule regarding travel expenses: "Everyone should behave as if he or she is spending his or her own money." Typical large organizations issue a special, sometimes more than twenty-page manual concerning travel expenses. The difference between the two approaches is that the hidden champions' reign generally reflects social or group norms that have a much stronger impact on behavior than detailed, written regulations which are not rooted in a value system. One reason for the absence or sparsity of rules is that small and medium-size companies haven't the personnel to write handbooks and manuals—a side effect of having more work than people to do it. And they obviously don't need such publications. This doesn't mean that control is less effective, it's simply different, self- and social control rather than formal pronouncements sent down from above to impose control. These observations are consistent with the findings of Rommel et al. (1995), who report that successful small companies generally delegate more responsibility to small groups and individuals.

A closely associated observation is that measuring performance in the hidden champion firms is oriented toward results rather than processes. People's achievements are more important than the ways they achieve them. Process control and monitoring are much less pronounced than in large firms. This may induce a certain degree of risk, but if a company has the right personnel, it ultimately leads to better performance. Of course, selecting the most qualified people is crucial to maintaining such a trust-based leadership style (see Chapter 9).

In my discussions with hidden champion employees, I often perceived an ambivalent attitude toward the leader. On one hand there were complaints about the authoritarian style, that leaders were found to be irritating, threatening, or disruptive. On the other hand, the same employees appreciated their leaders and had no desire to work for another company, because their identification and motivation were very strong. Such ambiguity reminded me of the attitudes of children toward their teachers. A demanding teacher can simultaneously be liked and disliked by pupils. The attitudes toward demanding leaders tend to be ambiguous. Successful leadership seems to involve a carrot-and-stick element.

MANAGEMENT SUCCESSION

Management succession is the most serious long-term problem facing the hidden champions. A sudden death or illness of a leader can cause a serious crisis in a company, but even without such unexpected events, succession presents an enormous challenge. To find good managers in a succeeding generation is a difficult task for any company, but for a family business it is the most challenging task of all. In traditional agricultural, craft, and small-business societies, it was seen as natural to pass a business on to the owner's children, and many hidden champion leaders still adhere to tradition. Wishing to keep the businesses they founded in their families, their preference is for having family members on the management team.

This attitude is one of the roots of the problem. I think that passing management to the next generation should be seriously questioned by leaders of small and medium-size companies for two reasons. First, one shouldn't assume that a son or daughter automatically inherits the ability to manage a business. If that happens to be true, so much the better, but otherwise a company should be prepared to pass the baton to a nonfamily person or team. Second, the assumption that children have to follow in their parents' footsteps limits their choices in a way that is becoming less and less acceptable to modern society. Children increasingly wish to choose their own professions.

The hidden champions present a mixed picture. In the context of Table 10.1, I provided patterns of successful management transition, an aspect that need not be reconsidered. Rather, I concentrate here on the role of the leader as an individual.

Many founder-leaders underestimate the time required to develop able successors. I discussed the succession problem with the heads of the sample companies. Those in their early or mid-fifties usually thought that they had plenty of time to select and develop the future management team. Only a minority in this age group had a definite opinion of who would follow them and when. Though there are exceptions, I think that by their mid-fifties, leaders should know whom they want to succeed them.

Yielding power is a second serious problem. Again a minority of hidden champion leaders seem to be willing, at a reasonable age, to yield power voluntarily to the next generation. Many leaders consider themselves irreplaceable and, perhaps subconsciously, do everything they can to make themselves irreplaceable. As intelligent as these leaders may be in running a business, they often fail to recognize their limits. One admitted, "Intelligence is halved when your own person is concerned." Their wish to ensure continuity becomes the very cause of discontinuity and crisis.

There are two common outcomes of such behavior: either a company encounters serious trouble or it is quickly sold to a concern. The second may be the worse outcome because the company might lose its independence and the advantages it has enjoyed as a hidden champion. Not all concerns are capable of managing hidden champions, which basically involves leaving them alone.

An attractive third option could be a management buyout. In several hidden champions, managers have, over time, acquired the company. Berthold Leibinger, who started as an employee of Trumpf, now owns the company. Dietrich Fricke of Tente Rollen, world leader in hospital bed casters, joined Tente as a manager and acquired the company when the second generation of the founder family lost interest in the business. In the realm of retaining the advantages of a small company, a management buyout seems to be a more attractive option than selling to a large organization. There are companies like Quadriga Capital Management that specialize in assisting hidden champions handle management buyouts.

Whatever the eventual outcome, hidden champion leaders are well advised not to assume from the very beginning that their managing duties can be passed on to a family member. If the reverse occurs, it should be considered as a positive surprise. The leaders must be aware that developing new leaders is the most difficult task and start early on to search out and groom successors capable of one day assuming control. They must be willing to yield true power to these people and pull out in a reasonable length of time. Since the danger of false self-assessment seems particularly threatening in these aspects, calling on neutral external consultants is eminently advisable.

Hidden champion leaders who consult external advisers they trust are better able to handle the succession problem than those who rely solely on their own judgment. Some hidden champion leaders are paragons in this area: Reinhold Würth of Würth, Werner Baier of Webasto, Heinz Dürr of Dürr, all passed on their leadership when they were in their fifties, but they represent the exception rather than the rule. I encourage all leaders not to deny the succession problem but to approach it proactively and creatively. I believe that many a former hidden champion could have survived or become a successful large company had this problem been handled earlier and more skillfully.

The hidden champions face a second management development problem, which originates with their small size and lean organizations. Unlike large companies, they can't afford to hire many employees who show leadership potential and vet them through a long selection process that ultimately produces a sufficient cadre of able executives. Neither can they offer many positions in which an employee can evidence general management capability. Large concerns command a huge advantage in this regard since they tend to have subsidiaries and business units that serve as training centers for young managers. The trainees can progress from less to more complex units, acquiring management know-how along the way.

Managing a foreign affiliate is an excellent learning opportunity, but many subsidiaries are confined to sales and service and do not offer sufficient breadth. On the other hand the sample companies' more holistic management approach encourages understanding a total business process even for those who are not in a formal general management position. I have found that hidden champion managers whose responsibility is limited to a function or division have a remarkably good overall view of a business. Some hidden champions systematically try to develop management expertise by dividing their companies into full-scale units designed to generate value-added. For instance, Grohmann Engineering projects are run like small temporary companies. The project manager, who has full responsibility from sales to completion, is expected to act like a small-business entrepreneur. He or she puts a team together, calls on common resources in R&D and production, and essentially has to be familiar with and handle all aspects like finance, marketing, and installation. Klaus Grohmann is optimistic that this organization can, over time, develop a sufficient number of knowledgeable and experienced general managers. A project-based business lends itself well to this type of learning organization. Similar results are achieved through the business unit organization of a world leader in special chemical-metallurgical products. This company, whose total revenue is $530 million, is organized into ten small business units, the smallest with a sales revenue of $8 million, which are run by people with comprehensive management responsibility.

The specific company situation affects the way the value-generation process can be allocated to various players. Many hidden champions must be aware that they are not as fortunate as Grohmann and the chemical company in its ease of developing managers, and there is no simple solution to their problem. Large companies may hire more trainees than they need and "store" them for some time, but this method runs counter to the hidden champions' lean philosophy. Hiring a specified percentage of managers from other companies might be an answer, but again, the idiosyncratic corporate cultures render integration of outsiders difficult. Companies must strive for a compromise between these methods.

LEADING CONCERN-OWNED HIDDEN CHAMPIONS

In my sample, 21.1% of the companies were owned by other companies or concerns. By definition, these hidden champions have professional hired managers. It is my impression that to attain hidden championship, it makes no difference whether a company belongs to a family or a concern as long as it meets certain conditions. (I considered only legally independent companies, not divisions of large corporations, to be hidden champions.) In almost all instances, the concern-owned hidden champions were acquired, not started, by the concerns. Originated as family companies, they developed their own corporate cultures and only after they attained hidden champion status were they taken over by the concerns.

Table 10.3 contains a number of examples of companies whose parentage is not only German but that of other nationals.

Many concern-owned hidden champions do very well. Belonging to a larger group obviously has advantages and disadvantages. Alfred K. Klein of Stabilus expressed both sides:

> Operationally and for short-term aspects it is disadvantageous to belong to a concern, but for the long term and surviving a crisis it can be highly advantageous to be part of a larger group. Also, financial power is increasingly important. More and more, we are becoming a systems supplier because our auto industry customers engage in global sourcing and want a strong, secure partner. In this regard the backing of our parent company is definitely a strength. Maneuvering between these two poles is an art. We are lucky that our parent is patient and allows us time, but sometimes the requirements of the concern can be annoying.

The remarks of the CEO of a hidden champion whose parent is a large chemical concern shed light on somewhat different pros and cons of concern ownership:

> We meet with our parent once a month for half a day. As long as the numbers are okay, we are largely left alone about how to conduct our business. Half a day per month—or say it's a day if we include preparation—is adequate. And we have the advantage of not having to spend time on handling investors, preparing road shows, and so on. I can't tell you what the net advantage is, but we live with our parent rather well.

After completing numerous interviews and gaining knowledge of both the concerns and the hidden champions, I candidly advise concerns, whenever feasible, to leave the hidden champions to their own devices. Normally I recommend one meeting every three months rather than one a month. The owner has to pay utmost attention to selecting appropriate leaders but beyond that should interfere as little as possible. Although it may be difficult for a typical concern and its corporate bureaucracy, no one should deceive himself regarding synergies. By trying to maximize

Table 10.3 A Sampling of Concern-owned Hidden Champions

| Company | Parent Company/Concern | | Primary Product | Sales in millions of U.S. $ | Employees | World Market Position | | |
	Name	Country of Origin				Rank	Share in Percentage	Relative Share
Tetra Gruppe	Warner-Lambert	U.S.	Fish food	266	650	1	50	5
Stabilus	Mannesmann	Germany	Gas-pressurized springs	330	2,400	1	n.a.	n.a.
Zanders	International Paper	U.S.	Art paper	580	3,300	1	15	3
Rofin-Sinar	Siemens	Germany	Industrial lasers	73	460	1	21	1.2
KBC	Dollfus-Miag	France	Printed textiles	466	1,500	1	8	1
Böwe Systec	Wanderer	Germany	Paper management	116	1,000	2	16	0.46
Schlafhorst	Saurer	Switzer-land	Rotor spinning machines	1,066	5,700	1	35	1.4
SMS	MAN	Germany	Rolling mills for flat products	566	2,550	1	30	1.5
Glyco	Federal Mogul	U.S.	Gliding rings	167	2,000	1[a]	40[a]	1[a]
Sabo	John Deere	U.S.	Lawn-mowers	73	250	1[a]	n.a.	n.a.

[a]Europe.

them, a concern is more likely to destroy the very strengths of its hidden champion units. A manager of a chemical concern admitted: "We are always acquiring small companies in hopes of retaining their strengths and avoiding our weaknesses. But too often, in about three years' time, we find that we have imposed our weaknesses on them and destroyed their strengths." This usually starts with apparently harmless standardization like imposing a concern's accounting system, information technology, and similar programs on a small company—and ends in paralysis.

Another important point is to leave as many functions as possible to a hidden champion. This company has been eminently successful in managing its own fate. If it is stripped of essential decision-making power in such departments as finance, R&D, sales, and information technology, it tends to lose its identity as a fully integrated unit of value creation. This counsel is likely to run against the grain of a concern's bean counters who calculate hard savings by sharing common resources. But at the same time these people often don't understand or are unable to quantify the value of entrepreneurship, flexibility, and identification in a small unit.

I think that operating hidden champion-style subsidiaries is a real art, which most concerns have not mastered well. But they must learn this skill not only to be able to acquire such companies but also, perhaps primarily, because large firms should aim to become a group of hidden champions. While some concerns of the past were similar to a huge supertanker, I envision large corporations of the future as groups of small, flexible speedboats loosely coordinated by a central authority but operating independently. It is obvious that the units of such groups require leaders who can emulate the leaders of the hidden champions rather than the traditional managers of large corporate bureaucracies.

SUMMARY

The leaders are the source of the hidden champions' success, for within them burn the fires that drive their companies. Leadership is the most important factor contributing to overall accomplishment. What the leaders of the hidden champions do and how they do it can teach other companies a great deal about effective direction:

- Leaders are normal people who reflect the full spectrum of humankind; they can be extroverts or introverts, good or bad communicators, whatever, for no single criterion characterizes a leader.

- Leadership structure, whether leaders are family members or not, is less important than the personalities and coherence of the management team.

- Most leaders emerge early in life. Overextended education and perhaps a long career path in a large company may burn out their energy, suggesting that leaders be spotted and selected when they are still young.

- In selecting leaders, one should give a lot of weight to energy, willpower, and drive, and perhaps relatively less weight should be placed on such factors as cognitive ability and "IQ intelligence."

- Continuity is an important aspect of leadership. The average tenure of the hidden champion CEOs is more than twenty years. If a company pursues ambitious long-term goals, it is usually to its advantage to have leaders who remain at the helm for many years.

- In considering personalities of leaders, one should seek unity of person and purpose, a certain degree of single-mindedness, fearlessness, stamina, and the ability to inspire others. Only leaders who can ignite a fire in others can guide a company to the horizon of success.

- Leadership styles may, or perhaps should, be ambivalent: authoritarian in the fundamentals, participative and empowerment oriented in the process and details of implementation. Leadership is not an either authoritarian or participative option but a both authoritarian and participative option. Leadership requires balancing apparently irreconcilable polarities.

- Management succession is a serious problem for every company, but for family firms it is "the" problem. Family firms are well advised not to assume that management should remain in family hands and must attempt to develop as many potential leaders as possible.

- Concern-owned hidden champions should be left alone as far as possible. Striving to force concern synergies upon small companies poses a major threat to hidden championship.

Although we may not understand what leadership involves, we can follow examples and learn from them. Again, the hidden champion leaders teach us elementary lessons. Leadership should focus on fundamentals authoritatively and leave details to employees. It is the task of leaders to leave no doubt as to the core values and goals of a company. Leadership must never playact, for it has to be genuine and based on the unity of person and purpose. Energy and willpower are indispensable characteristics of an effective leader. Continuity is necessary for the pursuit of long-term goals. Simple as they are, these lessons are difficult to adhere to because they require a person's full devotion to the leadership task. This is the ultimate challenge for each leader: to be, like the hidden champion CEOs, fully devoted to a company's cause.

11

The Lessons

A small company is not a little big company.

MANY BUSINESS ACADEMICS and practitioners continue to believe that the large corporation should be the role model for companies. Books ranging from *In Search of Excellence* (Peters and Waterman 1982) to *Built to Last* (Collins and Porras 1994) analyze and celebrate successful large enterprises, which, they imply, other firms should emulate.

The present book radically reverses this perspective. I hold that in terms of global market position and competitive performance, many of the best companies in the world are not giant corporations but largely unknown, inconspicuous, hidden firms. The latter behave differently both from suggested prototypes and from modern management teaching. Their sustained success indicates that other companies, particularly large organizations, can learn from their practices and experiences.

The assumption that learning is a one-way street from large to small companies is no longer tenable, and the time has come to turn the one-way sign around. But no one should naively attempt to replicate the hidden champions' experiences; rather one must assess them with a grain of salt. Not all markets and all situations lend themselves to the hidden champion approach. Large companies have retained and continue to retain their reason to exist because they possess certain requisite capabilities, which small firms do not possess, for operating in some markets. However, many markets are amenable to the hidden champion approach.

A challenging model envisions the large company of the future as either a big champion or a group of hidden champions. Going a step further, my findings also support the notion that instead of building ever larger and more complex concerns, it might be preferable to divide oversize organizations into truly independent companies that can operate like hidden champions. The first tendencies toward this philosophy are emerging as either staying small or becoming small appears to be a promising path for the future.

A second avenue to learning involves the issue of whether hidden champions are specifically a German phenomenon or whether their strategies can apply everywhere. I have found many hidden champions with remarkably similar characteristics in many other countries. In this chapter I provide a selection of them, discuss their characteristics, and draw conclusions applicable to companies around the world.

SMALL OR LARGE?

Large-corporation bashing has recently become a popular pastime. One of the most outspoken proponents of this trend, Percy Barnevik, CEO of the Swedish-Swiss conglomerate ABB, comments: "I believe that big organizations are inherently negative. They create so much delay, bureaucracy, and distance from customers, discourage employee initiative, and attract the sort of people who survive in such environments" ("ABB on the Move" 1994, 27; see also Knobel 1994). Peter Drucker (1991) agrees:

> The advantages of smaller size are becoming very great. When you look at who is exporting, it is not the big companies. Yes, GE has done very well with aircraft engines, and Boeing with aircraft, but other than that, practically all the exporters of manufactured goods are medium-size companies, highly specialized. I don't think big companies will disappear. But I see more and more businesses where medium size is much better and where it simply diffuses results and destroys profitability to try to be big. It is becoming increasingly important to think through what is the right size.

Considering the results from my survey of the sample companies, I find it difficult to argue with Drucker, but would add that his using the General Electric Aircraft Engine Group and Boeing as examples corroborates my arguments. While, by my definition, they are too large to be "hidden," these two are largely models of the hidden champion strategy in, among other strengths, their powerful focus, global market orientation, and innovation.

GE is particularly representative. I had hours of discussions with Dr. Gerhard Neumann, who, as its head for seventeen years, brought the GE Aircraft Engine Group to its world leader position. Dr. Neumann confirms practically all my findings on the hidden champions and says that he adhered to similar principles. An interesting aside is that he considers his years of apprenticeship in Germany as the most formative phase of his life, even unto his top-management practices. Neumann is a paragon of the leadership traits outlined in Chapter 10, and his operation of that GE group is a prototype for the management of such a unit within a large concern, namely, with a large dose of independence.

It is obvious and increasingly accepted that small firms adapt better and more quickly to changing environments. They make do with fewer but better-motivated employees. Only they seem to be capable of sustaining significant departures from the norm. Large corporations face a different challenge. Dr. Ronaldo Schmitz, now on the management board of Deutsche Bank, told me when he was a board member of chemical giant BASF, "With more than 100,000 employees, it is difficult for us to deviate from society at large. Basically our workforce duplicates the total society. If this is true, which I am afraid it is, it is hard for us to be much better than average." I tend to agree with him. While there are marked differences among big corporations, the risk of becoming a clone of society at large increases with the size of a company. Outstanding performance requires an elite, and an organization that wishes to reach and maintain that status must limit its size.

When I speak of small or medium size, my primary concern is not sheer size but the focus underlying it. If a world market represents sales of U.S. $25 billion, a company with a 40% share of that market realizes $10 billion. This company may not be small, but is probably well focused and adheres to the principles described in this book. Boeing falls into this category. On the other hand, a company of the same size that is active in many unrelated markets but has a weak market position in each of them definitely doesn't meet my criteria. Size always has to be judged in relation to the market, but focus can be applied to any market.

Certain enormous markets, such as telecommunications, infrastructure, and automobiles, which require large resources, will always be the domain of large firms. But even within these markets, the firm structure is not a given. Value creation can be organized in many ways. The fully integrated model of Ford's River Rouge plant encompassing the total value chain from ore mining to sale of a new car is less and less the model for the future. Large size may still be important in some large markets, but increasingly the motivational advantages of fewer personnel are compensating for the economies of scale inherent in large volume. Adjustments in division of labor allow companies to exploit these advantages.

REMAINING SMALL

If modest size provides certain advantages that are endangered by increasing size, small and medium-size companies should seriously consider remaining small. Although this runs counter to accepted knowledge and behavior, and partially to my statements about growth in Chapter 1, traditional growth patterns and goals must be questioned in view of my findings. Remember that most of today's large companies could not have achieved that size had they not once been successful medium-sized companies; somewhere along the way, many must have contracted "big company" disease. One wonders whether they could have avoided it had they consciously made and implemented the decision to stay small. Perhaps!

Always relating its size to its (preferably world) market, if a company can grow either by increasing its low market share or by regional expansion, it has no cause for concern. It can continue to focus on its market and competencies and adopt a growth strategy perfectly consistent with the hidden champion success route. If, however, its global market share is already high and diversification appears to be the only road to further growth, its shareholders should seriously consider investing their money elsewhere. The common—and in my opinion, often wrong—decision in such a case is to diversify. Such expansion can distract from the focus that made the company strong and leads to violation of the characteristic principles of a hidden champion. In that situation, the management and shareholders could opt to remain small and keep the narrow market focus to retain existing strengths, and individual shareholders can seek other ventures in which to entrust their company dividends. For a family-owned business, this may be a strange approach, but staying small and focused in an original enterprise deserves consideration as a strategic option. A person who has made great strides in one business tends to overestimate his or her ability to replicate success in new ventures.

A family-owned hidden champion faced such a situation. A profitable world market leader in an industrial sector, the business provided only limited reinvestment opportunities. Because of the long-term nature of its projects, its share moves only gradually and it is difficult to attain satisfactory growth within its current market. The company considered two alternatives, the first being diversification into a promising new field, which entailed substantial risk but also presented attractive opportunities. The new business would be supervised by the same top management team, but a new division within the company would be established. The second was simply to pay out the money not required for reinvestment to the shareholders and let them decide what to do with it. The decision to go with the second alternative, I believe, was correct. I am fairly sure that the strength, the focus, and the world market leadership in the existing business will continue since management's full concentration is guaranteed. But the decision also entails limits on the company's size and prospects for growth in the foreseeable future.

GROWING SMALL

The idea that companies should shrink in size is anathema to widely accepted growth and merger credos. Bigger is usually considered to be synonymous with better. However, the U.S. banking industry is challenging that view, as noted in the subhead of a *Wall Street Journal Europe* article (Hirsch 1995, 4): "Bigger Is Better but Narrower Is Even Nicer." Most entrepreneurs are aware that businesses which are units or divisions of large companies may not be doing well. If released to become true independent entities, many of these businesses have the potential to become hidden champions on their own merit. Essentially, they face the challenge of paring down and ridding themselves of the big companies' weaknesses.

Most mergers create ever larger organizations. I suggest that the opposite route, carving up companies, can have an important effect, but examples of this practice are rare. One such is ICI, the U.K. chemical manufacturer. In 1993, its pharmaceutical division was spun off as an independent public corporation and named Zeneca, and its industrial chemical businesses continue to operate under the ICI name. In a *Harvard Business Review* article, Owen and Harrison (1995) give a detailed report of the process leading led to this action and its results. They state that a 1980s acquisition spree had "increased the complexity of an already complicated and hard-to-manage portfolio of businesses" (133). The value of ICI's star products, pharmaceuticals, wasn't reflected in the price of the company's stock, resulting in a mismatch between the role of corporate and the requirements of the businesses.

Now Zeneca, with more than three-quarters of its profits derived from pharmaceuticals, can focus completely on its narrow core business. And the new ICI has already set its goal "to achieve world market leadership for the areas in which ICI has a technological advantage" (Owen and Harrison 1995, 139). After two years the evaluation of the two companies and the ensuing refocus is positive. Sir Ronald Hampel, CEO of the "new" ICI, offered some interesting comments in a 1995 interview.

- We now have more time to focus on our chemical business.

- One of my greatest worries before the split-up was: Are we going to make ICI too small? Too small to compete successfully in the technological race? After all, we had to relinquish some of the synergies between chemical and pharmaceutical production.

- Before the split-up I was responsible for more turnover than I am presently. Nobody likes to surrender a share of responsibility, but we took advantage of the opportunity for change. Our whole work life has changed to the better. I never thought it was possible. (*Wirtschaftswoche* 1995)

ICI-Zeneca's experience has encouraged other large companies to consider similar moves. In mid-1995, the Swiss chemical giant Sandoz starting selling its specialty chemicals business under its new name Clariant on the Zürich stock exchange. In the future Sandoz plans to focus on only two businesses, pharmaceuticals and food. Also in mid-1995, ITT announced a plan to divide itself into three independent, better-focused companies. AT&T followed a few months later announcing its breakup into three independent companies. The stock market responded positively. In November 1995, 3M announced the spin-off of its data storage business into a new company. And in December 1995, Baxter International, the hospital supply company, announced a split-up into two independent firms. These moves may be harbingers of a demerger wave to come.

It is interesting to imagine what would happen if there should be as many splits as mergers. It would most likely introduce a new, dynamic element into the economy. Some spin-offs imposed on companies by external forces point to this direction. The 1911 breakup of the Standard Oil trust led to the emergence of a number of extremely successful companies, Exxon, for one. After World War II, the German chemical monopoly IG Farben was divided into BASF, Bayer, and Hoechst. There can be little doubt that these three combined have outdone any possible world market achievement of a monolithic IG Farben. The 1984 split-up of AT&T provides further support for my thesis. Together, the baby Bells and the new AT&T combined have been eminently successful. It's interesting to speculate on what might have happened if IBM had been split into separate companies as planned by the Justice Department at about the same time. It doesn't seem too far-fetched to imagine the development of a number of highly focused, successful "baby Blues" in the 1980s. The traditional striving for bigness should be seriously questioned. Breakups, split-ups, spin-offs, and similar moves are likely to become highly attractive options for future strategy.

A less radical step than a total spin-off is establishing a legally independent firm. A good case in point is AgrEvo, a new company in the plant protection business formed by the former plant protection divisions of the German chemical companies Hoechst and Schering and the French company Roussel Uclaf. Dr. Gerhard Prante, AgrEvo's CEO, holds that the new firm has developed an identity of its own in a very short time. The company now focuses only on plant protection undistracted by problems of other chemical businesses. With a decidedly global market orientation, it is much closer to customers than it could ever be in the context of its giant parent corporations. Employee identification with AgrEvo has increased, and the advantages of a typical hidden champion are emerging. This is an almost ideal prototype for creating hidden champion companies from units of large corporations. In a mid-1995 move, Hoechst replicated this model by combining its textile dyes business with Bayer's respective division to form a new company called Dystar.

It is critical to a successful transition that each such newly formed company be granted maximum possible independence. The new entity takes care of itself and in an unbelievably short time reaches heights of achievement that seemed impossible in the larger whole. Ideally, a new unit should even be physically separated from its parent.

I see great opportunities for similar moves in many large corporations. Businesses that are parts of huge, diversified, unfocused organizations with unclear missions and identities can be forged into hidden champion units. For instance, a formerly unprofitable division of a large German chemical concern was sold to a Swiss parent, which, unlike the former parent, granted the company a great deal of independence. In one year it turned a loss of $46.5 million into a profit of $26.5 million. The CEO who had retained his position explained that his only real problems were the restrictions imposed by the former owner, whose structure and business ideas were totally different from what was necessary to make this unit successful. This company has become a hidden champion and world market leader.

Large corporations are also well advised to sell off businesses that are too tiny in their context. Such units may be highly attractive for small niche-oriented companies. Siemens sold its pacemaker business, a relatively small unit in the Siemens context, to St. Jude Medical, a specialist and hidden champion in the cardiology field (see Table 11.1 on page 260). The pacemaker business is likely to receive more management attention and focus at St. Jude Medical than it could have ever hoped to attract at Siemens. The same is true for Bayer's dental business, which was sold to Heraeus Kulzer, a specialist in this field, in mid-1995. With 560 employees and $134 million in sales, this unit was too small to play a significant role in the large Bayer concern, as Dr. Manfred Schneider, Bayer's CEO, explained to me. And Juergen Heraeus, CEO of the acquiring Heraeus concern, thinks that this business fits perfectly into the culture of his company, which is accustomed to running niche businesses and has several hidden champions.

A small business unit that is likely to be neglected in a large corporation can become the core and focus of attention when it is either given its independence or sold to a smaller company. The size of a business should be consistent with the size of its parent company. Small businesses do better in the hands of small companies, so large companies may be well advised not to hold on to them. First, they do not operate them well, and second, these ventures distract them from their larger core businesses.

LESSONS FOR LARGE COMPANIES

Can the findings on the hidden champions be applied to large, multibillion-dollar companies? Of course, it's an oxymoron to attach the label "hidden" to large, prominent corporations, and one should refrain from naively recommending that large companies adopt small-firm strategies. It seems useful, in applying the lessons, to distinguish between two types of large corporations. The first type, the focused organization that essentially confines its activities to one market, in which it strives for a leading position, I call a big champion. The other type, the large firm that is active in several different but more or less related businesses or markets, I call a diversified corporation.

LESSONS FOR CHAMPION CORPORATIONS

It is obvious that the champion corporation pursues a strategy similar to that of the hidden champions, though on a larger and more noticeable scale. Therefore the lessons contained in this book can readily and largely be adopted by this kind of company. Boeing belongs to this category. Its focus is on airplanes, and it is a world leader in its market. Whirlpool, already the world's leading manufacturer of large household appliances, has declared that it wants to become the leader in each of the world's main regions. Otto-Versand, the world's largest mail-order company, is systematically building its position in all major countries of the world.

Other companies that historically had such a focus but deviated from the "path of virtue" are recentering. A case in point is Kodak which, after selling its pharmaceutical and diagnostic businesses, is returning to its traditional core. *Business Week* (Maremont 1995, 65) comments: "The massive sale transformed Kodak from a conglomerate to a narrowly focused imaging company." Interestingly, George Fisher, Kodak's new CEO, suddenly detects plenty of growth opportunities in the narrower market. How is this possible? Because he has redirected Kodak's attention to global markets. According to *Business Week* (63),

> Fisher is convinced that Kodak's traditional film and paper business can grow at 7% to 9% annually for the next decade. How? In part, through expansion in the fast-moving economies of Asia, where Kodak has been badly lagging behind archrival Fuji Photo Film Co. And he sees dramatic growth in barely tapped developing markets such as Russia, India, and Brazil.

With its new focus, Kodak started, in March 1995, to do the hitherto unthinkable, namely, sell private label films in Japan. This is an ideal type of case. Nothing has changed in the reality of these markets. Only the perspective has been refocused along the lines of the hidden champion archetype.

Many large diversified corporations have enacted or are considering similar moves. Schering is another company that has totally refocused its business on pharmaceuticals. Starting in 1992 all nonpharmaceutical businesses were either sold or organized into separate companies, as was done with AgrEvo. Schering has become a purely pharmaceutical company with a clear focus. After three years it gives a positive evaluation to its recentering. Disposal of all but its pharmaceutical units led to a sales decline of more than $785 million, but half of this decline was made up by improved growth in its first year as a newly focused company.

Many other large companies seem to pursue similar routes by shedding marginal businesses and concentrating on fewer units. What I haven't seen as often is an accompanying realignment of goals, market scope, and competitive advantages. A company that withdraws from some markets and focuses on one or a few others should simultaneously set more ambitious goals, expand its regional market scope, move closer to its customers, and improve its competitive strength. Almost everything I have reported about the hidden champions applies to the focused corporation.

LESSONS FOR DIVERSIFIED CORPORATIONS

Diversified corporations present a more complex category. It is less evident whether and what these firms can learn from the hidden champions. Aren't they pursuing the opposite of what the hidden champions exemplify by engaging in many different businesses to balance risks, exploit synergies, and so forth? Most of these businesses have at least a marginal relation between technology and markets, but such interdependence usually allows substantial scope for a strong focus on technology or market.

The latter aspect offers the opportunity to run divisions or business units somewhat in the style of hidden champions. This means giving them a clear mission to strive for strong market positions and much autonomy in deciding how to achieve this goal. Hewlett-Packard and 3M belong to this category of modern decentralized corporations. Hewlett-Packard, with sales of more than $20 billion, organizes around business units that are operated like small businesses and have full profit-making responsibility. A business unit may have sales of hidden champion magnitude, say $100 million. The same can be said of 3M, whose constant innovation depends essentially on this kind of decentralization.

In Europe, ABB, with several thousand business units that are supposed to be run like small firms, is probably the corporation that has most systematically implemented this concept. However, one has to wonder about ABB whether it has too many such units and whether market leadership goals and focus are sufficiently pronounced. How can a group of hundreds or thousands of hidden champion-type companies be kept focused, managed, and controlled? Beyond the individual unit focuses, the corporation as a whole needs bonds and a central focus.

I discern similar tendencies toward establishing groups of hidden champions among other large corporations. For many years General Electric has had a distinct mission that its divisions strive to be world number one or two. *Fortune* calls GE's divisions "lithe units that dominate their global markets" (Grant 1995, 74). The Aircraft Engine Group, mentioned earlier in this chapter, is an impressive model of champion strategy. Siemens is pursuing a similar path, though its process of decentralization is in an earlier stage. It is interesting to observe that some Siemens divisions are developing their own identity, as AgrEvo has done.

Is the hidden champion approach suggested here for the diversified corporation different from the omnipresent recommendations to decentralize? Not fundamentally! But the hidden champions suggest that decentralization should be more radical than is customary today. Newly formed units must be empowered with all, not only parts, of a business's core functions.

The issue of what is or remains common among divisions that belong to a diversified corporation is extremely complex and cannot be answered naively. There must be some sharing of resources and synergies, whether related to technology or market. I fully agree with a statement in a 1995 *Harvard Business Review* article: "As we have come to learn, the relatedness of businesses is at the heart of value creation in diversified companies" (Collis and Montgomery 1995, 125). The optimal compromise between centralized and decentralized competencies is difficult to find and not static. In the context of a diversified corporation, a hidden champion strategy cannot be duplicated to the letter. But divisions should observe the lessons nevertheless. The synthesis of authoritarian and participative leadership discussed in Chapter 10 can be applied to the relation between a center and its decentralized units. The center should be authoritarian in the fundamental aspects it determines, but those should be few. In all details, leadership should be highly participative, with the units having their say. In most corporations, in spite of lip service to the contrary, there is still too much centralization. The center doesn't confine itself to setting the fundamental goals and values but engages in too much micromanagement, which prevents the units from pursuing a true hidden champion strategy. The center must continually and critically ask itself what value it contributes to the business of the units.

A further requisite for hidden championship is comprehensive functional responsibilities. The business units must be defined so that they are given full responsibility for the core functions and value-added of their business. According to the Siemens experience, this should be the governing criterion for the definition of a business unit. It implies that both market aspects and internal resources have to be included, as exemplified in the hidden champions' balance of external market opportunities and internal resources or competencies. Only if both aspects are handled by a business unit's management can it pursue a strategy of striving for global market leadership. What is currently being practiced is a violation of this condition: sales and production are allocated to different business units or sales and service are separated. Such division of responsibilities that belong to the same value chain is unthinkable for the hidden champions. Units from which core functions have been amputated are unlikely to become or remain a champion. However, in industries that require close integration of manufacturing and research (e.g., chemicals and electronics), it is almost impossible to realize the pure model of full delegation of core functions.

The art of finding an optimal middle way between the two poles of centralization and decentralization determines the future of a large corporation. I imagine the diversified corporation of the future as a group of companies that share a few core resources but, beyond that, operate like independent champions with explicit missions, focused markets, global orientation, and so on. Small autonomous units are most likely to achieve the kind of specialization, integration of technology and marketing, and employee identification that meet the competitive requirements of the future. Large companies may find it hard to replicate some hidden champion characteristics because the skills and personalities of those in top management are such vital assets. Leaders who are technically competent, unify person and purpose, know the nuts and bolts of a business, are willing to get their hands dirty, and are fully devoted to their job are key to creating an atmosphere in which employees are motivated and involved. These are underdeveloped traits in many corporations.

This implies that the transition from a centrally managed company to a hidden champion corporation is not only organizational. The greater challenge lies in changing leadership styles and corporate culture. It takes time and energy to modify these characteristics, but as AgrEvo and Zeneca illustrate, this change is much more likely to come about in smaller units than in the context of a large corporation.

On many occasions in diversified corporations, I have witnessed the enthusiastic reception of the hidden champions' approach. I have the impression that many people in large companies would prefer to work in smaller, more clearly focused, less regulated units. A manager in a huge concern described the situation pointedly. After having worked for three years in a rather independent subsidiary of a hidden champion type of corporation, he had returned to the parent company, where he attained a senior management position. He commented: "I was three times as effective in the hidden champion unit as I am in the large corporation. There I devoted seventy-five percent of my energy to the market, but here I devote seventy-five percent of it to internal fights and activities." A way to restore efficiency in large corporations is to decentralize into hidden champion-style units.

LESSONS FOR SMALL COMPANIES

Not every small company can be or should strive to be a world market leader, for many markets are local or regional. The fact that we excluded such markets from our study doesn't mean that there are no excellent firms within them. The reverse is true. Companies similar to the hidden champions operate in all markets. Participants in my seminars frequently turned my attention to local companies that were champions in their smaller regional markets.

Regardless of market scope, successful companies exercise similar principles, and my conclusions are equally relevant to small firms with local or regional scope. The lessons on goal setting, motivation, and leadership are directly transferable to them. The most specific recommendation, however, is to remain narrowly focused and to grow through regional expansion. Instead of diversifying, as my friend did (see Chapter 4), from supermarket to hotel in the same town, it is preferable to stick to supermarkets and expand into a neighboring town. A person who has done really well with supermarkets in one location can probably repeat the results in other locations. Excelling in supermarkets (apples), however, does not necessarily carry over to excelling in hotel management (oranges), because one has to deal with a totally different clientele. The instruction for a regional company is that, no matter how small a market, it has to have a leader, the position for which an entrepreneur should aim. Hidden championship does not depend on the size of a market.

Another case of a high-tech supplier to the banking industry illustrates the relevance of internationalization. This $100 million company holds 80% of the very demanding German market but so far has refrained from going international. It took me some time to convince the management that if they are able to get 80% of a market as difficult as Germany, then they should be able to conquer their share in other countries. Each small company that is excellent in one regional market should seriously consider going international.

BEYOND GERMANY

The research project on which this book is based focused on hidden champions from Germany, although I occasionally injected insights gained from other countries' hidden champions. The question of whether hidden champions exist and whether their experiences can be applied outside Germany is interesting and relevant.

Even without a systematic search, I discovered hidden champions in many countries, from Europe and the United States to South Africa and New Zealand. In 1989, French world market leaders even formed an organization called *Club de numéros 1 mondiaux français à l'export* (Club of Global Number One French Exporters). The majority of the 139 members are large companies, but many hidden champions are included. In some smaller countries a hidden champion may well be the largest multinational. A case in point is Corticeira Amorim of Portugal, by far the world's largest maker of cork stoppers and other cork products. Of this company, which perfectly displays our hidden champion traits, it is said, "The company has emerged as the dominant force in the production and distribution of cork and its derivatives worldwide. It is the only Portuguese multinational to have such a large share of its market" (Vitzthum 1994b, 4). The non-German hidden champions listed in Table 11.1 provide evidence, at least as far as objective criteria like size and market position are concerned, that hidden champions are plying their trades around the globe.

While it is informative to know of their existence, it does not necessarily follow that the non-German hidden champions exhibit the same strategic traits as their German counterparts. Location can play an important role in a company's strategy and global success. I have no conclusive, 100% scientific proof that the companies named in Table 11.1 can benefit from the examples or model themselves on the German hidden champions.

But I have investigated and visited a good number of the non-German hidden champions. In workshops and seminars with them I heard many comments on their methods and those of the German prototypes. The information I gleaned leads me to conclude that hidden champions are remarkably similar across countries, employing almost identical strategies. They share similar attitudes toward publicity, hold the same core values, and have excellent employee motivation. On a visit to SAPPI-SAICCOR in South Africa, world leader in dissolvable pulp (its U.S. subsidiary, S. D. Warren, is world number one in coated wood-free paper), I sensed exactly the same intense atmosphere that prevails among the German companies. I had the same experience in the U.S. Midwest, where I visited a hidden champion—a world market leader for a special machine product—that prefers anonymity.

In my experience, hidden champions are more alike from country to country than they are in relation to large companies within their own countries. I believe that Kärcher in Winnenden, southern Germany, is more similar to Melroe in Gwinner, North Dakota, than Kärcher is to Volkswagen or Melroe to General Motors.

My observations were validated in many conversations with international businesspeople. Bill Gallagher, CEO of Gallagher in New Zealand, the world leader in electric agricultural fences, confirmed in our discussion that his strategy is practially congruent with the German hidden champions' approach. And the following quotation, from an *Interna-*

Table 11.1 Hidden Champions around the World

Company	Country	Primary Product	Sales in Millions of U.S. $	Employees	World Market Position		
					Rank	Absolute Share in Percentage	Relative Share
Swarovski	Austria	Cut-crystal jewelry	990	9,200	1	67	>2
Fischer	Austria	Cross-country skis	79	860	1	40	2.8
Mayr-Melnhof	Austria	Cardboard boxes	1,000	4,800	1[a]	25[a]	1.5[a]
Trierenberg	Austria	Cigarette paper	370	900	1[a]	45[a]	1.5[a]
Veitsch-Radex	Austria	Magnesia-bonded refractories	540	4,000	1	15	1.3
Nyco Minerals	Denmark	Wollastonite	30	120	1	60	3
Rockwool	Denmark	Rockwool, mineral wool	928	5,600	1	n.a.	n.a.
Babolat	France	Natural strings for tennis rackets	28	200	1	75	5
Eurocopters	France	Helicopters (nonmilitary)	1,700	n.a.	1	51	>2
Manitou	France	Rough terrain forklift trucks	270	1,200	1[a]	35[a]	n.a.

Rossignol	France	Alpine skis	410	2,000	1	25	2.4
Sofamor	France	Instruments for back surgery and implants	47	n.a.	1	28	1.2
DeLonghi	Italy	Portable air conditioners	800	2,000	1[a]	30[a]	1.5[a]
Mabuchi Motors	Japan	Small electric motors (e.g., for VCRs)	n.a.	n.a.	1	40	4.4
Minibea	Japan	Miniature bearings	n.a.	n.a.	1	65	>3
Nideq	Japan	Spindle motors for Winchester drives	n.a.	n.a.	1	85	>5
Nikon	Japan	Lithography equipment for semiconductor production	n.a.	n.a.	1	50	n.a.
Eurocomposites	Luxembourg	Comb panels	17	110	1[a]	50[a]	1.4[a]
Gallagher	New Zealand	Electric agricultural fences	100	650	1	45	2

[a]Europe.

Continued on next page

Table 11.1 *continued*

Company	Country	Primary Product	Sales in Millions of U.S. $	Employees	World Market Position		
					Rank	Absolute Share in Percentage	Relative Share
Amorim	Portugal	Cork products	293	n.a.	1	Fuzzy market	>3
SAPPI-SAICCOR	South Africa	Dissolving pulp	300	1,200	1	17	1.4
Chupa Chups	Spain	Lollipops	275	n.a.	1	Fuzzy market	n.a.
Freixenet	Spain	Sparkling wine	300	1,100	1	5	1.2
Gambro	Sweden	Dialysis machines	1,400	9,000	1	30	1.5
Ares Serono	Switzerland	Biotech products	650	n.a.	1	70	>2
Cerbérus Guinard	Switzerland	Fire-alarm systems	n.a.	n.a.	1[a]	50[a]	n.a.
Flytec	Switzerland	Instrumentation for hang gliders	3	n.a.	1	60	>1.5
Uwatec	Switzerland	Scuba diving instruments	14	n.a.	1	60	>1.5
Giant	Taiwan	Mountain bikes	400	1,500	1	3	1.1

De la Rue	U.K.	Money printing	1,000	n.a.	1	60	>3
Molins	U.K.	Mid-range cigarette makers	475	3,000	1	65	2
Vinten Group plc	U.K.	Accessories for TV cameras	n.a.	n.a.	1	In many segments 80–90	>10
Meiko	U.K.	Massively parallel processing	223	180	1[a]	25[a]	n.a.
BE Avionics	U.S.	Passenger control units for airplane seats	n.a.	n.a.	1	70	>2
Brush Wellman	U.S.	Beryllium-engineered products	346	n.a.	1	65	>2
Cray Research	U.S.	Supercomputers	921	n.a.	1	66	n.a.
Institute for International Research	U.S.	Conferences, seminars	200	1,200	1	Fuzzy market, n.a.	n.a.
Loctite	U.S.	Anaerobic adhesives	417	n.a.	1	80	>5
Medtronic	U.S.	Pace-makers	1,600	10,000	1	46	2.1
		Defibrillators	n.a.	n.a.	1	33	n.a.

[a] Europe.

Continued on next page

Table 11.1 *continued*

| Company | Country | Primary Product | Sales in Millions of U.S. $ | Employees | World Market Position | | |
					Rank	Absolute Share in Percentage	Relative Share
Melroe	U.S.	Skid-steer loaders/ multipurpose loaders	n.a.	n.a.	1	75	>4
Morton International	U.S.	Air bags	225	2,000	1	55	1.5
Nordson	U.S.	Hot melt equipment	500	3,000	1	60	>1.5
Rohr Industries	U.S.	Commercial nacelles	907	n.a.	1	85	>6
Sensormatic Electronics Corp.	U.S.	Electronic article protection	890	5,500	1	Fuzzy market	>2
St. Jude Medical	U.S.	Artificial heart valves	253	725	1	60	9.1
Superior International Industries	U.S.	Aluminum wheel rims for automobiles	456	4,500	1	20	1.8
S. D. Warren	U.S.	Coated wood-free paper	1,144	4,500	1	7	n.a.

aEurope.

tional Management article about Chupa Chups, a Spanish hidden champion, world leader in lollipops, reveals astonishing similarities (Webster 1992, 55).

> Chupa Chups is dynastic and rooted in a guild system of crafts that survived into this century.
>
> In this strategy and personnel, Chupa Chups is thoroughly international. Three-fifths of Chupa Chups's turnover now comes from outside Spain. Soon after Enrique Bernat took over the company in 1957, he made his first big decision, to cut the 200 products it was then manufacturing to just one: the lollipop. Bernat patented his product. Over the years he has consistently invested in new technology to stay ahead of the competition.
>
> More than 80% of the machinery that Chupa Chups uses is designed internally and guarded jealously from competitors.

The description of the strategy of Amorim, the Portuguese world market leader in cork products, reflects the hidden champion pattern equally well with regard to global presence, closeness to customer, market dominance, and full control (Vitzthum 1994b, 4):

- 50 manufacturing and distribution units located in 15 countries . . .
- We know our markets well, there's a strong link between distribution and production . . .
- dominant in cork and its derivatives . . .
- we are always willing to buy out distributors . . .

These could be descriptions of almost any German hidden champion: traditional values, globalization, focus on one product or market, innovation, competitive advantage, and reliance on one's own strength. All of which suggests that the lessons outlined here are not limited to Germany but offer valuable advice for companies throughout the globe. The fundamental principles of good management are equally pertinent across countries and cultures. Doesn't the hidden champions' global success almost require that companies find common denominators for conducting business on a worldwide scale?

I do not mean to denigrate the relevance of local conditions. Demanding customers, strong competitors, support industries, and other favorable factors are all helpful in attaining global market leadership, as outlined in Michael Porter's *Competitive Advantage of Nations* (1990a). The same is true of the general educational, technological, and international orientation of a society as emphasized by Horst Albach in *Culture and Technical Innovation* (1994).

Therefore, American companies may have better opportunities than European firms to become hidden champions in fields like computers, software, biotechnology, entertainment, and multimedia. The conditions for these industries seem to be most favorable in the United States. Mabuchi is the world leader in small electric motors for CD and video players because the greatest, most urgent demand is in Japan owing to the Japanese leadership position in CD players and tape and video recorders. World leaders in skis like Fischer (cross-country) and Rossignol (downhill) operate in mountain regions where skiing has traditionally been popular. Some of the companies mentioned in Table 11.1, such as Gallagher, the New Zealand maker of electric agricultural fences, are also beneficiaries of favorable locations. The number of sheep in New Zealand is about twenty times higher than the number of humans, and all grazing sheep have to be controlled by fences.

But this is only a partial, and diminishing, picture. Both German and non-German hidden champions prove that there are always exceptions to a rule. Many of these firms are situated where they shouldn't be according to international competitive wisdom. Why should a company like Melroe, maker of a relatively simple device like the Bobcat skid-steer loader, be in Gwinner, North Dakota? Or why is St. Jude Medical in Minneapolis? Beyond tradition, are there specific reasons for the German locations of Grohmann Engineering when most of its customers are American electronics companies, or Fischer Labor- und Verfahrenstechnik, which derives 90% of its turnover from international oil companies? Then there's SAP, the world leader in client/server standard business software. Would it not be better off with a U.S. rather than a German base? With so many different markets and niches, so many potential competitive advantages and competencies, and with their determination and corporate culture, many hidden champions could establish themselves anywhere in the industrial world, flourish, and retain their leading positions.

My opinion is seconded by many of the respondents. Peter Barth, CEO of the world market leader in hop products, thinks the company could carry on its business from almost anyplace in the world. His view is shared by Klaus Grohmann, who suggested that a North American location would be as good a site for his company's headquarters as the current one in Germany. And when I visited the American subsidiaries of Dürr, the world leader in paint finishing systems in Detroit, I couldn't detect much difference in spirit from its Stuttgart headquarters, even though there were hardly any Germans in the Detroit plant (the CEO is South African). I believe that many people, particularly Americans, overestimate the country-specific aspects of management.

My investigation of the hidden champions inside and outside of Germany suggests that the ultimate factor is not location but the ability of a company to develop the competencies and competitive advantages required in its specific market. While this may not be independent of location, environment is only one determinant of success. The hidden champions' global orientation and for many their multilocations make them increasingly independent of a specific country. The upper echelons of the hidden champions are among the most cosmopolitan people I have met, and becoming a cosmopolite is both a requisite and a consequence of hidden championship independent of one's country of origin. A shrinking world offers every company willing to transcend its cultural and national limitations great opportunity for growth.

LESSONS FOR INVESTORS

The hidden champions are tempting targets for investors. Market focus, global market leadership, and continuity are attractive criteria that smart investors seek. Investors like uncomplicated, single-minded companies and dislike conglomerates that dilute their results and responsibilities (see Owen and Harrison 1995 for the example of ICI-Zeneca). The hidden champions' having remained largely unknown makes it unlikely that they have realized their full value in capital markets. This is intensified by the fact that the German stock market for small companies is in an early stage of development with only a small minority of the hidden champions (a selection is shown in Table 11.2) being publicly traded.

These companies deserve closer examination as potential investment targets. Their long-term development promises attractive returns to stockholders, particularly through long-term appreciation of stock. In the short term, hidden champion share prices are likely to be more volatile than those of large corporations. Their focus indicates that the sample companies' development depends closely on the fluctuations of their product markets. They are strongly affected by single causal factors like

Table 11.2 **A Selection of Publicly Traded Hidden Champions**

Company	Primary Product	Sales in Millions of U.S. $	Employees	Stock Price, December 1995, in U.S. $
Aqua Signal	Illumination systems for ships	34.5	229	60
Barmag	Machines for the fiber industry	480	3,700	113.3
Biotest*	Pharmaceutical specialties	175.3	939	213.3
Böwe Systec	Paper management	116.7	1,000	200
CeWe	Photo finishing	1,106.7	2,400	303.3
CS-Interglas	Technical fabrics for the electronic industry	166.7	1,150	93.3
Dräger*	Incubators	590	5,278	146
Dürr	Paint finishing systems	800	3,000	301.3
Edding	Felt markers	130	250	430
eff-eff Fr. Fuss*	Security products	117	1,000	36.4
Ex-Cell-O	Track-mining and grinding machines	200	1,300	84
Fielmann*	Eyeglasses at retail and wholesale	580	5,000	48.6
Fresenius*	Dialysis instruments	446.7	1,749	1040
Garny	Safes, fittings for banks	200	1,100	307.7
Grohe*	Sanitary fittings	652	4,000	216.7
Hegener + Glaser	Chess computers	60	500	52.7
Herlitz	Stationery	486.7	2,800	170

*Particularly attractive.

Company	Primary Product	Sales in Millions of U.S. $	Employees	Stock Price, December 1995, in U.S. $
Hermle	Universal milling and boring machines		566	92.7
Hohner	Mouth organs and accordions	126.7	1,050	46
Jado	Designer door hardware	66.7	700	9.1
Jungheinrich	Electric material-handling equipment	1,100	6,000	157.3
KHS	Bottling systems for the beverage industry	682	5,719	142.6
Kiekert*	Car locking systems	400	2,700	57.2
Koenig & Bauer	Money-printing presses	383.3	2,000	158
Kögel	Truck chassis	146.7	1,000	188
Krones*	Bottling systems	657.3	4,515	356.6
KSB	Centrifugal pumps	1,353.3	13,800	163.3
Kühnle, Kopp & Kausch (KKK)	Turbo chargers	210	2,000	140
KWS	Sugar-beet seed	173.3	700	408.6
Plettac	Scaffolding	433.3	1,000	244
Revell	Plastic model kits	60	250	190
Röder	Tent rental	100	550	61
SAP	Client/server applications	1,200	5,000	155
Sartorius	Balances, filters	120	1,400	112

Continued on next page

Table 11.2 *continued*

Company	Primary Product	Sales in Millions of U.S. $	Employees	Stock Price, December 1995, in U.S. $
Schenck	Balances	666.7	7,000	82.7
Schön & Cie.	Shoe machines	76.7	500	64
Schumag	Combined drawing machines	126.7	1,100	386.7
SGL Carbon	Carbon and graphite products	956.7	5,300	70.1
SKW Trostberg*	Specialty chemicals	2,266	11,000	32.3
Turbon	Ribbon cassettes	93.3	1,000	28.3
Villeroy & Boch	Ceramic products	966.7	12,000	152.3
Weinig	Molders for machining solid wood	197.3	1,100	353
Windhoff	Track repair machines	63.3	450	213
Zanders	Art paper	580.7	3,300	97.7

*Particularly attractive.

currency rates since they rely heavily on exports. But this type of volatility may make the stock of these companies even more appealing to investors with short-term profit goals.

Many of the hidden champions listed in Table 11.2 went public relatively recently, and more are planning to follow suit. This development offers attractive investment opportunities for the future.

Besides their being publicly traded, the hidden champions are sought-after targets for takeovers, management buyouts, and private investment. A number of institutional investors prefer to buy equity positions in firms with leading market positions. Among those are national funds from Kuwait or Singapore, special funds, and investment banks. Because such investors usually shun publicity to protect their niches, I refrain from naming them here.

GENERAL QUALITATIVE LESSONS

The hidden champions present some significant general lessons. Their basic ingredient is a large degree of common sense: giving value to customers, reliability, building long-term relationships, delivering good quality and service. Their practices illustrate that many modern management buzzwords like "outsourcing," "strategic alliances," and "time competition" may be either short-lived fashions or one-sided exaggerations of a single aspect of business. Many of the leaders I interviewed emphasized that they have been remarkably little influenced by such new management fashions. In their opinion, those buzzwords come and go and shouldn't influence one's thinking too strongly.

Fundamentally good and successful management practices don't change much over the years. Instead of following each new management fad, a company is well advised to adhere to simple but proven principles such as those of the hidden champions. Remain sober and don't flip over the most recent article on the newest business wonder medicine!

Another general point boils down to the fact that good management means performing many minor details better than one's competitors do rather than getting just one or a few elements right. Most hidden champion leaders said that they don't have a unidimensional success formula for fighting competition. They conceded that their competitors are also strong, often excellent. But through the sum of the many aspects in which they outperform their rivals, they achieve superiority. This should not preclude a certain concentration, as suggested by EKS, the bottleneck-concentrated strategy described in Chapter 10. But it certainly requires that no relevant aspect of the business be handled carelessly. It also calls for continual improvement in every aspect of company business. In this regard the hidden champions adhere to the Japanese *kaizen* philosophy. They constantly achieve improvements less through formal suggestion systems than through the active participation and involvement of employees who, in turn, are driven by sincere motivation and identification with their company.

An implicit lesson reposes in the focus of the hidden champions, which posits that no one can be a champion in many trades. Those who are focused beat those who spread themselves thin. This message is particularly relevant for small companies with limited resources. But it applies equally to large companies, which frequently deceive themselves in thinking they can develop many different competencies and handle many different businesses—a dangerous illusion. The single-minded specialist usually beats the generalist.

Simplicity is yet another guide the hidden champions hold for us. Simplicity is related to both organizational processes and structure. The discussions of both the lean and the reengineering philosophies of the recent years are tied to simplicity. Many hidden champions have never been anything but lean. Authors like Rommel et al. (1995) suggest simplicity as a promising path to increased productivity. Large organizations have developed so much artificial complexity that they are paralyzing themselves. An essential ingredient of simplicity, in my opinion, is a company's having more work than it can comfortably handle. This condition prevents people from devising new complexities and keeps them focused on the tasks that must be done.

But simplicity also refers to people's views of the world. Many hidden champion leaders hold a rather simple, though not simplistic, view. They focus on the essentials of a situation, refusing to be distracted and misguided by its many irrelevant intricacies. Large organizations and groups, on the other hand, trying to grasp all contingencies of a situation, build complex models, are overwhelmed by seas of data, and sometimes lose the view of the essentials, overlooking the forest for the trees. The ability to reduce conditions to their essentials without oversimplifying gains in importance with the increasing complexity of the environment.

BOTH-AND LESSONS

It was Heinrich Flik of W. L. Gore, Inc., who first directed my attention to the importance of a "both-and" philosophy in management (Flik 1990). Gore's corporate culture is built around this concept, not an "either-or" notion. The company motto, "To make money and have fun," emphasizes two elements. Two company principles are "freedom" and "waterline." While the former encourages all employees to develop their full potential, the latter limits them with the warning not to bore holes below the waterline. Gore strives to be both tough about the principles and flexible about the details.

The same attitude pervades the behavior of the hidden champions, as has been stressed in each chapter. Table 11.3 outlines some both-and examples. The market definition, for instance, is both narrow with regard to product and technology and wide with regard to regional scope; leadership is both authoritarian on fundamentals and participative when details are concerned.

Both-and is a recurrent theme in the management literature. Barry Johnson, in *Polarity Management* (1992), emphasizes the need to find compromises between opposites and warns of the danger in opting for extreme solutions, appealing as they may seem to be. In *Built to Last,* Collins and Porras (1994) speak of the "tyranny of the *or*" and suggest that one "embrace the genius of the *and.*" They relate this problem to the yin and yang of dualistic Chinese philosophy.

Reconciling apparently irreconcilable aspects is an essential ingredient

Table 11.3 **The Hidden Champions' Both-And Philosophy**

Aspect	Both . . .	And
Market	Narrow: product, technology	Wide: world, regional
Driving Force/Innovation	Customer-driven	Technology-driven
Strategy	External opportunities	Internal resources/ competencies
Innovation	Product	Process
Time Horizon	Short-term: efficiency (doing the right thing)	Long-term: effectiveness (doing the thing right)
Competitive Advantage	Product quality	Service/interaction
Creation of Value-Added	Core activities in-house	Outsourcing of noncore activities
Job Turnover	High: early in the selection phase	Low: long-term personnel
Leadership	Authoritarian in core values, goals	Participative in details, process

in the art of management. Although I have emphasized simplicity, the world is hardly so simple that it suffices to consider only one side of a coin and go for an extreme solution. One should realize that both-and does not necessitate a naive fifty-fifty or midpoint compromise. As I illustrated in Figure 6.3, the issue is not either technology or market orientation but both technology and market orientation. The two are not mutually exclusive alternatives but dimensions to be pursued simultaneously. To a lesser or greater degree, the same holds for the other aspects in Table 11.3. It warns against one-sidedness, which is one of the most prevalent errors in management success formulas. Difficult choices and trade-offs are unavoidable in management, even though managers may dislike them. Michael Porter (1994, 273) says, "Managers, I have found, have been all too eager to embrace one or more of these notions as the solution because they promised to eliminate the need for difficult choices." This is an illusion. Good management always involves difficult choices. Dr. Hans-Joachim Langmann, since the early 1960s CEO of Merck KGaA, a company that holds several world market leader positions, and one of the most considerate managers I know, suggested to me that making these difficult choices intelligently constitutes the true art of management.

THREE CIRCLES AND NINE LESSONS

This section summarizes the hidden champion's nine most significant lessons, each reflecting the essence of one chapter of this book. Figure 11.1 portrays, in a systems context, the nine lessons embedded in three nested circles: the core, the inner circle reflecting internal competencies, and the outer circle relating to external opportunities.

The core is defined by strong leadership, which sets ambitious goals that in turn define and align the competencies of the company. The competencies comprise well-selected and motivated employees, continuous innovation in product and process, and reliance on one's own strength. The internal competencies are translated into external strengths. The outer circle includes narrow market focus in product, technology, and application, which fosters closeness to customer and clear competitive advantages and is complemented by a global orientation that creates a large enough market. While the lessons proceed in a causal order from

Figure 11.1 The Hidden Champions' Three Circles and Nine Lessons

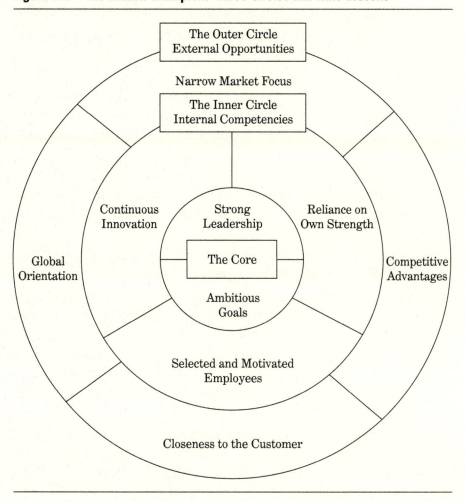

core to outer circle, no one aspect dominates another. The combination of all is what leads to success.

The nine specific lessons are:

1. Set clear and ambitious goals. Ideally a company should strive to be the best and to become the leader in its market.

2. Define a market narrowly and in so doing include both customer needs and technology. Don't accept given market definitions but

consider the market definition itself part of strategy. Stay focused and concentrated. Avoid distractions.

3. Combine a narrow market focus with a global orientation involving worldwide sales and marketing. Deal as directly as possible with customers around the globe.

4. Be close to customers in both performance and interaction. Make sure that all functions have direct customer contacts. Adopt a value-driven strategy. Pay close attention to the most demanding customers.

5. Strive for continuous innovation in both product and process. Innovation should be both technology- and customer-driven. Pay equal attention to internal resources and competencies and external opportunities.

6. Create clear-cut competitive advantages in both product and service. Defend the company's competitive position ferociously.

7. Rely on your own strengths. Keep core competencies in the company, but outsource noncore activities. Consider cooperation a last resort rather than a first choice.

8. Try always to have more work than heads. Select employees rigorously in the first phase, then retain them for the long-term. Communicate directly to motivate people and use employee creativity to its full potential.

9. Practice leadership that is both authoritarian in the fundamentals and participative in the details. Pay utmost attention to the selection of leaders, observing their unity of person and purpose, energy and perseverance, and the ability to inspire others.

A HIDDEN CHAMPION AUDIT

The nine lessons suggest that companies evaluate themselves against these criteria. I have carried out such hidden champion audits in a number of companies. The first step is to assess the importance of the nine lessons, which may vary from market to market. Second, evaluate the company's performance with respect to the lessons. Managers can do this individually by completing a questionnaire (see Table 11.4) or in a group discussion or workshop setting, the latter being preferable. To compare importance and performance and to judge how well a company adheres to the hidden champions' lessons, use the matrix developed in Chapter 6 for the analysis of competitive performance and internal competencies. My method depicts the importance rating on the vertical axis and the performance rating on the horizontal axis of the matrix. The most desirable result is the more important the criterion, the better the performance should be. This is illustrated by the shaded diagonal in Figure 11.2, which shows such an audit for two companies. A true hidden champion's matrix is on the left; the matrix of a large diversified corporation is on the right. For each firm, ten high-level managers completed the questionnaire.

The hidden champion audit on the left reveals that this company adheres closely to the lessons. There is consistency between importance and performance, the most important factors showing a high performance. The reverse is true for the diversified corporation. Its performance is rated low on the most important lessons, and vice versa. It is also interesting to compare the importance rankings for the two companies. The hidden champion obviously does not feel strong competitive pressure

Table 11.4 **Hidden Champions Audit Questionnaire**

Lesson	Importance 1 = less important 5 = very important	Performance 1 = very low 5 = very high
1. Ambitious Goals	1 2 3 4 5	1 2 3 4 5
2. Narrow Market Focus	1 2 3 4 5	1 2 3 4 5
3. Global Orientation	1 2 3 4 5	1 2 3 4 5
4. Closeness to Customer	1 2 3 4 5	1 2 3 4 5
5. Continuous Innovation	1 2 3 4 5	1 2 3 4 5
6. Competitive Advantages	1 2 3 4 5	1 2 3 4 5
7. Reliance on Own Strength	1 2 3 4 5	1 2 3 4 5
8. Motivated Employees	1 2 3 4 5	1 2 3 4 5
9. Strong Leadership	1 2 3 4 5	1 2 3 4 5

Figure 11.2   **A Hidden Champion Audit of Two Companies**

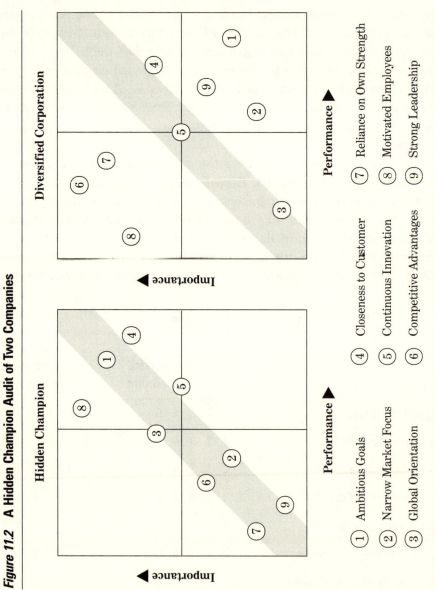

and ranks competitive advantages only below average; in the diversified corporation, competitive advantages is the most important criterion. The reverse is true for ambitious goals, rated high in importance by the hidden champion and low by the diversified company.

These two companies see and experience the world very differently, but the hidden champion seems to be on a much more purposeful and effective track. This audit and the comparison led to major consequences in the large diversified corporation. It has become determined to reforge itself into a group of hidden champions.

THE ULTIMATE LESSON

The hidden champions go their own ways. Their procedures are quite different from those of other companies and of modern management teaching. Essentially, their only secret success formula is common sense. So simple, but so difficult to achieve! This is the ultimate lesson.

References

"ABB on the Move." 1994. *International Management,* April 26–29.

Abell, Derek F. 1980. *Defining the Business—The Starting Point of Strategic Planning.* Englewood Cliffs, N.J.: Prentice-Hall.

Adamer, Manfred M., and Günter Kaindl. 1994. *Erfolgsgeheimnisse von Markt- und Weltmarktführern* (Success secrets of market and world market leaders). Munich: Rainer Hampp Verlag.

Albach, Horst. 1994. *Culture and Technical Innovation.* Berlin/New York: de Gruyter.

Albaum, G. 1989. *International Marketing and Export Management.* Boston: Addison-Wesley.

Andersen, Otto. 1993. "On the Internationalization Process of Firms: A Critical Analysis." *Journal of International Business Studies* 2: 209–231.

Arrufat, Miguel A., and George H. Haines. 1992. "Market Definition for Application Development Software Packages." Carleton University School of Business, Working Paper 93–02.

Ascarelli, Silvia. 1994. "How Germany's Krones Slipped on a Big Order and Just Kept Falling." *Wall Street Journal Europe,* December 16.

Attiyeh, R. S., and S. L. Wenner. 1981. "Critical Mass: Key to Export Profit." *McKinsey Quarterly,* Winter, 73–87.

Australian Manufacturing Council and McKinsey & Company. 1993. "Emerging Exporters: Australia's High Value-Added Manufacturing Exporters." Canberra: Australian Manufacturing Council.

Ayal, Igal, and Jehiel Zif. 1979. "Competitive Market Choice Strategies in Multinational Marketing." *Journal of Marketing* 43 (Spring): 84–94.

Bennis, Warren. 1989. *Why Leaders Can't Lead.* San Francisco: Jossey-Bass.

Biallo, Horst. 1993. *Die geheimen deutschen Weltmeister: Mittelständische Erfolgsunternehmen und ihre Strategie.* (The secret German world champions: Mid-sized success firms and their strategies). Vienna: Wirtschaftsverlag Ueberreuter.

Burke, Jeffrey. 1994. "Bad Impressions." *Wall Street Journal Europe,* November 30.

Buzzell, Robert D., and Bradley T. Gale. 1987. *The PIMS Principles: Linking Strategy to Performance.* New York: Free Press, 1987.

Cavusgil, S. T. 1980. "On the Internationalization Process of the Firm." *European Research,* November, 273–281.

Clifford, Donald K., Jr. 1973. "Growth Pains of the Threshold Company." *Harvard Business Review* 51 (September–October): 143–154.

Clifford, Donald K., and Richard E. Cavanagh. 1985. *The Winning Performance: How America's High-growth Midsize Companies Succeed.* New York: Bantam Books.

Collins, James C., and Jerry I. Porras. 1994. *Built to Last: Successful Habits of Visionary Companies.* New York: Harper Collins.

———. 1995. "Die Besten der Besten: Zwölf Managementmythen" (The best of the best: Twelve management myths). *gdi-impuls.* Zurich: Gottlieb Duttweiler-Institut, January, 23–29.

Collis, David J., and Cynthia A. Montgomery. 1995. "Competing on Resources: Strategy in the 1990s." *Harvard Business Review* 73 (July–August): 118–128.

Cooper, R. G. 1979. "The Dimensions of Industrial New Product Success and Failure." *Journal of Marketing* 43 (July): 93–103.

Davenport, Thomas H. 1993. *Process Innovation: Reengineering Work through Information Technology.* Boston: Harvard Business School Press.

Drewes, C. 1992. "Euro-Kommunikation" (Euro-communications). In H. G. Meissner, ed. *Euro-Dimensionen des Marketing.* (Euro-dimensions of marketing). Dortmund: Fachverlag Arnold, 84–96.

Drucker, Peter F. 1978. *Adventures of a Bystander.* New York: Harper Collins.

———. 1988. "Management and the World's Work." *Harvard Business Review* 66 (September–October): 65–76.

———. 1989. "Lest Business Alliances Become Dangerous." *Wall Street Journal Europe,* September.

———. 1991. *Fortune.* December 30. Quoted in Thomas J. Peters. 1992. *Liberation Management.* New York: Alfred A. Knopf.

"Ein echter Braun wird mit Nüssen und Kirschkernen beschossen" (A true Braun will be exposed to tough tests). *Frankfurter Allgemeine Zeitung,* August 21.

Flik, Heinrich. 1990. "The Amoeba Concept: Organizing around Opportunity within the Gore Culture." In Hermann Simon, ed. *Herausforderung Unternehmenskultur* (Corporate culture as a challenge). Stuttgart: Schäffer-Verlag, 91–129.

Ford, Henry. 1922. *My Life and Work.* New York: Doubleday.

Foster, Richard. 1986. *Innovation: The Attacker's Advantage.* New York: Summit Books.

"Geht Karl Mayer nun auch den Weg nach China?" (Does Karl Mayer go to China?) 1993. *Frankfurter Allgemeine Zeitung,* November 22.

"Gillette hat ehrgeizige Ziele und eigenwillige Grundsätze" (Gillette has ambitious goals and headstrong principles). *Frankfurter Allgemeine Zeitung,* March 25.

Glouchevitch, Philip. 1992. *Juggernaut: The German Way of Business: Why It Is Transforming Europe—and the World.* New York: Simon and Schuster.

Grant, Linda. 1995. "GE: The Envelope Please." *Fortune,* June 26, 73–74.

Hamel, Gary, and C. K. Prahalad. 1994. *Competing for the Future.* Boston: Harvard Business School Press.

Hammer, Michael, and James Champy. 1993. *Reengineering the Corporation: A Manifesto for Business Revolution.* New York: Harper Collins.

Helmer, Wolfgang. 1995. "Noch gelten die Grundsätze der Firmengründer" (The principles of the company founders are still valid). *Frankfurter Allgemeine Zeitung,* May 30.

Henderson, Bruce D. 1983. "The Anatomy of Competition." *Journal of Marketing* 47 (Spring): 7–11.

Heskett, James L., Christopher Hart, and W. Earl Sasser, Jr. 1990. "The Profitable Art of Service Recovery." *Harvard Business Review* 68 (July–August): 148–156.

Hippel, Eric von. 1988. *The Sources of Innovation.* New York/Oxford: Oxford University Press.

Hirsch, James S. "For U.S. Banks, It's the Niche That Counts: Bigger Is Better but Narrower Is Even Nicer." 1995. *Wall Street Journal Europe,* August 29.

Homburg, Christian. 1995. "Kundennähe von Industriegüterunternehmen: Konzeptualisierung, Erfolgsauswirkungen und organisationale Determinanten" (Closeness to customers of industrial firms: Conceptualization, success effects and determinants). Wiesbaden: Gabler.

Informationsdienst des Instituts der Deutschen Wirtschaft. 1988. October.

———. 1994. September 28.

Institut der deutschen Wirtschaft. 1994. *Industriestandort Deutschland* (Germany as an industrial location). Cologne: Deutsche Instituts-Verlag.

Jacobson, Robert, and David A. Aaker. 1985. "Is Market Share All That It Is Cracked Up to Be?" *Journal of Marketing* 49 (Fall): 11–22.

Johnson, Barry. 1992. *Polarity Management: Identifying and Managing Unsolvable Problems.* Amherst, Mass.: HRD Press.

Knobel, Lance. "The ABC of ABB." *World Link.* September–October, 31–34.

Landrum, Gene N. 1993. *Profiles of Genius.* Buffalo, N.Y.: Prometheus Books.

Learned, Edmund P., C. Roland Christensen, Kenneth R. Andrews, and William D. Guth. 1965. *Business Policy: Text and Cases.* Homewood, Ill.: Irwin.

Levitt, Theodore. 1960. "Marketing Myopia." *Harvard Business Review* 38 (July–August): 24–47.

———. 1983. "The Globalization of Markets." *Harvard Business Review* 61 (May–June): 92–100.

———. 1988. "Betterness." *Harvard Business Review* 66 (November–December): 9.

Lloyd, Sam. 1994. "Western Europe." In *World Science Report.* Paris: UNESCO.

Loeb, Marshall. 1995. "Ten Commandments for Managing Creative People." *Fortune,* January 16, 83–84.

Maremont, Mark. 1995. "Kodak's New Focus: An Inside Look at George Fisher's Strategy." *Business Week,* January 30, 62–68.

McQuarrie, Edward F. 1993. *The Customer Visit: A Tool to Build Customer Focus.* San Francisco: Sage Publications.

Miesenbock, K. J. 1988. "Small Business and Exporting: A Literature Review." *International Small Business Journal* 6, no. 2: 42–61.

Mintzberg, Henry, and James A. Waters. 1985. "Of Strategies, Deliberate and Emergent." *Strategic Management Journal* 6: 257–272.

Montaña, Jordi, ed. 1994. *Marketing in Europe.* London.

"Nach dem Schock über den Kursrutsch zeigt der Vorstand Einsicht—Getränkemaschinenbauer Krones will Controlling und Finanzwesen verbessen" (After the stock price shock the management of Krones wants to improve controlling and finance). 1995. *Frankfurter Allgemeine Zeitung,* January 2.

Ohmae, Kenichi. 1985. *Triad Power.* New York: Free Press.

Ortega y Gasset, José. 1960. *What Is Philosophy?* New York: Norton.

Owen, Geoffrey, and Trevor Harrison. 1993. "Why ICI Chose to Demerge." *Harvard Business Review* 73 (March–April): 133–142.

Penrose, Edith T. 1959. *The Theory of the Growth of the Firm.* Oxford: Basil Blackwell.

Peteraf, Margaret A. 1993. "The Cornerstone of Competitive Advantage: A Resource-Based View." *Strategic Management Journal* 14: 179–191.

———. 1994. *The Tom Peters Seminar: Crazy Times for Crazy Organizations.* New York: Vintage Books.

Peters, Thomas J., and Robert H. Waterman. 1982. *In Search of Excellence: Lessons from America's Best-Run Companies.* New York: Harper & Row.

Porter, Michael E. 1980. *Competitive Strategy.* New York: Free Press.

———. 1985. *Competitive Advantage.* New York: Free Press.

———. 1990a. *Competitive Advantage of Nations.* London: Macmillan.

———. 1990b. "Competitive Advantage of Nations." *Harvard Business Review* 68 (March–April): 73–93.

———. 1994. "Competitive Strategy Revisited: A View from the 1990s." In *The Relevance of a Decade: Essays to Mark the First Ten Years of the Harvard Business School Press,* edited by Paula B. Duffy. Boston: Harvard Business School Press.

Prahalad, C. K., and G. Hamel. 1990. "The Core Competence of the Corporation." *Harvard Business Review* (May–June): 79–91.

Rohwedder, Cacilie. 1996. "Teen Tycoon Gives Risk-Averse Germans a Lesson in Survival." *Wall Street Journal Europe,* January 4, 1996.

Rommel, Günter; Jürgen Kluge, Rolf-Dieter Kempis, Raimund Diederichs, and Felix Brück. 1995. *Simplicity Wins: How Germany's Mid-Sized Industrial Companies Succeed.* Boston: Harvard Business School Press.

Root, Franklin R. 1987. *Entry Strategies for International Markets.* Lexington, Mass.: Lexington Books, D. C. Heath.

Saporito, Bill. 1994. "The Eclipse of Mars." *Fortune International,* November 18, 50–58.

Schares, Gail E., and John Templeman. 1991. "Think Small—Midsize Companies Give Germany's Export Powerhouse Its Punch." *Business Week,* October 7, 24B-J.

"Schering will weltweit Spezialmärkte beherrschen" (Schering wants to dominat specialty markets worldwide). 1994. *General-Anzeiger Bonn,* November 15.

Schlender, Brent. 1995. "What Bill Gates Really Wants." *Fortune International,* January 16, 16–33.

Scientific American. 1993. May, 62.

Selznick, P. 1957. *Leadership in Administration.* New York/Tokyo.

Simon, Hermann. 1982. *International Expansion: Theoretical Concepts and Experiences in a Medium-sized Company.* Berlin: Erich Schmidt.

———. 1988. "Management strategischer Wettbewerbsvorteile" (Managing competitive advantages). *Zeitschrift für Betriebswirtschaft* 58, no. 4: 461–480.

———. 1992. "Lessons from Germany's Midsize Giants." *Harvard Business Review* 70 (March–April): 115–123.

Simon, Hermann, Kai Wiltinger, Karl-Heinz Sebastian, and Georg Tacke. 1995. *Effektives Personalmarketing* (Effective personnel marketing). Wiesbaden: Gabler.

Simon, Kucher & Partner. 1995. "Strategic Analysis and Action." Bonn: Simon, Kucher & Partner. Brochure.

Slater, Robert. 1993. *The New GE: How Jack Welch Revived an American Institution.* Homewood, Ill.: Business One Irwin.

Smith, Lee. 1994. "Stamina: Who Has It. Why You Need It. How You Get It." *Fortune,* November 28, 67–75.

Statistisches Bundesamt (Federal Statistical Office). 1993. *Tourismus in Zahlen, 1993.* Wiesbaden.

Statistische Jahrbücher der Bundesrepublik Deutschland (Statistical yearbooks of the Federal Republic of Germany). 1986–1995. Stuttgart: Schäffer-Poeschel.

Staudt, Erich, Jürgen Bock, and Peter Mühleneyer. 1992. "Informationsverhalten von innovationsaktiven kleinen und mittleren Unternehmen" (Information behavior of innovative small and medium-sized companies). *Zeitschrift für Betriebswirtschaft* 62: 989–1008.

Treacy, Michael, and Fred Wiersema. 1995. *The Discipline of Market Leaders.* Boston: Addison-Wesley.

Vitzthum, Carla. 1994a. "Spain Urges Firms to Be Export-Minded." *Wall Street Journal Europe,* August 20.

———. 1994b. "Amorim of Portugal Pops Out a Corker." *Wall Street Journal Europe,* September 9–10.

Wallace, D. B., and H. E. Gruber, eds. 1989. *Creative People at Work, Twelve Cognitive Case Studies.* New York/Oxford: Oxford University Press.

Wall Street Journal Europe. 1994. December 29.

Warnecke, Hans-Jürgen. 1992. *Die fraktale Fabrik: Revolution der Unternehmenskultur* (The fractal factory: Revolution of corporate culture). Heidelberg/New York: Springer.

Webster, Justin. 1992. "Taste for World Markets: Lollipop Manufacturer Chupa Chups." *International Management,* June, 55.

Wells, L. T. 1972. *The Product Life Cycle and International Trade.* Ed. Louis T. Wells, Jr. Cambridge, Mass.

Wirtschaftswoche. 1995. June 29.

Index

About the Author

Hermann Simon is the chairman and CEO of Simon, Kucher & Partners, Strategy & Marketing Consultants in Bonn and Boston and a visiting professor at the London Business School. He has also held positions as a professor of management and marketing at the Johannes Gutenberg-University in Mainz, the scientific director of USW—The German Management Institute in Cologne, and the chair of management and marketing at the University of Bielefeld. Fellowships and visiting professorships have taken him to the Harvard Business School, the Sloan School of Management, Stanford University, INSEAD, and Keio University.

A former president of the European Marketing Academy, Simon is a member of several supervisory boards and a trustee of numerous corporations and foundations. He also sits on the editorial boards of the *International Journal of Research in Marketing, Recherche et Applications en Marketing,* and several scientific journals in Germany. Simon has written *Price Management: Theory, Strategy, Implementation* (in German and in English), *Simon for Managers, Goodwill and Marketing Strategy, Pricing Strategy for New Products, Thinking Management: Companies with Visions* and *Price Management* (co-authored in Korean with Professor Pil H. Yoo), and *Thinking Management: Companies with Visions* (in Japanese). He is also the editor of numerous books published in Germany. Simon's articles have appeared in American, British, Dutch, French, German, Hungarian, Italian, Korean, Japanese, Polish, Russian, and Spanish journals.